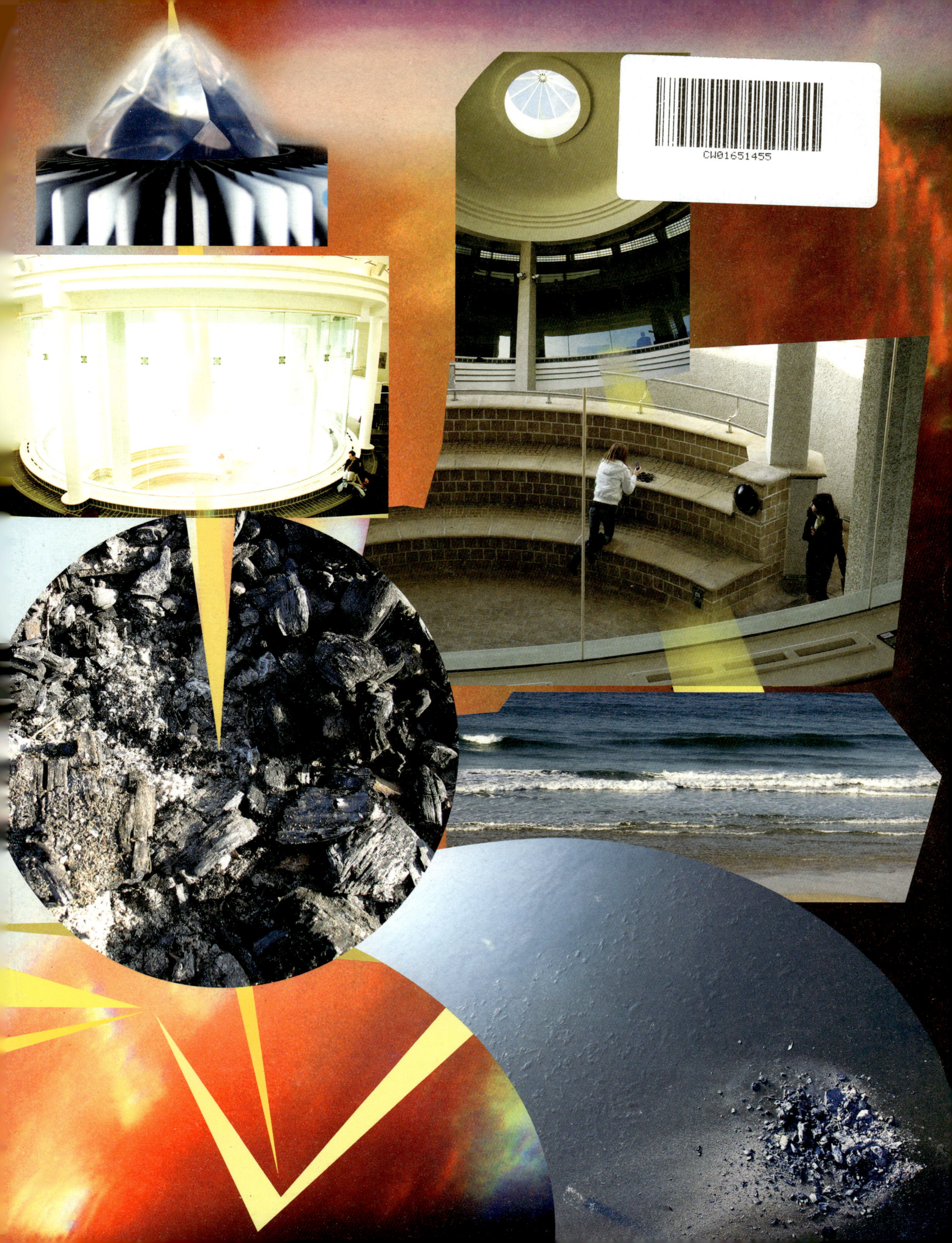

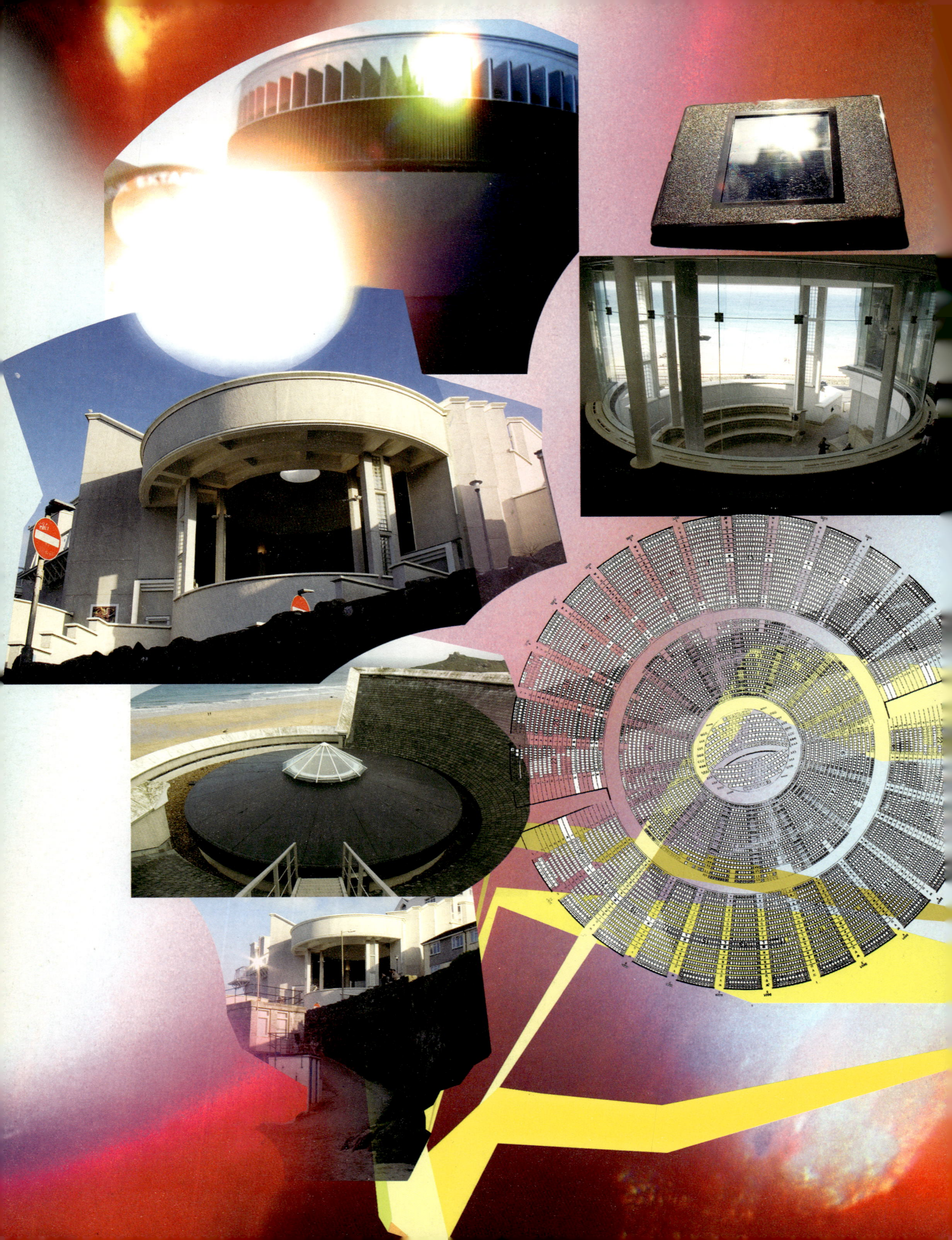

# Adam Chodzko

## Proxigean Tide

## Works



## Words

# 4

**The God Look-Alike Contest** 1992

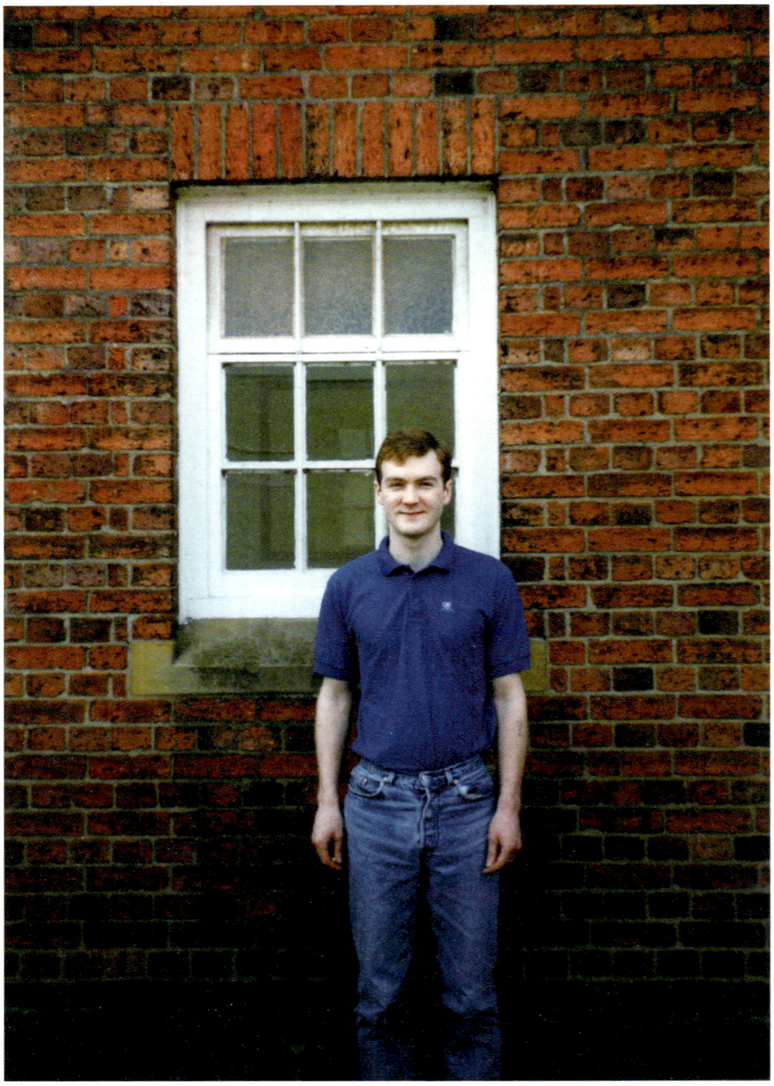

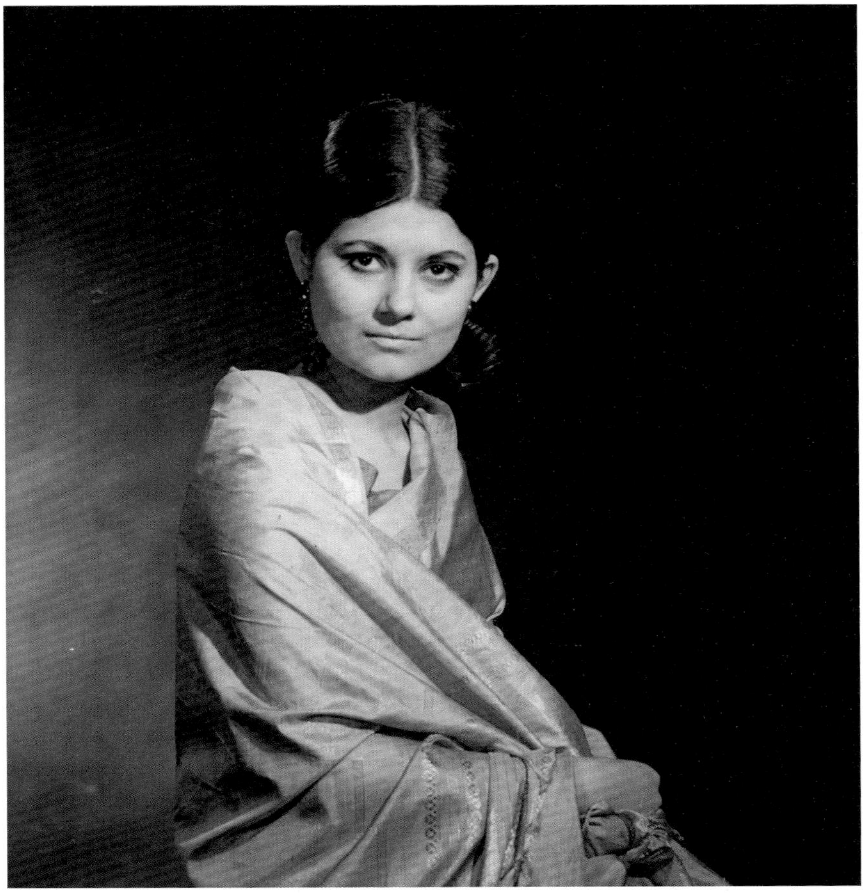

## Foreword

This exhibition at Tate St Ives, Proxigean Tide, is the most comprehensive survey to date of the work of Adam Chodzko, one of Britain's most respected contemporary artists. Since 1991 Chodzko has been making works that consistently challenge our preconceptions of the possibilities and place of artistic practice, and the very nature and mutability of the world around us.

Chodzko's art takes various forms and occupies numerous kinds of spaces both inside and outside the museum or gallery: from video and slide installations to adverts placed in newspapers and magazines; from posters appearing on city centre hoardings to an exchange of clothing, a removal or a gift. In his work the conventions of the everyday and the ubiquity of the visible world are gently destabalised and disrupted, opening up possibilities for entirely new and previously unimagined perspectives, positions and interactions. His works are invariably performative, they enact rather than simply represent; every aspect of their production, dissemination and reception is brought into play through his complex, holistic, but open-ended approach. Works are set in the past as well as the future, they oscillate precariously between fiction and fact, documentary and fantasy, as objects, images and actions become obscure catalysts for enigmatic rumours, extraordinary stories and unstable, intricate mythologies.

For Proxigean Tide Chodzko has created three new works: Borrowed Cold Lodge, a major new installation produced for the very special environment of the Heron Mall at Tate St Ives; Next Meeting: The car park of the plywood factory, just north of the town of Tolhóin …, a new addition to an ongoing poster project located on the coastal path between St Ives and Zennor; and Memory Theatre (which appears as a special project in Tate Etc. magazine and as the end-papers in this book). He is also presenting another work for the first time, Test Tone for Landscape, installed in the building's iconic Loggia. Elsewhere in the galleries we have brought together works spanning the last 17 years including videos, sculpture, photography, posters, sound works, drawings, slide projections and photographs. Through the non-linear, non-chronological juxtaposition of these works in the procession of spaces at Tate St Ives, various dialogues are initiated and explored. In his approach to the show – as well as the very particular location and history of this extraordinary place – Chodzko has responded in a typically insightful and unconventional way, engaging with the unique context of the building, the community and the landscape.

This publication, produced to accompany the exhibition, has been beautifully designed by Claudia Schenk and Silke Klinnert. Three new essays cover various aspects of Chodzko's practice and present a number of original readings and references in relation to his work. Andrew Wilson explores ideas of ritual and sacrifice, both spiritual and secular, in a text that ranges from Chodzko's earliest exhibited works through to his most recent. Lisa Le Feuvre offers a close and perceptive reading of the social and performative interactions evoked and enacted across a number of Chodzko's works, in particular in relation to his various and varied posters. Martin Herbert focuses on Chodzko's recent video and slide works, opening up a territory that encompasses British science fiction writing and 20th-century European cinema. Also included is a recent conversation with the artist, a dialogue that touches on the exhibition at Tate St Ives and the new works produced for the show. We are indebted to Rosa Ainley who has worked so diligently and creatively in editing the texts for the book. The exhibition has been generously supported by Tate St Ives Members and Tate Members, and the production of Borrowed Cold Lodge by Arts Council England. We are enormously grateful to all at Tate St Ives and at Tate who have worked so hard on the production of this ambitious exhibition. In particular Sara Hughes and Matthew McDonald; Susan Lamb, Georgina Kennedy and Peter Hutchinson who worked on the production of Borrowed Cold Lodge; Simon Pollard and his technical team at Tate St Ives as well as Alistair Ashe at Tate Stores and Simeon Corless who provided expertise and assistance on the installation of the video, slide and sound works; and Katherine Lockett from Tate Paper Conservation. We are grateful to all those who have kindly supported the show through the loan of their works, as well as the individuals, groups and societies who contributed to the creation of Borrowed Cold Lodge by lending their winter clothing. We would also like to thank Russell Osborne at Trevalgan Farm who responded so generously to the proposition of siting the Meetings poster on his land and assisted in the installation of the work. Finally, our sincere thanks to Adam who has given such commitment and dedication to the whole project. It has been a hugely pleasurable and stimulating experience for everyone who has worked with him on this show and his engagement, generosity and warmth at every stage have been an inspiration.

Martin Clark, Artistic Director
Mark Osterfield, Executive Director

# 8

**Test Tone for Landscape**
2005 (Sketch for location in
Tate St Ives Loggia, 2008)

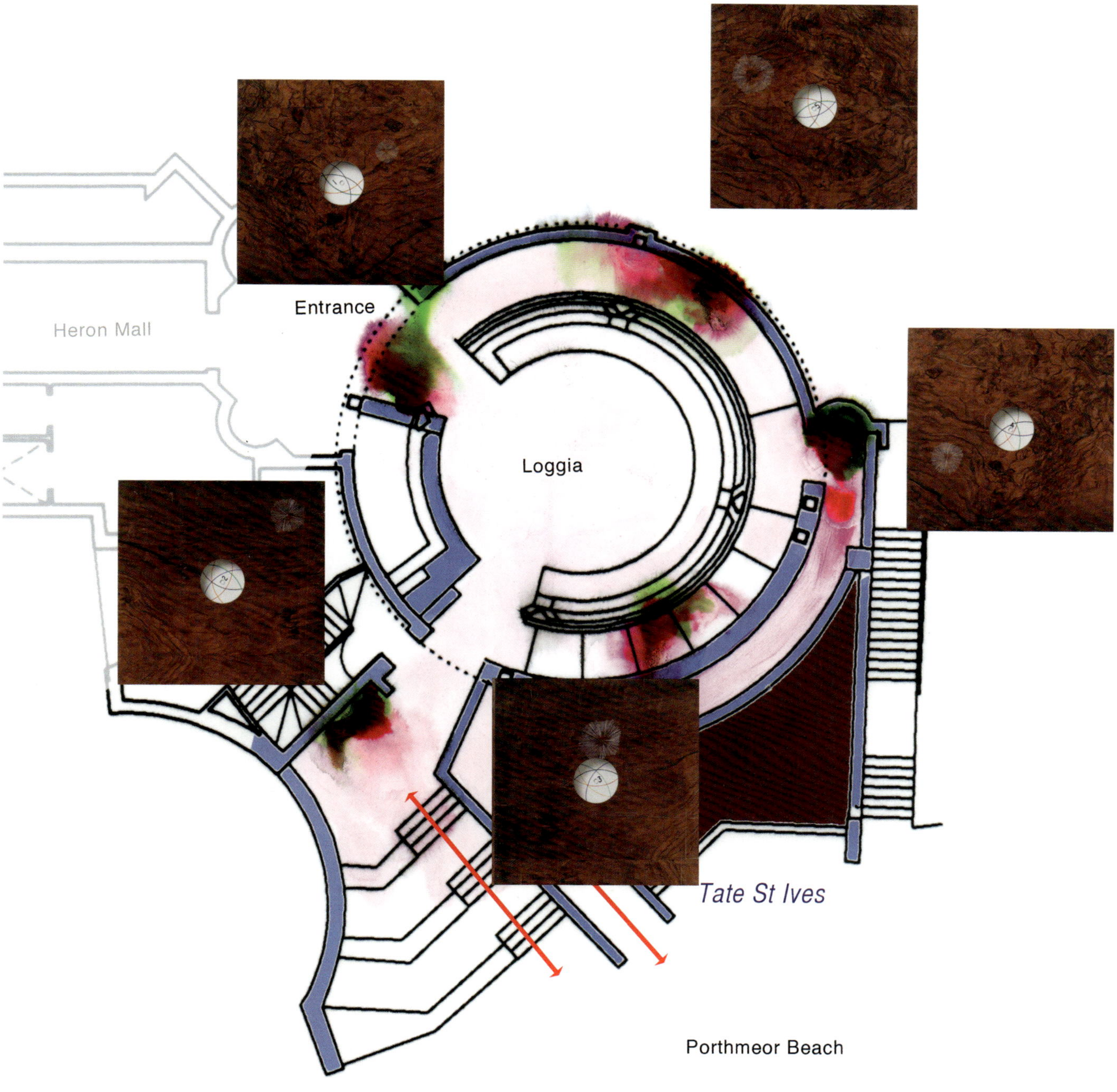

Entrance
Heron Mall
Loggia
Tate St Ives
Porthmeor Beach

# 10

**Test Tone for Landscape**
2005

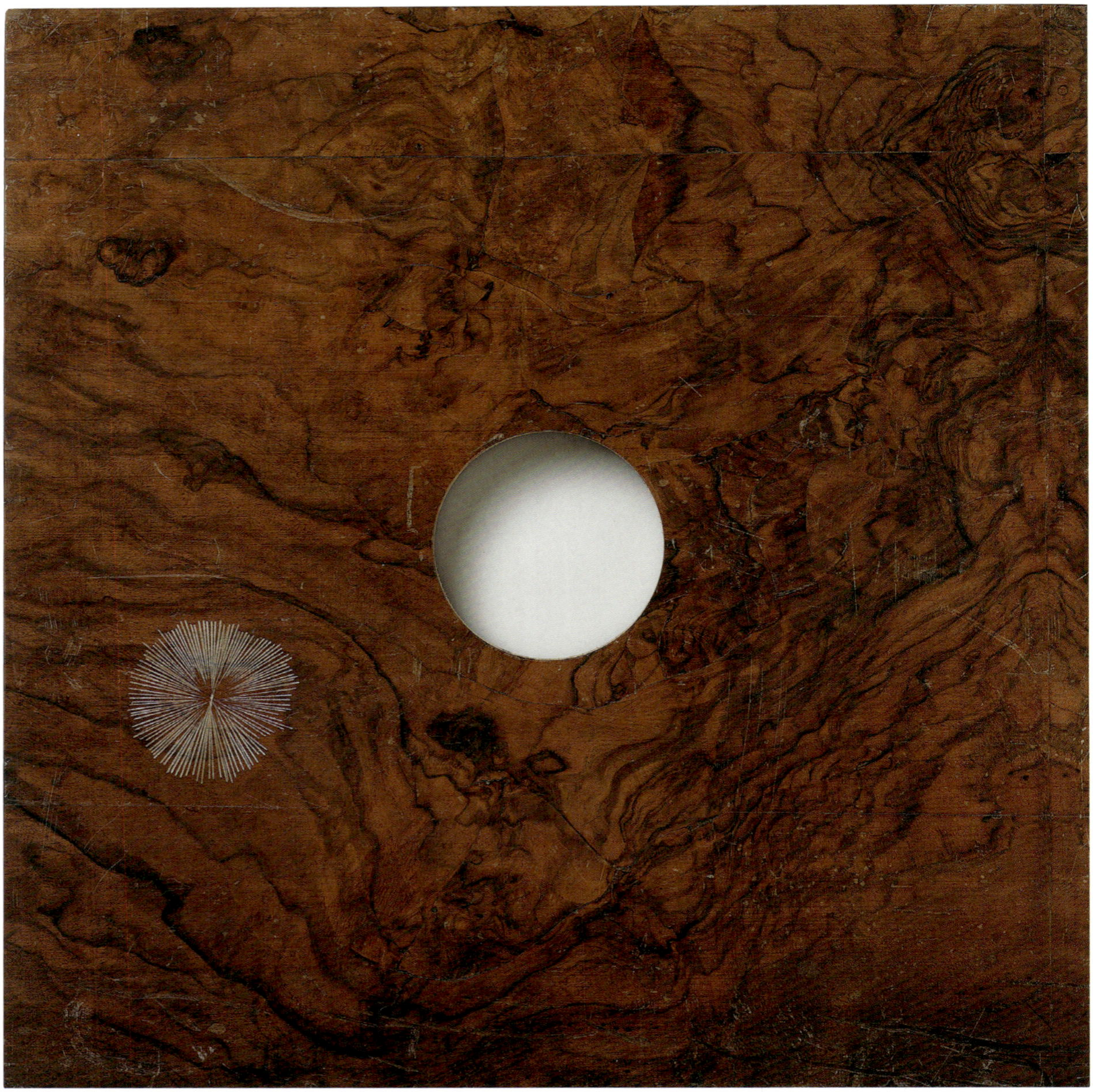

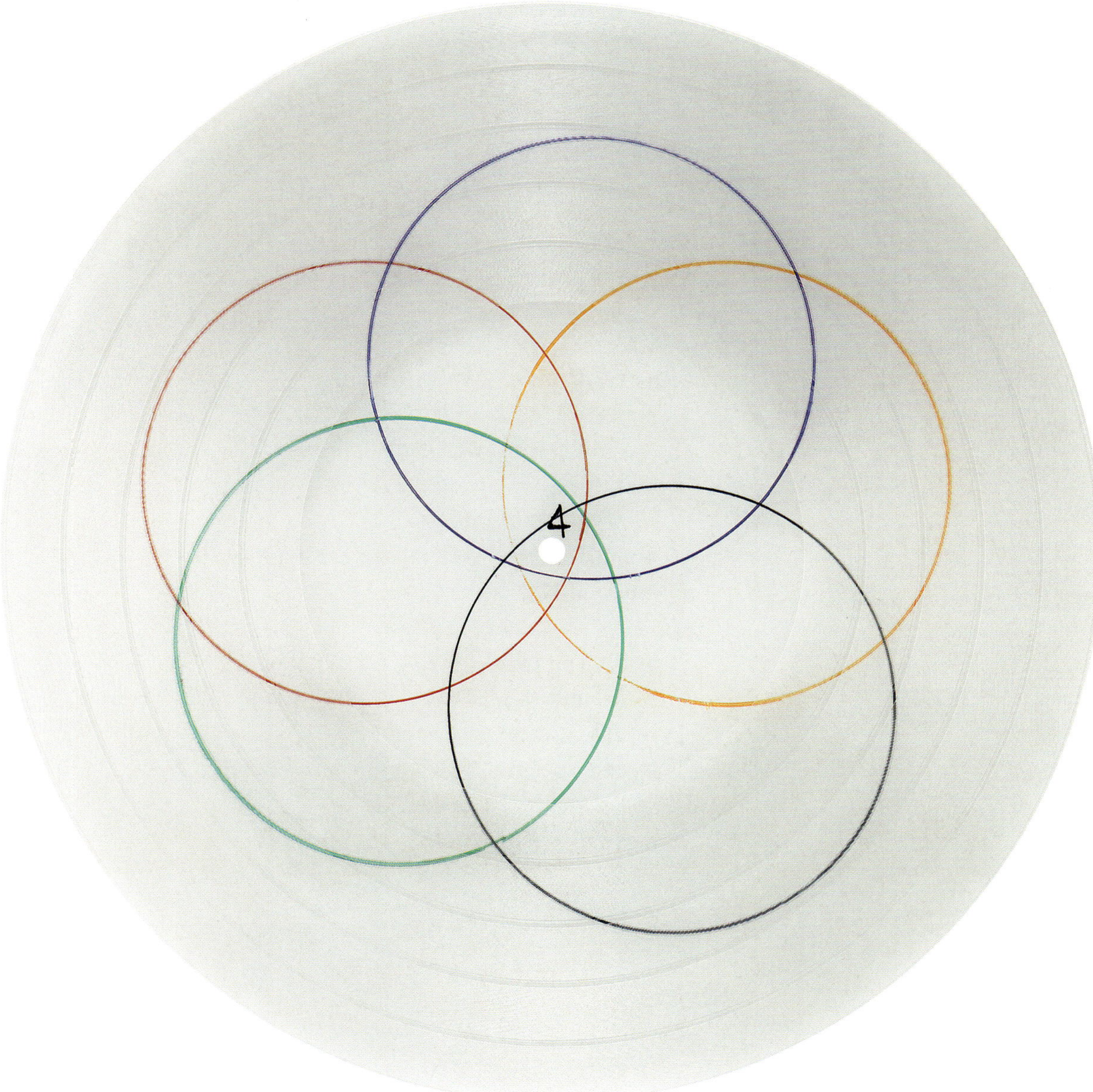
4

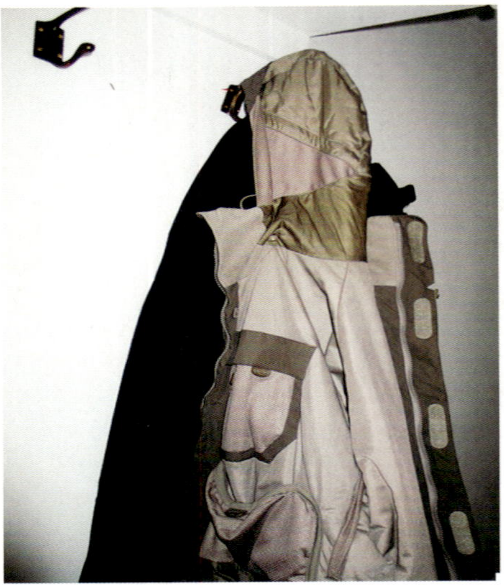

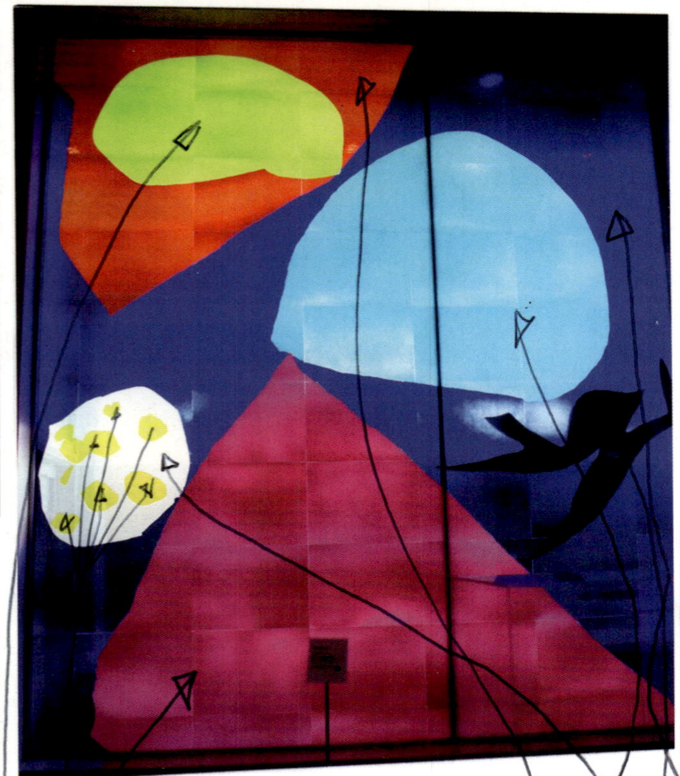

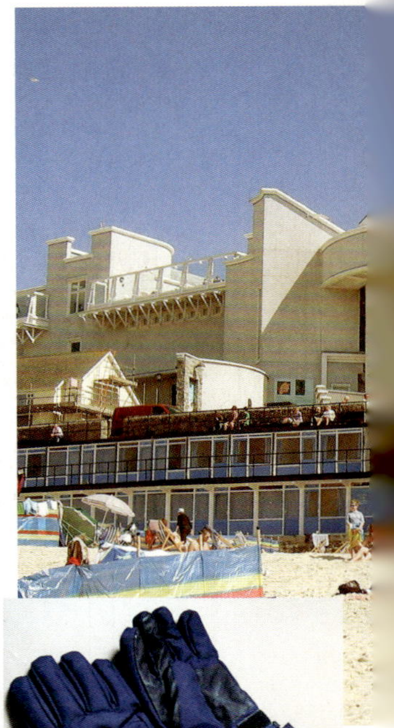

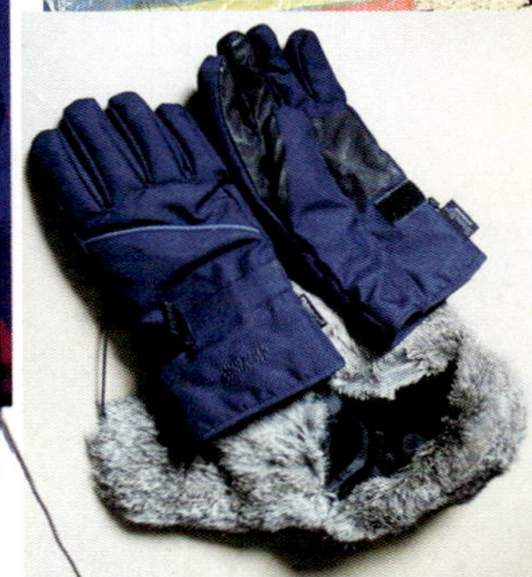

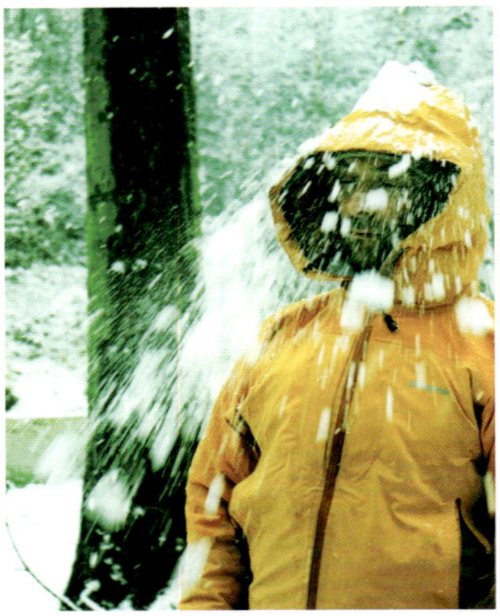

— 27 items of cold-weather,
protective, outer clothing for water use
— 37 items of cold-weather,
protective, outer clothing for walking
— 27 items of cold-weather,
protective, outer clothing for subterranean use
— 27 winter stable rugs
— 17 items of cold-weather,
protective, outer clothing for building use
— 97 winter coats from primary school children
— 27 items of cold-weather,
protective, outer clothing for field use
— 27 items of cold-weather,
protective, outer clothing for snow use

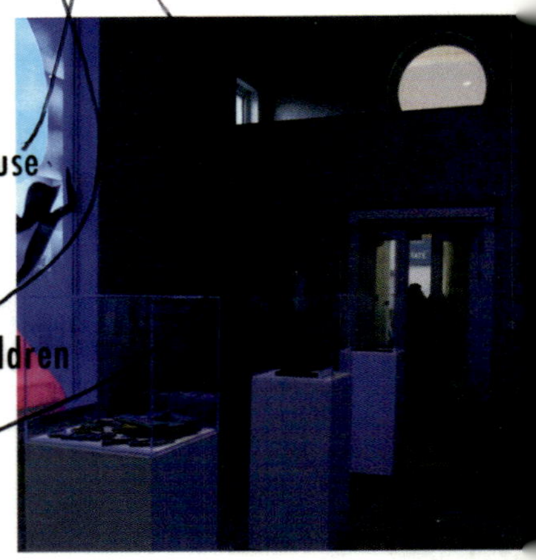

— In summer borrow

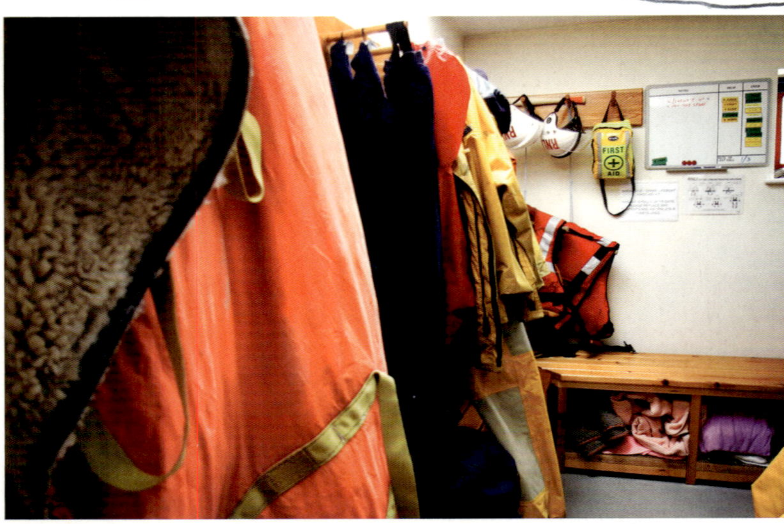


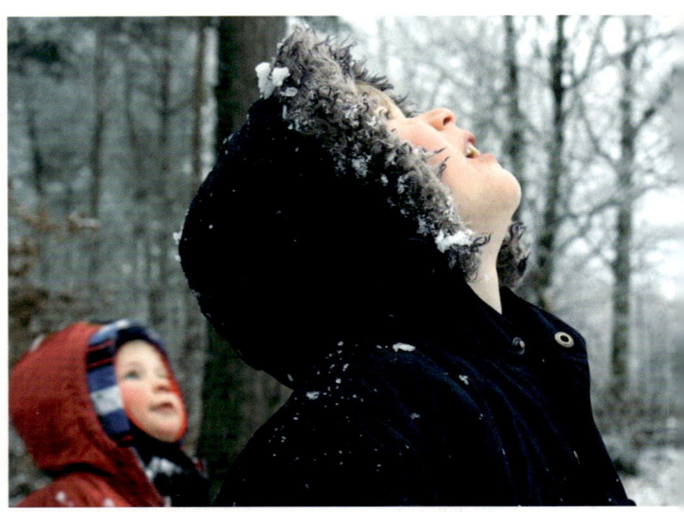

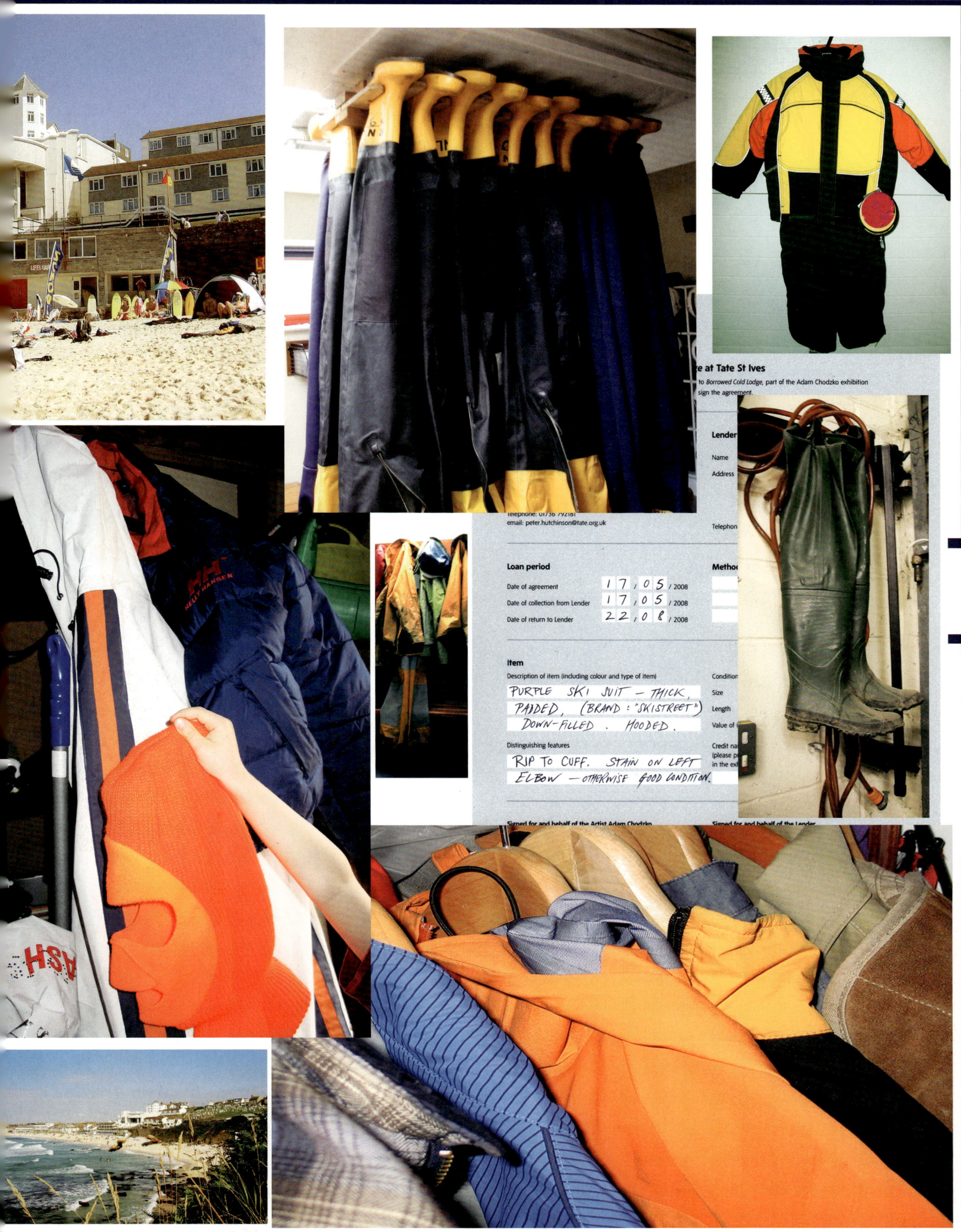
e at Tate St Ives
to *Borrowed Cold Lodge*, part of the Adam Chodzko exhibition
sign the agreement.
Lender
Name
Address
Telephone: 01736 792181
email: peter.hutchinson@tate.org.uk
Telephon
Loan period
Date of agreement 17 / 05 / 2008
Date of collection from Lender 17 / 05 / 2008
Date of return to Lender 22 / 08 / 2008
Metho
Item
Description of item (including colour and type of item)
PURPLE SKI SUIT – THICK, PADDED, (BRAND: "SKISTREET") DOWN-FILLED. HOODED.
Condition
Size
Length
Value of
Distinguishing features
RIP TO CUFF. STAIN ON LEFT ELBOW – OTHERWISE GOOD CONDITION.
Credit na
(please p
in the ex
Signed for and behalf of the Artist Adam Chodzko
Signed for and behalf of the Lender
HELLY HANSEN

# 14

**The music from Float 17, as it stops briefly under the fly-over, as it makes its way in to the city** 2003

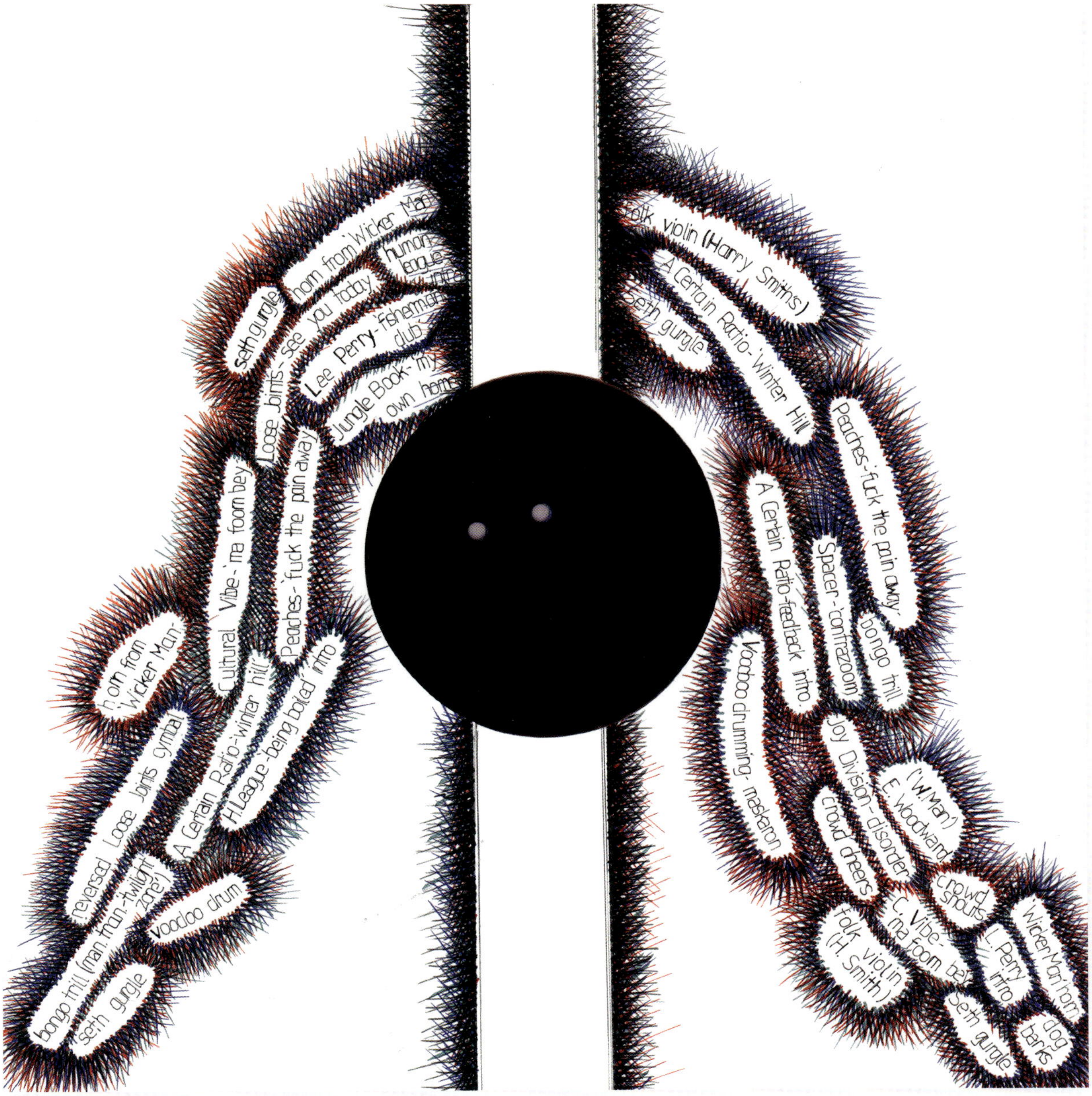
horn from 'Wicker Man'
human league intro
seth gurgle
Loose Joints - see you today
Lee Perry - fisherman club
Jungle Book - my own home
Cultural Vibe - 'ma foom bey'
Peaches - 'fuck the pain away'
horn from 'Wicker Man'
A Certain Ratio - 'winter hill'
H.League 'being boiled' intro
reversed Loose Joints cymbal
bongo trill (man. train - 'twilight zone')
Voodoo drum
seth gurgle
folk violin (Harry Smith's)
A Certain Ratio - 'winter Hill'
seth gurgle
Peaches - 'fuck the pain away'
A Certain Ratio - feedback intro
Spacer - 'contrazoom'
bongo trill
Voodoo drumming - masteron
Joy Division - disorder
crowd cheers
crowd shouts
C. Vibe - ma foom bey
folk violin (H. Smith)
L. Perry intro
Wicker Man horn
Seth gurgle
dog barks

# 16

**Baseball Hat Pyre** 2003

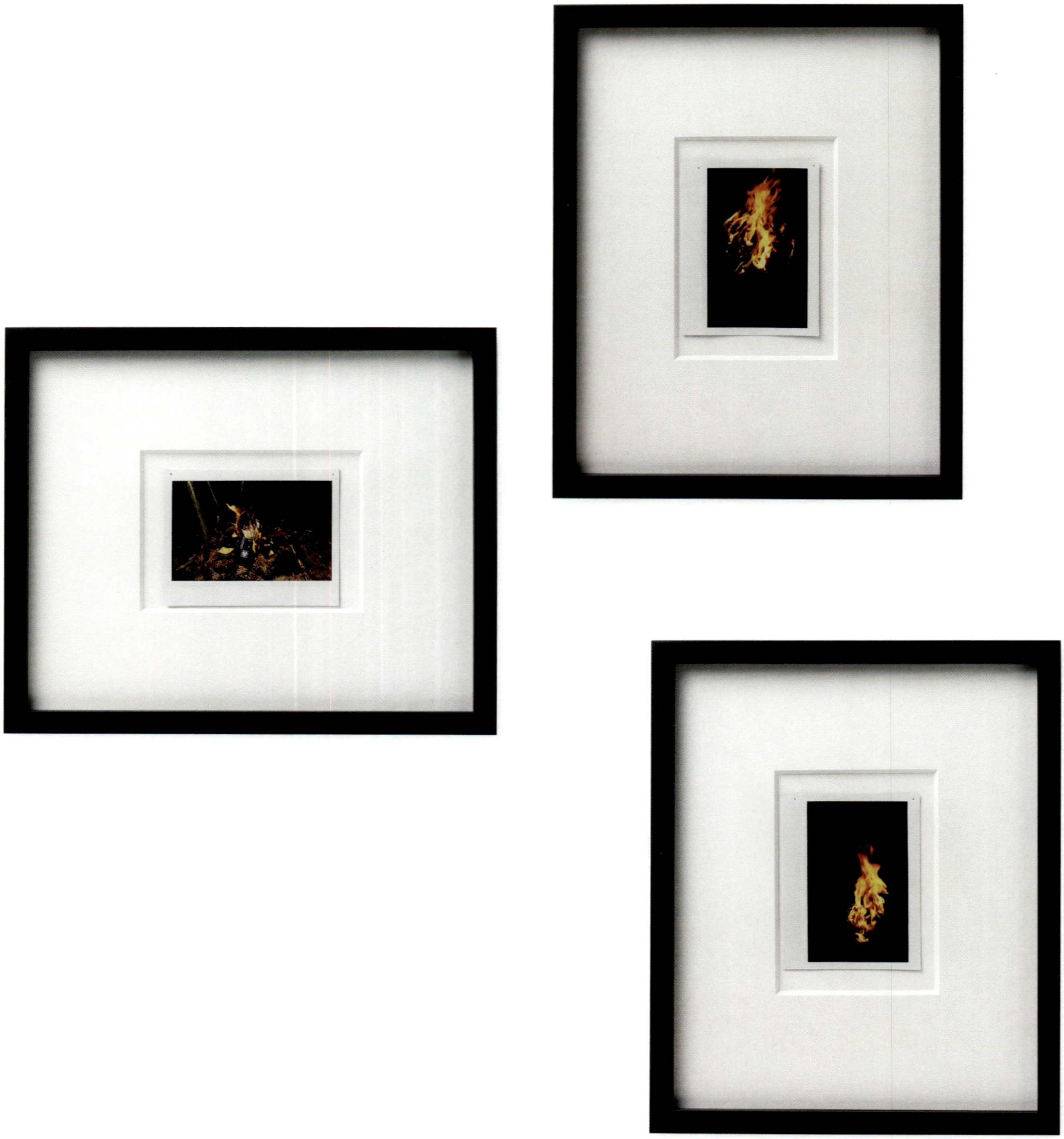

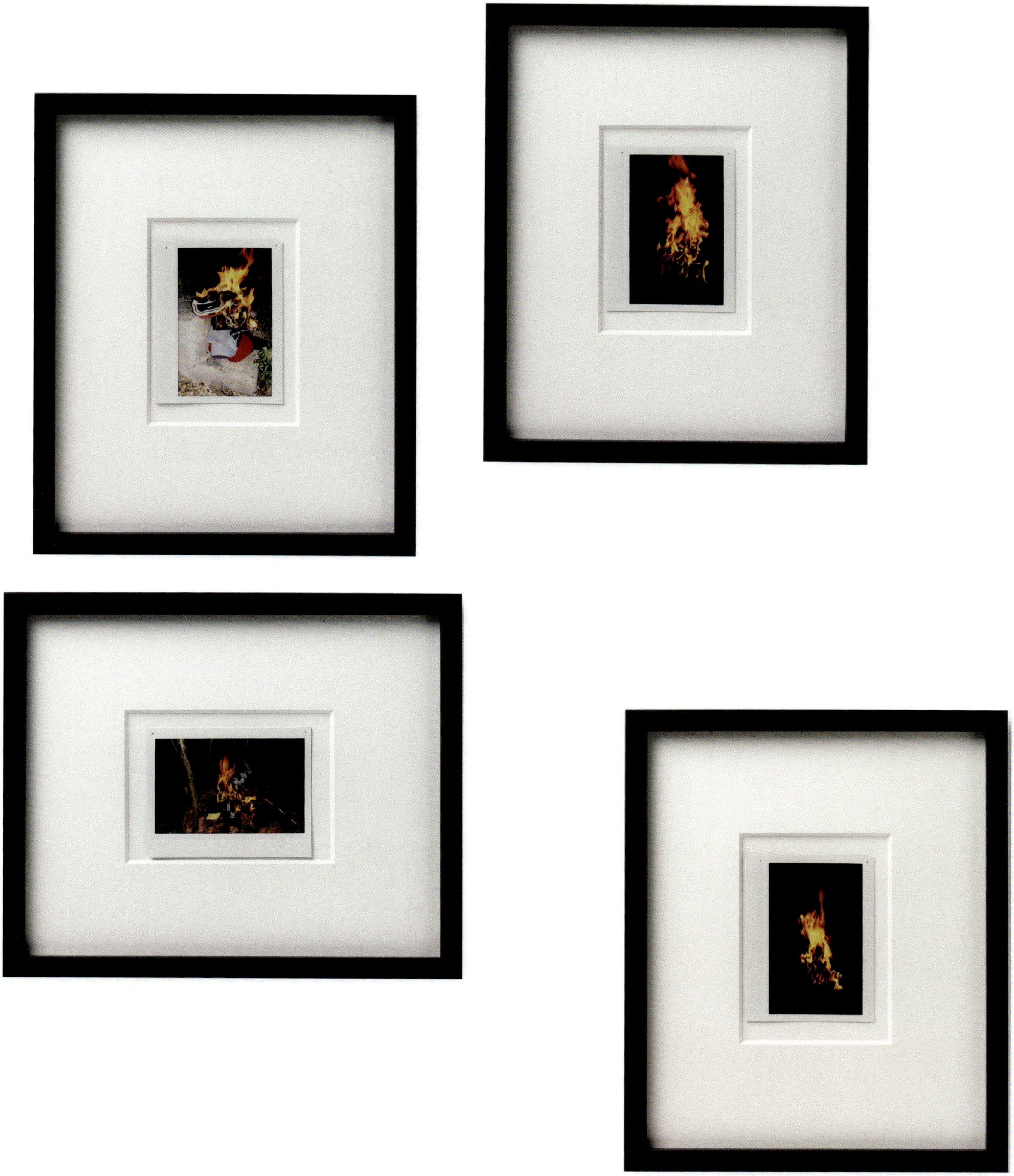

# 18

**Flasher no. 22**
**(Light Levellers)** 1996 –

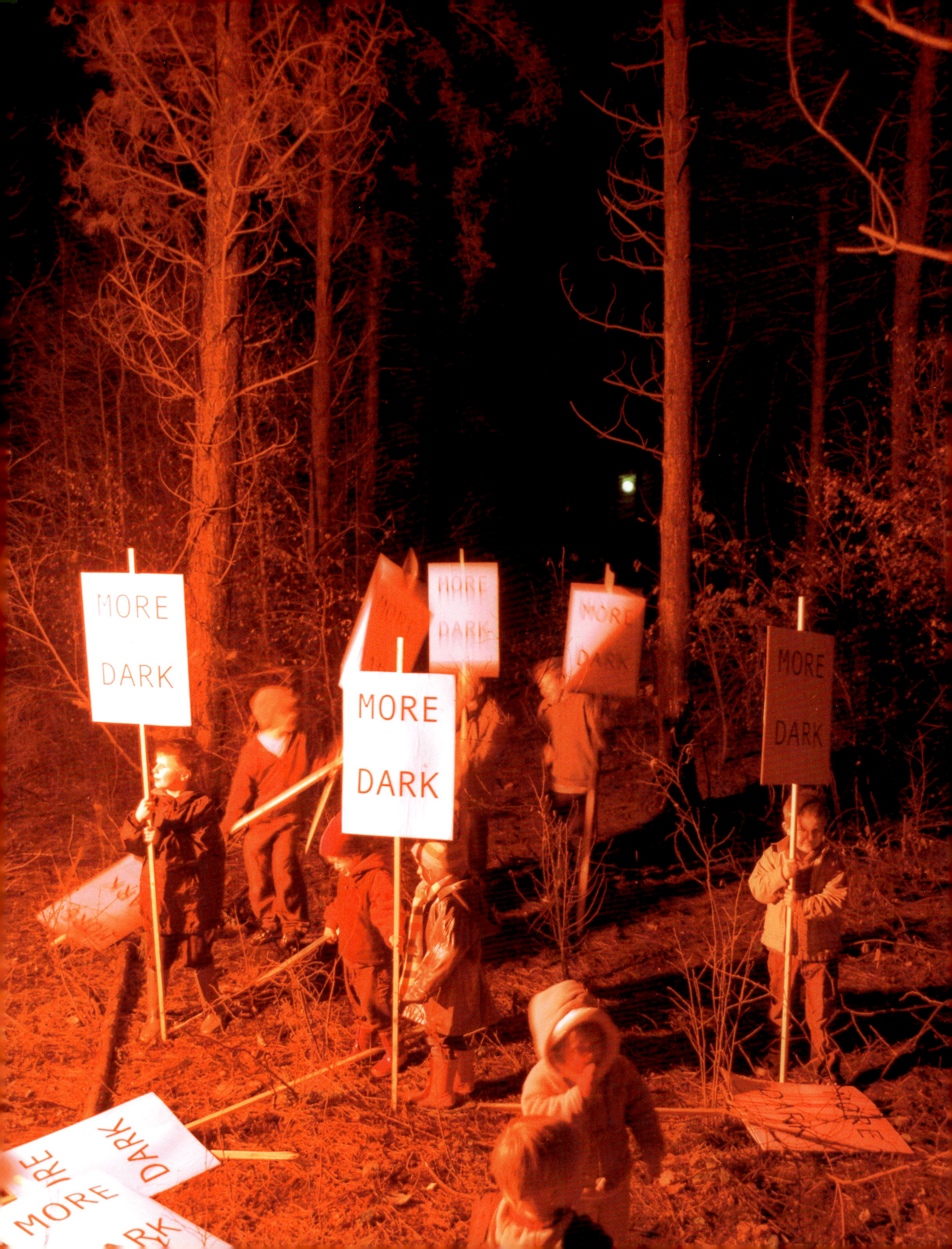
MORE
DARK
MORE
DARK
MORE
DARK
DARK
MORE

# 20

**This is it** 1992

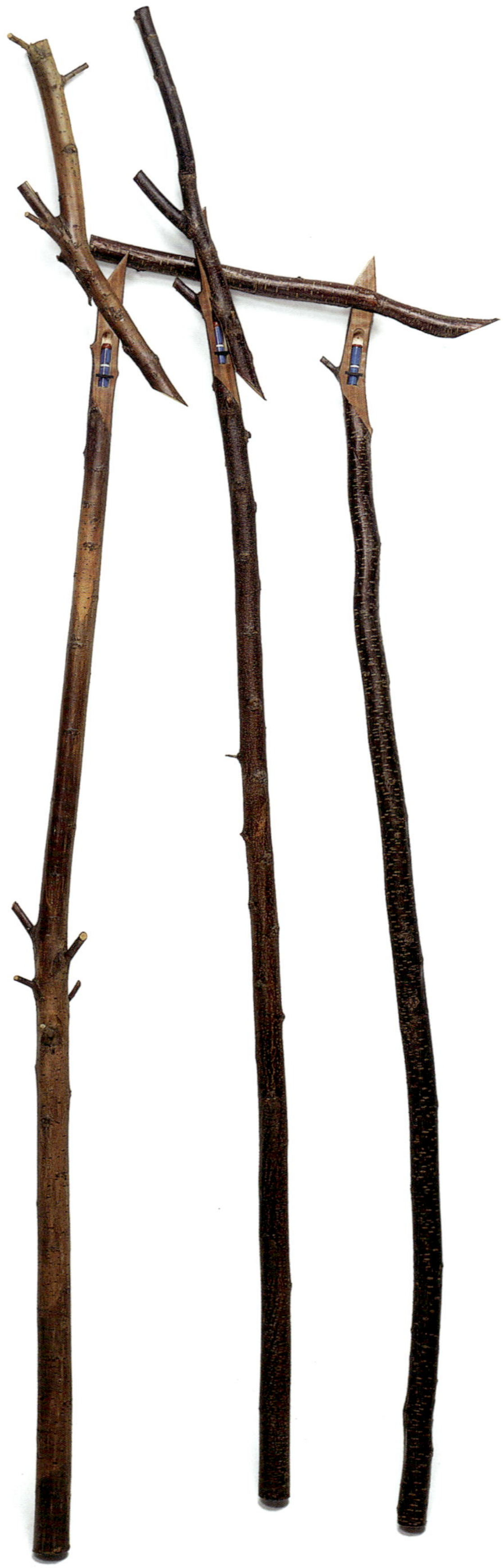

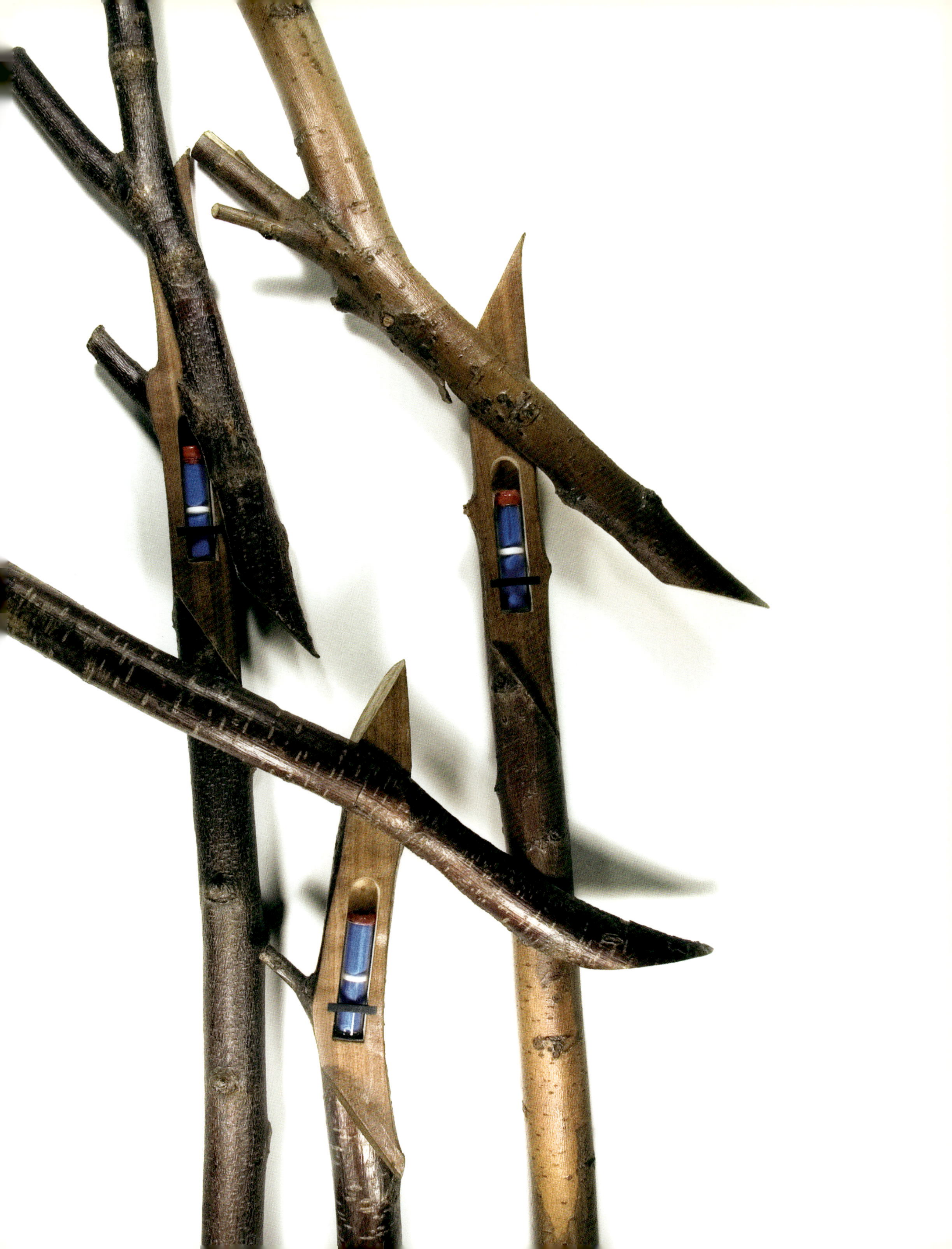

# 22

**Night Shift** 2004

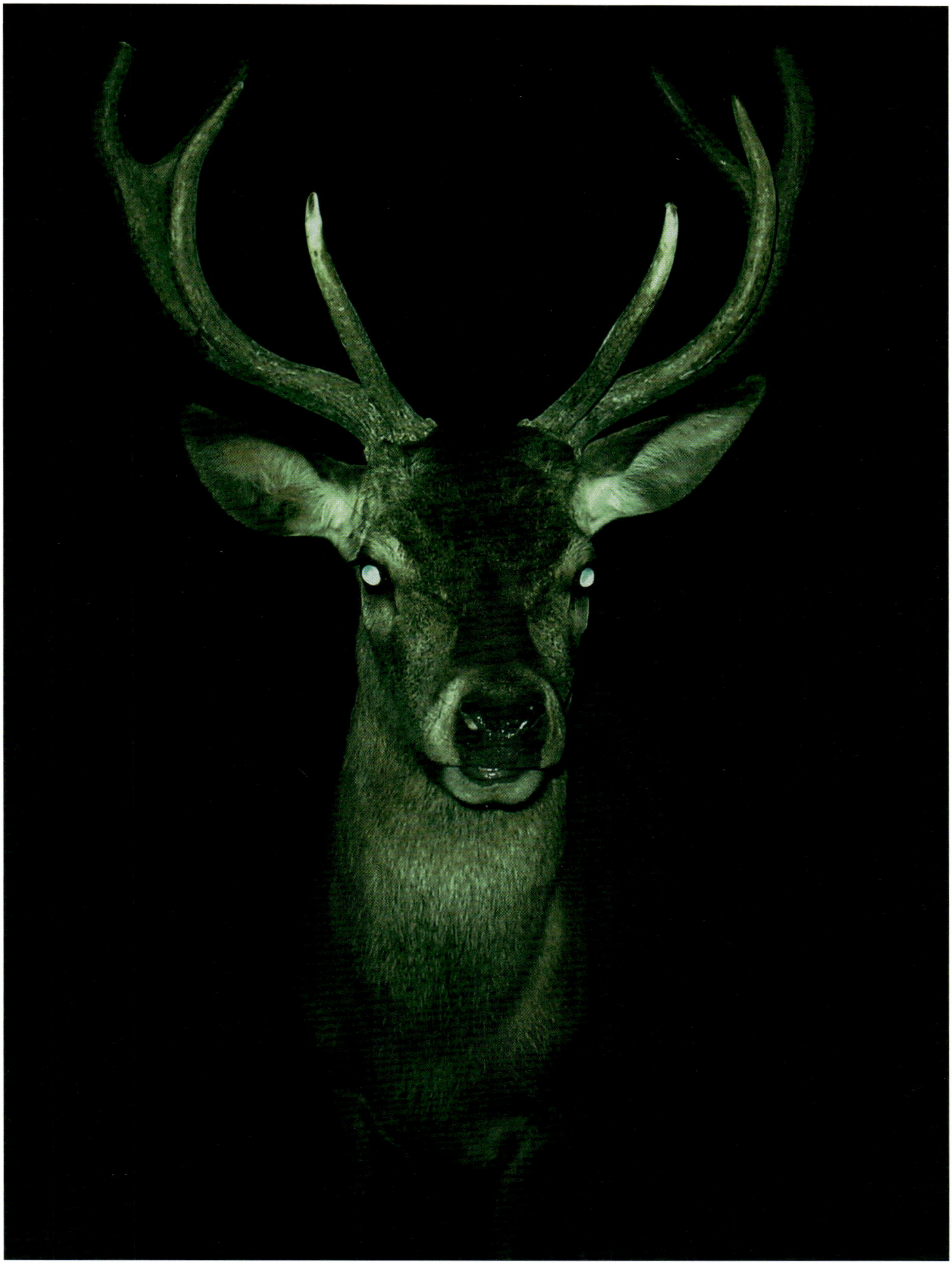

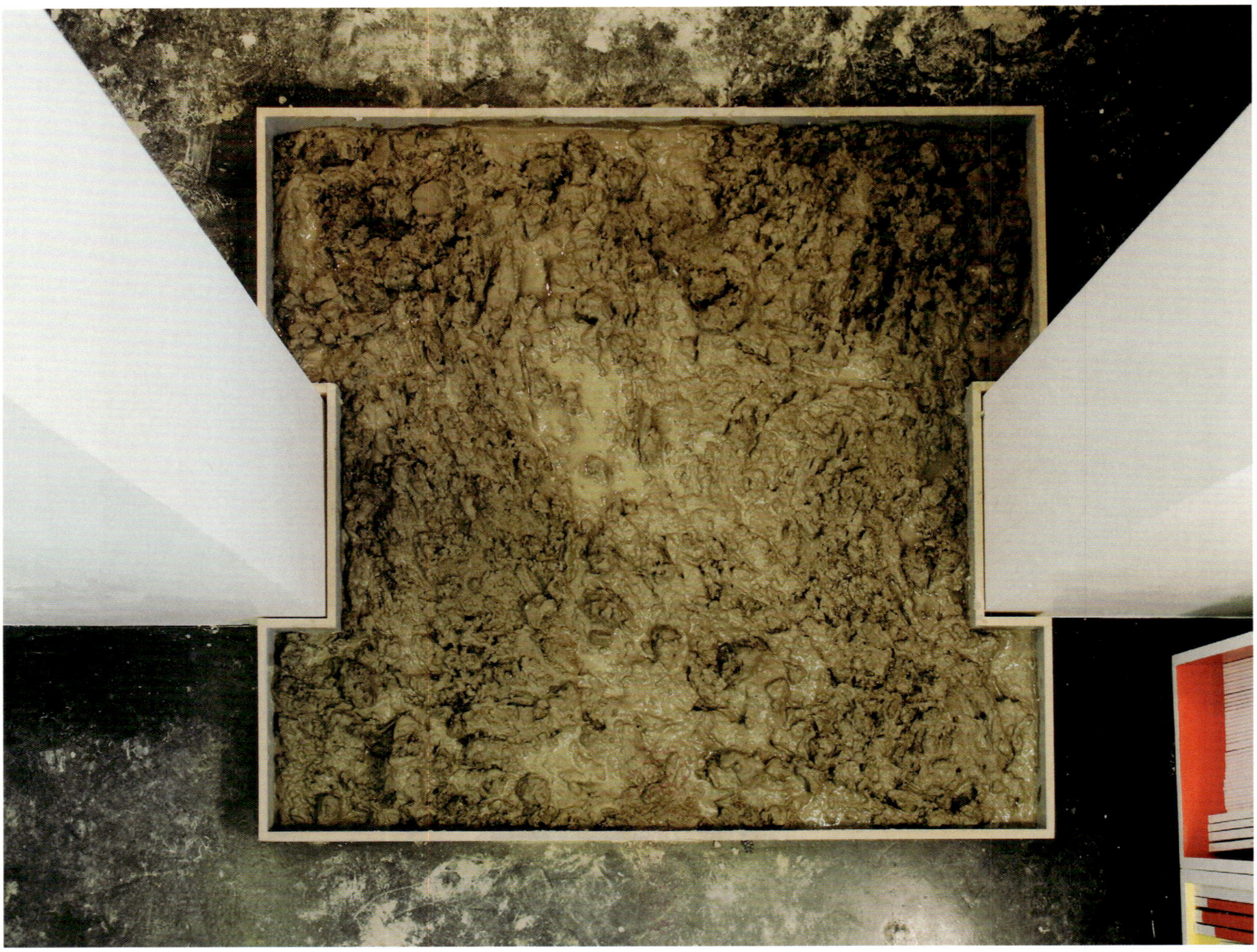

Sowmat 2007

## The Sacred and the Traversal of Social Space

Andrew Wilson

In his 1934 book L'Afrique Fantôme – part ethnographic study and part autobiography – Michel Leiris, in his record of Marcel Griaule's coast-to-coast ethnographic expedition from Dakar to Djibouti, described his observation of a sacrificial offering: 'It is an amorphous mass which, as the four men lift it with great care from its niche, turns out to be a sack of coarse patched canvas, covered with a sort of pitch made of congealed blood, stuffed with what one guesses to be an assortment of dusty things, with a protuberance at one end and a small bell at the other.' This was both an extraordinary object imbued with complex symbolisations and yet fabricated from rather ordinary and mundane materials. Leiris then provides a commentary to the object and its purpose: 'Great religious effusion brought by this simple, dirty object whose abjection is a fantastic force because men have condensed into it their own sense of the absolute, and that they have imprinted their own power in it, as in the little ball of earth a child rolls between his fingers when playing with clay.'[1] The act of a child at play making a ball of earth from clay has the power to project sacred symbolisations, even to form the beginnings of a ritual mask for life.

In his work Adam Chodzko has sought out those areas of everyday life – artifacts, activities and occurrences – that could perhaps offer a means of identifying the feelings and emotions surrounding the construction of such myths that, through an attention to ritual, put a fissure into understandings of what reality might be and mean in a lived sense. The works that have resulted are concerned with negotiation and traversal. They describe movements and meetings where exchanges of sorts are enacted. Such an equation as this builds a symbolic matrix which grounds life both individually, in a personally contained sense, and socially, as a form of exchange that is registered as both a description of, and building block for, communal society. In this respect, myth throws a spotlight on those events and beliefs that variously operate on the public stage of a shared communal identity, in the personal sphere of exchange as a form of magic, and also within a terrain that refuses to give up its secrets. In the modern world myth has been defined as something false – something that you do not even need to prove as false. Further, its falsity is assumed to be self-evident to notions of rational thought that have evolved beyond the need to mediate responses to the natural world through ritual. This loss of myth entails the emasculation and eventual disappearance of collective and communal forms of ritual, and ultimately a breakdown of a truly social fabric. Chodzko's work gives the lie to such a collapse and is affirmative without offering any solutions or answers to anyone. These are works of proposition.

One way of approaching this might be through those structures that contain or otherwise map a negotiation of territory. The fence or barrier marks out land in terms of property and use, restriction and safety; the countryside is formed by a lattice of such structures. Punctuating these fences, walls and hedgerows are paths that mark rights of way to those in pursuit of a supposedly natural experience; they are an indication of free time – of holidays. These paths are well trodden and their domestic nature can be registered by the thoughtful amenity that greets those whose path meets with a wall or fence: the stile. Chodzko's Untitled Stile (Teenage Version) (1992) is a sculpture of a stile. Isolated in the gallery it is without fence or wall, it is devoid of function and divorced from its place in the symbolic order as the crossing point of a boundary separating two areas from each other that can be traversed by a pathway. The stile has been

1 Michel Leiris, L'Afrique Fantôme, Editions Gallimard, Paris, 1981 [first published 1934], p.78. Cited in and translated by Michèle Richman, 'Leiris's L'Age d'homme: Politics and the Sacred in Everyday Ethnography', Yale French Studies no. 81 On Leiris, Yale University Press, London, 1992, pp.91, 92

2 Michel Leiris, 'The Sacred in Everyday Life', in Denis Hollier, ed., The College of Sociology 1937–39, University of Minnesota Press, Minneapolis, 1988, p.24

3 Ibid

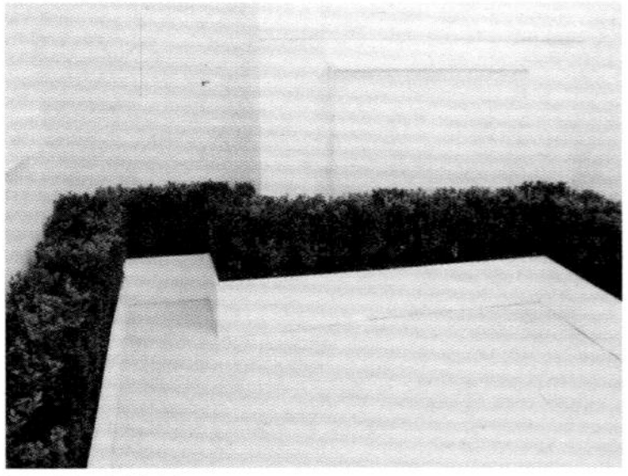

Untitled 1991

carved and then lacquered with turquoise paint. Both carving and lacquer encourage the object to be seen as removed from the realm of the everyday exchange; this is an object we walk around rather than over, its signifying function has shifted. In the countryside a stile is a useful object that provides a structure for acting out the permeability of space. Untitled Stile (Teenage Version) is a hard fetish object; it is also, true to itself, an urban or even properly suburban construct.

Its counterpart, Untitled (1991), is a knee-high box hedge that runs against the walls of the room in which it is installed and across its doorway to form a barricade against entrance which needs to be negotiated and which, once stepped over, provides a dubious sense of protection. Where the stile denotes a passage through the farmed and domesticated nature that exists as a grid of enclosures, the low box hedge is not so much a barrier or marker of property but the basis of an ornamental garden – a place of leisure, contemplation and secret messages – not so much a sacred grove but still a place bearing arcane symbolisations, an expression of interest in science, mathematics, philosophy and belief.

By isolating a stile or hedge Chodzko scrutinises them to the extent that they become other than they were. Such a 'making strange' might be at the heart of Chodzko's work, but it is by no means the whole story. These are both objects that can be recognised as signs of interaction and connection but have had their functionality stripped from them, so that their social meanings – their relevance to leisure and holiday – can be apprehended in a much clearer way. The strategies that Chodzko follows in making his work find echoes in the purpose followed by the Collège de Sociologie during its short history between 1937 and 1939. In its meetings, held in the back room of a Paris bookshop, members – among them Georges Bataille, Roger Callois, Pierre Klossowski, Alexandre Kojève, Michel Leiris, Jean Paulhan and Jean Wahl – proposed a notion of sacred sociology as a way of exploring those phenomena that draw people together in voluntary communal activity.

I am not thinking here so much of the convulsive, excessive view of festival for which Bataille argued, but rather of a sacred sociology that was more clearly described by Leiris. In 1938, at a session of the Collège, he asked 'What, for me, is the sacred? To be more exact: what does my sacred consist of? What objects, places, or occasions awake in me that mixture of fear and attachment, that ambiguous attitude caused by the approach of something simultaneously attractive and dangerous, prestigious and outcast – that combination of respect, desire and terror that we take as the psychological sign of the sacred?'[2] He proposed that this was a matter of 'searching through some of the humblest things, taken from everyday life and located outside of what today makes up the officially sacred (religion, fatherland, morals). It is the little things that are required to discover what features would allow me to characterise the nature of what is sacred for me, and help establish exactly the point at which I know I am no longer moving on the level of the ordinary (trivial or serious, pleasant or painful) but rather have entered a radically distinct world, as different from the profane world as water.'[3]

Chodzko's exhibition at Tate St Ives, Proxigean Tide, evokes a state where those 'little things' – objects as much as narrated events and staged situations – have been arranged by an extreme proxigean tide. This tide sets off an uncontrolled intervention into the creation of meaning found in the matrix provided by these things. It is the result of an exceptional event – such tides occur every 20 to 30 years – but it also arises from a structure that is regular and measured. The tides, like the seasons, form the basis of myth and belief structures. The architecture of the building becomes a memory theatre (where aspects of the building act as prompts for its inhabitants or guides) and the projection of a sun temple's sacrificial altar. The recovery of a notion of sacrifice as enacting a form of exchange or gift was an important aspect of the Collège's wish to identify the sacred elements of contemporary society and especially when seen at the heart of 'festival' (as was registered by Leiris's experience in Africa). Where a magazine artwork produced by Chodzko for Tate Etc. magazine maps out the architecture of Tate St Ives in just this way, Test Tone for Landscape (2005) provides a way of negotiating these spaces using the harmonies produced by five domestic ambient sounds while moving across the gallery's Loggia threshold. The sounds emanate from five different locations in the Loggia and so the frequencies and harmonies change with the movement through the building – closer to one sound, further away from another. Not all tones can be heard at once as they each play for no more than a minute and at differing intervals. This is one of an evolving grouping of works designated as existing under the umbrella of Design for a Carnival, and proclaim not just the importance that such, often celebratory, events have in knitting together communities, but also that these events draw their strength and relevance from their basis in the everyday. These ambient sounds of home are placed here as a way of negotiating public social space. It is an offer to each visitor stepping through the gallery's threshold to make themselves at home within this act.

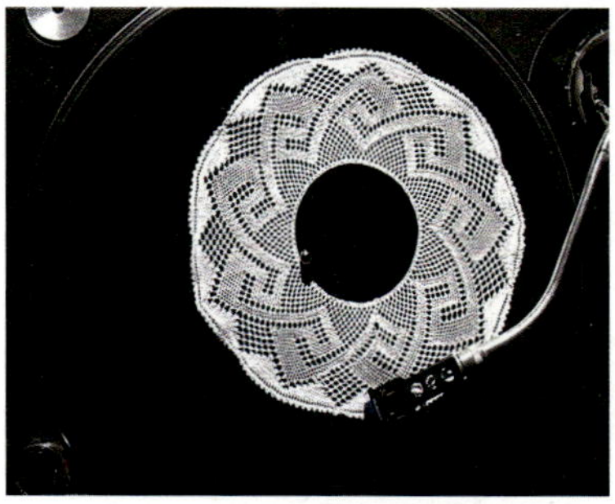

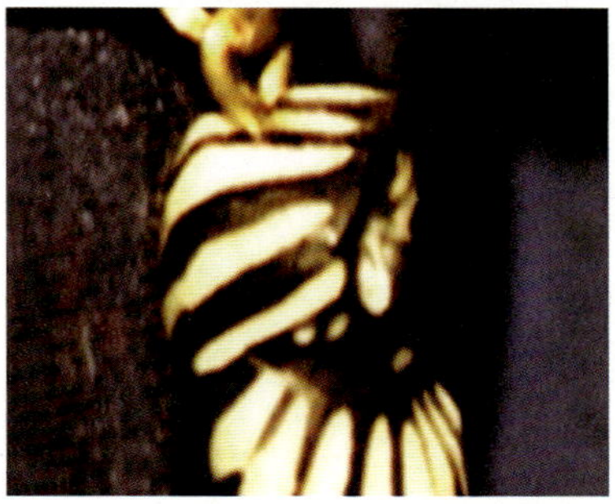

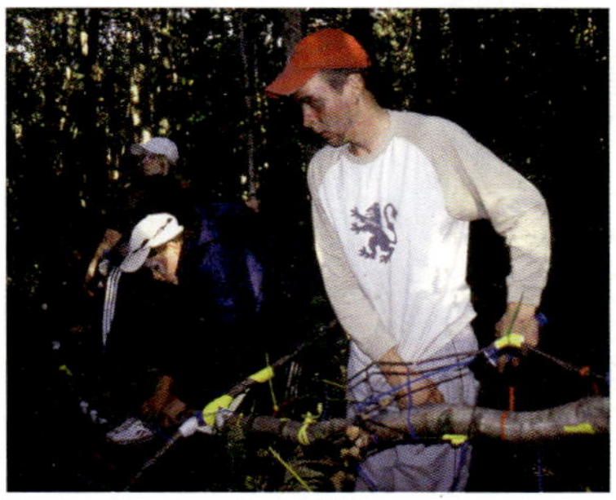

Design for a Carnival 2003

On entering the gallery, the visitor passes a permanently installed large stained-glass window by Patrick Heron. This space will, for the duration of Chodzko's exhibition, also hold Borrowed Cold Lodge (2008). This work is made up of a large number of cold weather clothing items that Chodzko has sourced from the local community and, like Test Tone for Landscape, provides a threshold for visitors to pass over, from one world to another. One aspect of the gift here is to see a gallery space as a storeroom, filtering the way in which the gallery might be experienced. This exists as another type of proposition. The element of masquerade also presents itself here in the ordering of cold weather clothes during the summer holiday season and by the speculative way in which the window provides a key for this ordering (a key that is not immediately obvious and demands negotiation). The mall space, housing the stained-glass window, is a depository for the clothes that make up the work, itemised by Chodzko as: '27 items of cold weather protective outer clothing for water use, 37 items of cold weather protective outer clothing for walking, 27 items of cold weather protective outer clothing for subterranean use, 27 winter stable rugs, 17 items of cold weather protective outer clothing for building use, 97 winter coats from primary school children, 27 items of cold weather protective outer clothing for field use and 27 items of cold weather protective outer clothing for snow use'. However, this organising 'map' that the stained glass window provides for the work, perhaps only functions in a poetic sense as another level of masquerade – as an analogy to the ways in which Heron himself playfully suggested that the landscape of West Penwith could be perceived in his abstract paintings: 'that the enormously powerful rhythmic energies of the granite outcrops beneath my feet transmit certain rhythms straight up through the soles of my shoes every day.'[4]

4 Patrick Heron, The Colour of Colour, University of Texas at Austin, 1979, p.26

5 Adam Chodzko, 2002, www.foundationforcontemporaryarts.org/grant_recipients/adamchodzko.html

These three works – Memory Theatre (2008), Test Tone for Landscape and Borrowed Cold Lodge – each provide a pointer towards themes that the exhibition unfolds: how history and narrative can be unlocked or prompted by almost any object; how changes to the specific character of spaces affects the way we negotiate our passage through them, while sound can also function to guide as well as disorientate, and that such a function is as much symbolic as actual; and that through the transaction of a gift or potlatch, social relations can be realised and that such gifts are therefore viewed to have symbolic power. Whether we realise it or not, ritual of one kind or another can be identified as governing most aspects of the way we lead our lives. There are those things that we do habitually, that describe certain routines, and then there are those other acts connecting that personal routine with a communal purpose. Certainly, the reasons why Chodzko isolates objects, phenomena and attitudes suggest possible ways in which society can be remade in fully social ways; as a statement he made in 2002 makes clear: 'If you look at anything too hard it begins to disintegrate, dissolving to the point where everything can be linked yet nothing is stable. I make art to explore this experience of perception (which feels like it hovers between joy and fear). The gallery installations (from video to drawings) are a series of propositions as to how our culture might be – how else might we coincide and communicate? What else might we value? – if reality shifted in the way it feels that it might, at any minute.'[5]

Chodzko made this statement at a time when the emphases within his work were already starting to shift and change. Although his work has always manifested itself in different ways, the core idea that ran through it was the intention to inhabit a social arena – a message board, a contact magazine, for instance. Within these spaces a barely noticed disturbance would be created from which a process might unfold, more often than not resulting in the enaction of a meeting, reunion or convention that wouldn't otherwise have happened and also might suggest a new basis for social relations – both actually and metaphorically. The extent to which these meetings might be more or less choreographed or even fictional did nothing to lessen their thrust. Posters such as those for the series Meeting (1999) might not have led to a meeting but their regard for displacement of meaning (and other forms of displacement) and temporal ephemerality (the flickering fire, the elisions of speech taking place at a time and place that, when specified, is impossible or incongruous; just 'Here / Everyone Welcome' – hence the potency of the idea of meeting rather than the meeting itself) was to take on increasing importance in his work. Other potential meetings, or at least exchanges, such as those for the Transmitters (1990-) series where Chodzko placed advertisements in Loot magazine for items offered or wanted, such as within the section Scientific Equipment in 1993, the offer for sale of 'Millenarian heterogenous apparition, 3 metres, unstructured model, reasonable condition, £75 ono', or in 1992 the notice for a 'Look-alike contest, artist seeks people who think they look like God, for interesting project'. The apparition took its place between an unused 12-volt invertor and a Tecktronix oscilloscope and most likely remained unsold. The notice for the look-alike contest did however result in an exchange and a coming together. The wording of Chodzko's notice is as matter-of-fact as the responses. He is not documenting delusion but belief, self-will and the understanding that a cohesive society relies on manifestations of the sacred – whether religious or not (and in this respect the god, as the project underlines, can be any sort of god).

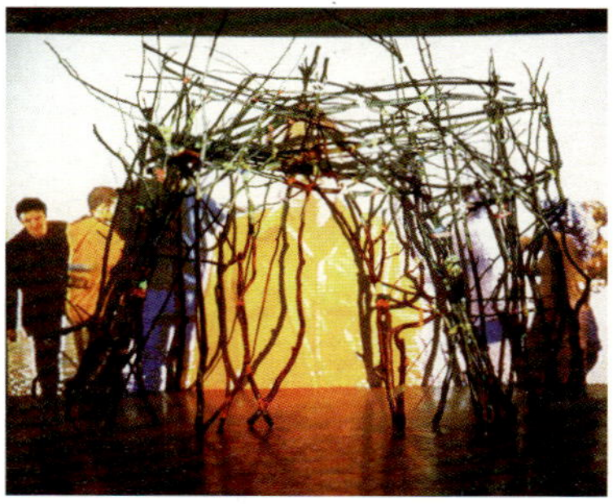
Recall: Strange Child 1997

For another project, under the banner 'Recall' (a term usually used for the recovery of faulty and defective, perhaps even dangerous, goods), Chodzko asked 'Were you a strange child? All people who were strange children are invited together to make a beautiful place for ourselves.' The resulting work, Recall: Strange Child (1997), was a film showing the meeting of these now grown-up, one-time strange children, relating their various individual strangenesses while, together, making a rudimentary hide structure from branches and tape. For Leiris, the world of the child was one arena of experience where everyday objects were positively imbued with the beginnings of an organisation of life according to sacred mythologies – the shelter or hide (a special and safe place) being part of this. He describes his memories of the bathroom as just such a place, free from the conventions in force elsewhere and offering a contrast to those attributes of power surrounding the father figure: 'the bathroom can be looked at as a cavern, a cave where one comes to be inspired by contacting the deepest, darkest subterranean powers. There, opposite the right-hand sacred of parental majesty, the sinister magic of a left-hand sacred took place.'[6]

Given Chodzko's attention to those areas of life that might otherwise go unremarked or remain unregarded, or even forgotten, and also given his weaving of narrative into these areas (symbolic, whether actual and real or fictional and constructed), it is telling that he organised a reunion of extras from Ken Russell's film The Devils (From Beyond, [1996]) as well as reunions of those children who appeared in Fellini's City of Women (The Return from The City of Women, [1996]) and in Pier Paolo Pasolini's Salò (Reunion: Salò, [1998]). This latter film had to be choreographed with doubles as only one adolescent from the film took part in the reunion (and even that one had absented herself from the final death scene). Chodzko had also, in a similar vein, recorded sequences over the trailers of rented film videos that were then returned, altered, to the video shop (Flasher, [1996-]) from where they could then be rented by unsuspecting customers. The results of such works displace reality whereby you think that you are watching something only to find you are watching something quite different. In the case of the Flasher series you finish watching a movie only to watch footage of a flare being let off in a wasteland setting, the disjunction between the two films – that rented and that unexpected and unlooked for – in effect forming the gift exchange. The gift, or spell that is cast here, is not just the Flasher film but the passage between the two films: one that has been given and one that has been rented; and yet the gift has then to be returned to the video rental store for others to receive. With the reunions of film extras, the marginalised inhabit and drive the narrative. It is just this inversion – what Mikhail Bakhtin, the philosopher of the carnivalesque, termed 'turn-about' – against a backdrop of play that is at the heart of shifts that were occurring within Chodzko's work.

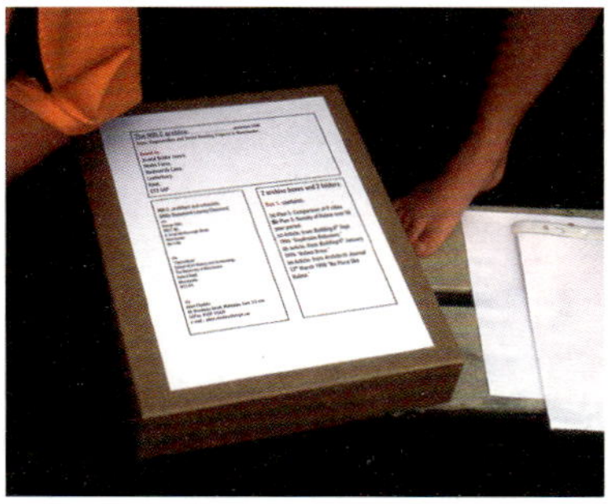
The Gorgies Centre 2002

A similar interruption to that enacted through Flasher where different codes and conventions are 'turned-about' is carried through in narratives of archival displacement told through two slide-projection works Cell-a (2002), that documents how the archive of the London art gallery Cubitt was given to a group of Kurdish asylum seekers for safe keeping, and The Gorgies Centre (2002), documenting the transfer of the archive of a Manchester architectural practice specialising in social housing to a group of gypsies in Kent who were being forced off their land by local property developers – the gypsies both storing the archive and making it available to researchers. In both

6 Michel Leiris, 1988, op. cit. p.26

# 30

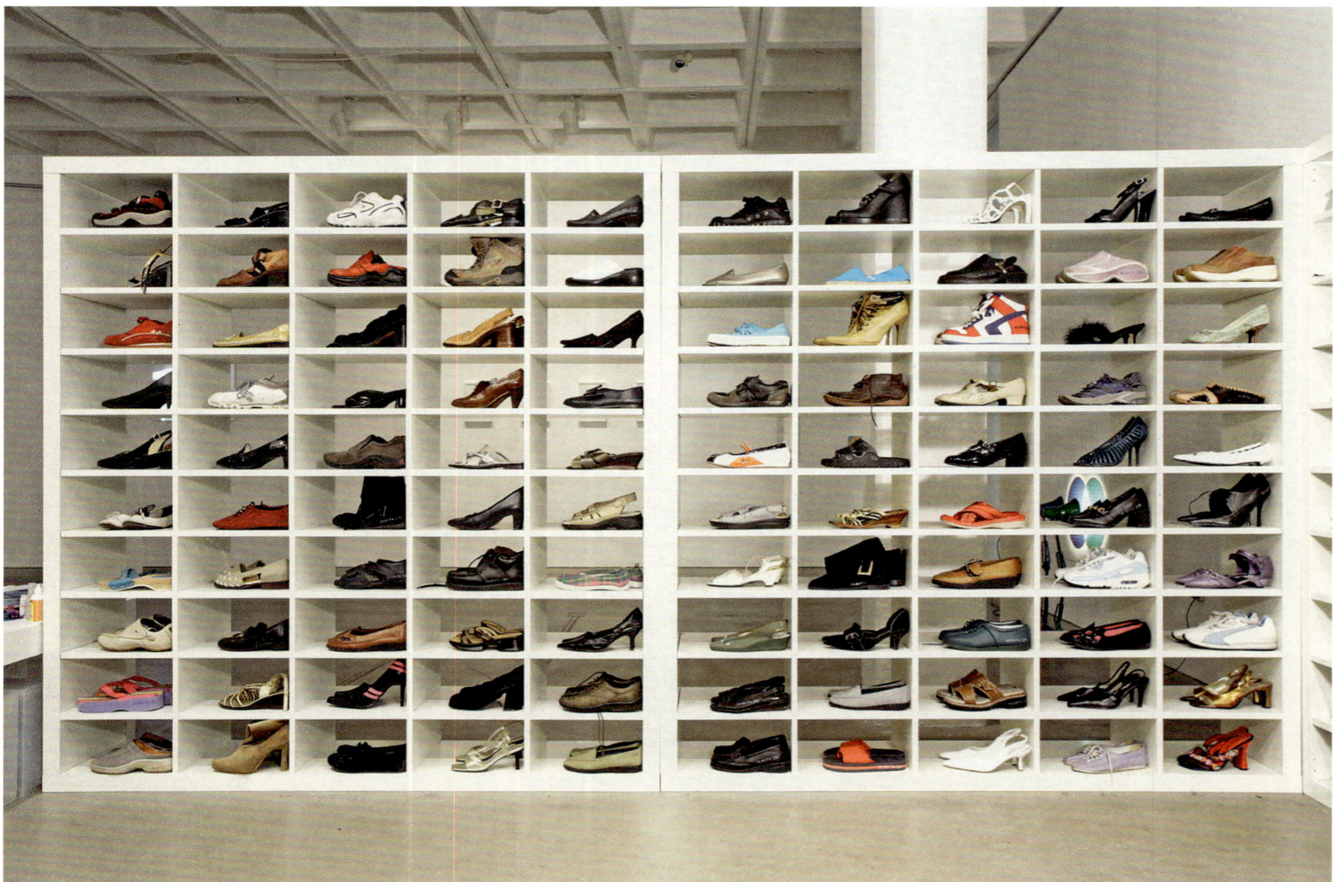

M-path 2006

works the initial gift of the archive entails a function or activity that would ordinarily seem unexpected given the recipients' cultural marginality within society. It is also a ritual and symbolically laden handing over of a sense of history and identity. The stark conjunction of different social groupings between whom ordinarily no contact would exist serves to underline the basic social need for culture and shelter. To whatever extent these two situations might be fabricated does not lessen their significance. In a more playful sense the need for safety and warmth through clothing is one strand underlying the function of a gift culture highlighted by Borrowed Cold Lodge and that was first signalled by successive versions of M-path (2006) and the earlier slide projection piece White Magic (2005).

White Magic exists as a kind of spell that is cast and spread using the most mundane and yet useful of materials: clothes from charity shops. Going to a local charity shop near where Chodzko lives in Kent, he bought up all the clothes in the store that were coloured green. These clothes were then taken by him to Brooklyn and donated to a thrift store there, and at that store he bought all the clothes that were coloured red. He then took these red clothes back to Kent and donated them to the same charity shop he had bought all the green clothes from. Over time these clothes disperse in a manner uncontrolled by the artist beyond the introduction of those clothes to the two shops. The spell's effect is this movement and transformation of coloured clothes (not unlike the blue dye released into water near the end of Around (2006), a film about the discovery and dissemination of an archive). The clothes suggest a kind of uniform for an unstated event that is unwittingly enacted by the purchasers of the green and red garments who unknowingly form a community, however dispersed.

It is in these respects – dispersal, transformative gift, costume, masquerade, play and spell – that this work forms one part of an evolving series Design for a Carnival. The series is made up of films, slide projections and objects. Its subjects are largely ordinary but have the capacity, the promise, to deliver something extraordinary. The series was introduced by Plan for a Spell (2001) a film with no beginning, no middle and no ending; a film that randomly shuffles sequences of images of vernacular expressions of cultural events/local festivals with text, so that the work is different at each viewing. The subtitled text seems to describe what we are looking at – 'This motion is really good' – only to ask questions of it – 'Is it too chaotic' – only to suggest that things are stable – 'So, I can see there must be ... something special about this too' – or maybe it does it another way (it does). It also describes the purpose of the film in providing a spell (or at least its plan) and how this might occur. For a brief moment, notations in red – a star map perhaps or a school physics exercise (or neither) – flashes up to overlay the footage of a street scene. Is this part of the plan? The film continues and continues. There are of course repetitions, rewindings and fast forwardings (at least that is what they seem like) – but never in the same order.

This is not a spell though but a plan for one; there is no carnival, only a multifaceted design for one. The transformations and displacements that Chodzko weaves – movement, chaos, disorder, fluidity, the uncharted – are preparatory, unresolved, contingent and still to be realised. They are not, however, rehearsals but propositions. The carnival is taking place, the spell is being cast and the movement is going somewhere. Why? Because we already see things differently in that the accepted ordering of an understanding of what constitutes society is already being flipped over by these works.

The short film Design for a Carnival (2003) concentrates on three stages or 'houses' that build on ephemeral moments in life: the sight of ants organizing sequins; a lace doily as a form of label for a record (designated as 'lace making for vinyl') and the reconfiguration of a woodland sapling ('tree smash/fix' – shades of Recall: Strange Child). The particular form of festival proposed here is constructed through play, where any certainty of identity or hierarchy, sense or reason, is ignored. The festival exists for spectator and subject as well as for those documenting it through the tangible existence of masks that are both to be looked at and a means of identifying play, and also to be looked through, attached to a camera the mask acts as a filter to create a semi-translucent veil full of incident and colour. Through these filters all participants, whatever their purpose, can fulfill their role within the masquerade. By using these filters, Chodzko has created a number of slide projections documenting the activity surrounding a Guide for a Parade with Two Masks (2004) (taking place at the Isle of Sheppey in Kent and Roosevelt Island in New York); Plan for a Parade with Two Masks (2004) (at Blean in Kent and Sepolia, Athens in Greece); as well as a Pattern for a Procession with Two Masks (2007) (at Whitstable, Kent and Vozdovac, Belgrade). All of this allusion resists definition, as might be expected of true festival, and its excessive ambiguities await decoding.

To return to the beginning, This is it (1992) joins with Untitled and Untitled Stile (Teenage Version) to form a particular matrix concerning a view of the outdoors in the process of being made sacred as preparation for festival. These are three staves cut from saplings and carefully prepared. Each is cut in two and hinged to open and reveal a secret compartment containing a single ecstasy tablet. These are for walking and for experiencing that which cannot be defined or represented (indeed can only be recognised in terms of an inability to be contained by representation): the enormity of the sublime in the world around us. The tablet hidden within each staff symbolically describes the potential for a momentary mask for such an experience, and the fragile promise of yet another turn-about – the commencement of convulsive joy and play. It is, like Leiris's mundane, yet extraordinarily powerful sacrificial object, an invitation to, and declaration of an exchange from which social relations are built.

Andrew Wilson is Curator of Modern and Contemporary British Art at Tate.

# 34

**Mask-Filter** 2004 –

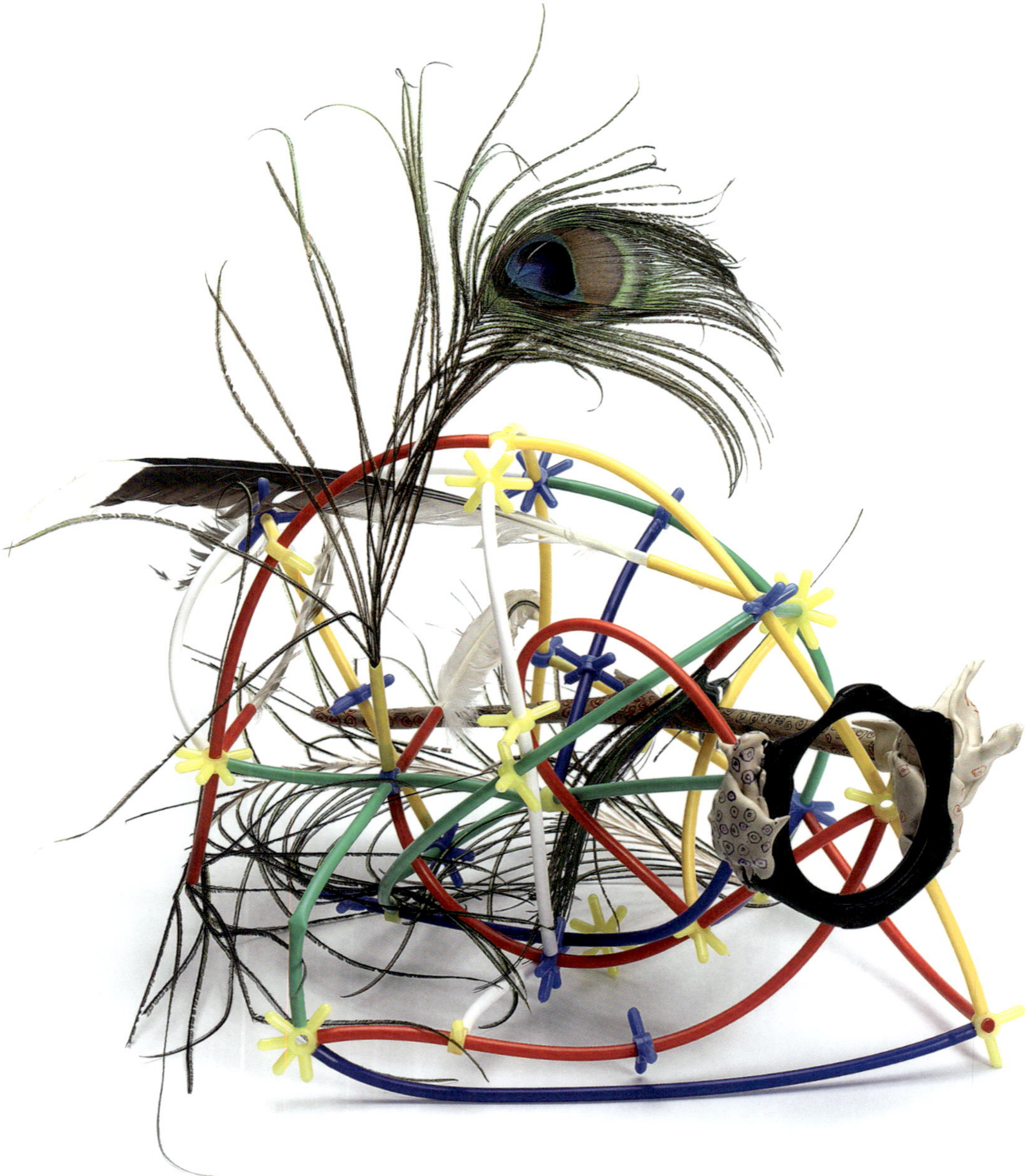

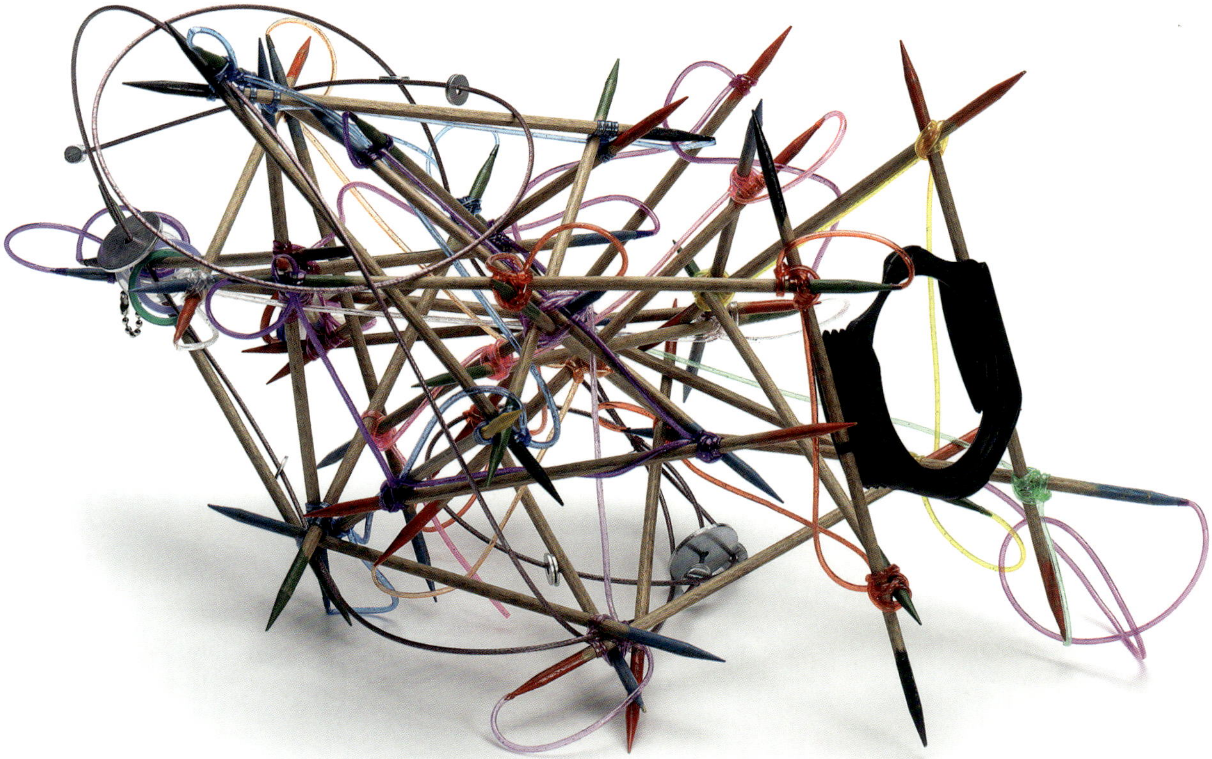

36

**Mask-Filter** 2004 –

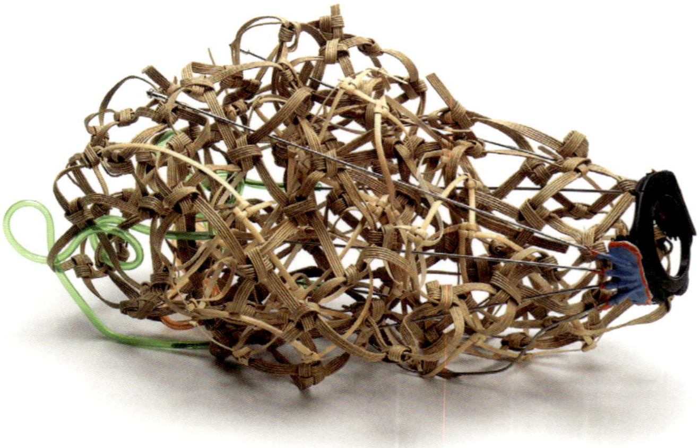

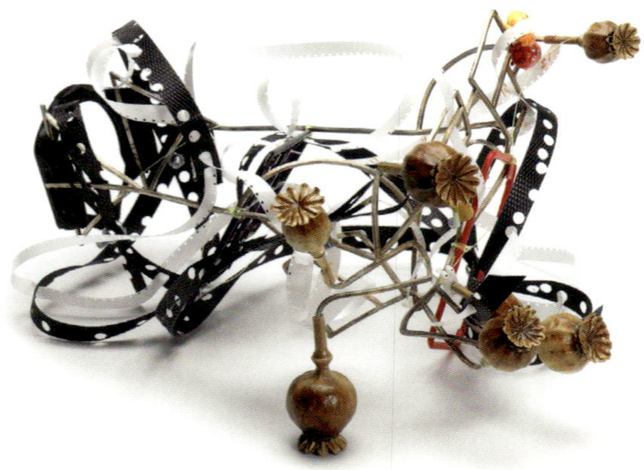

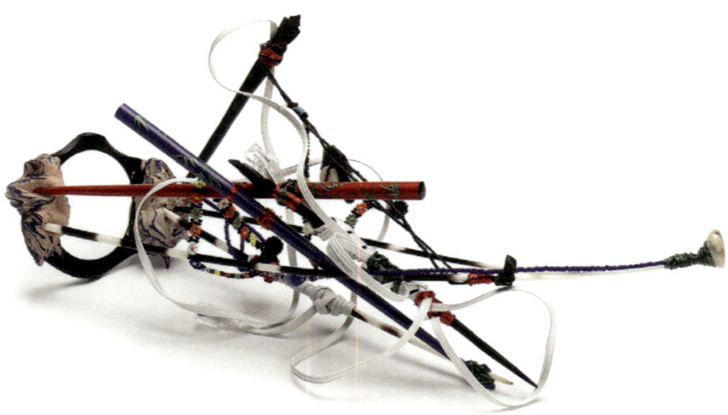

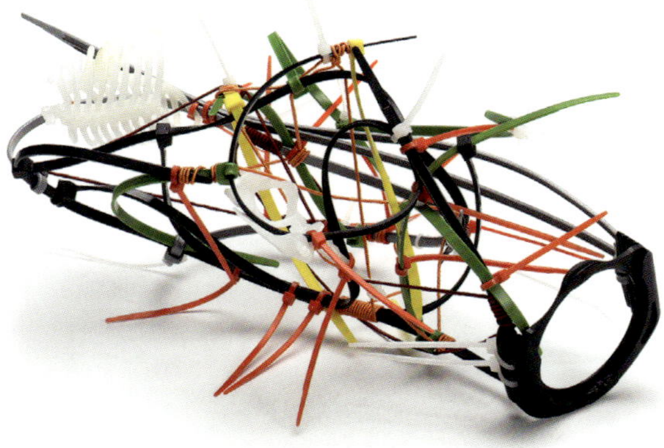

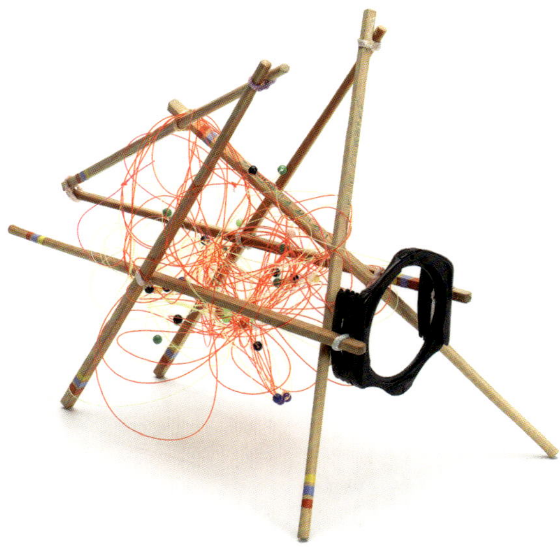

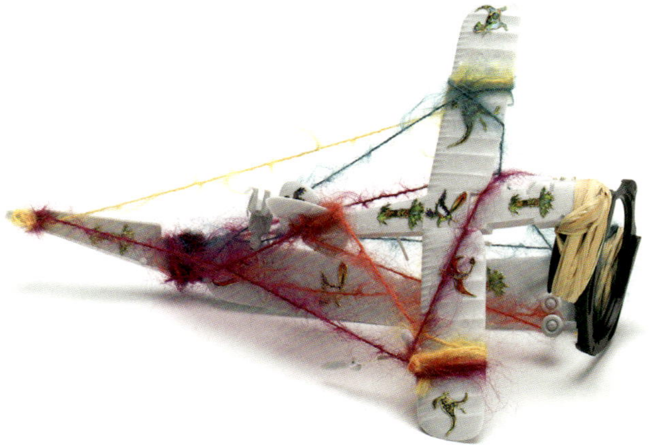

# 38

**Plan for a Parade with Two Masks** 2004

opposite page:
**Guide for a Parade with Two Masks** 2004

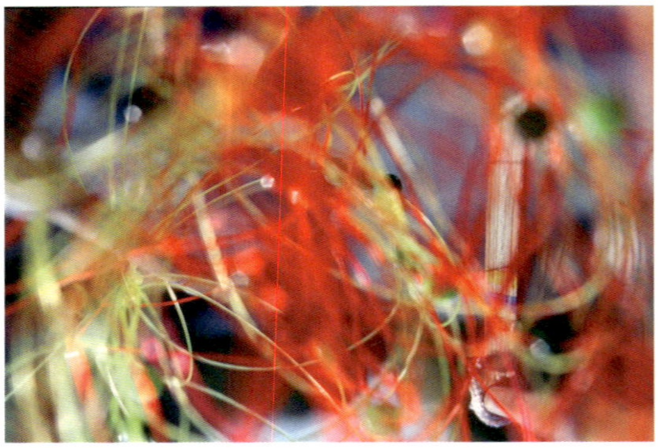

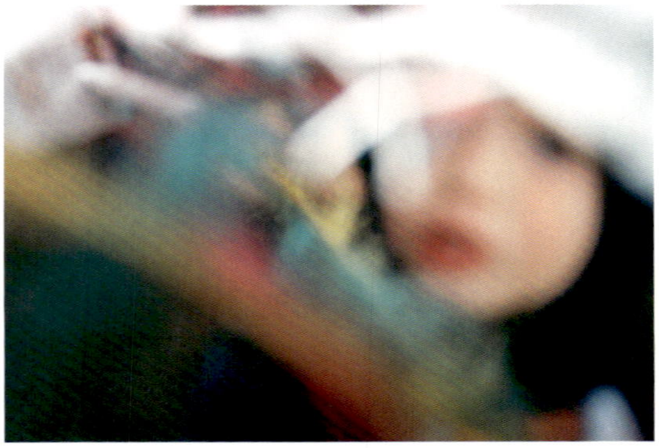

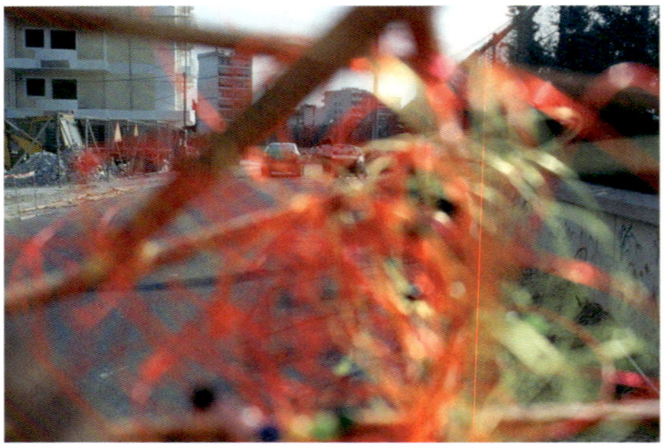

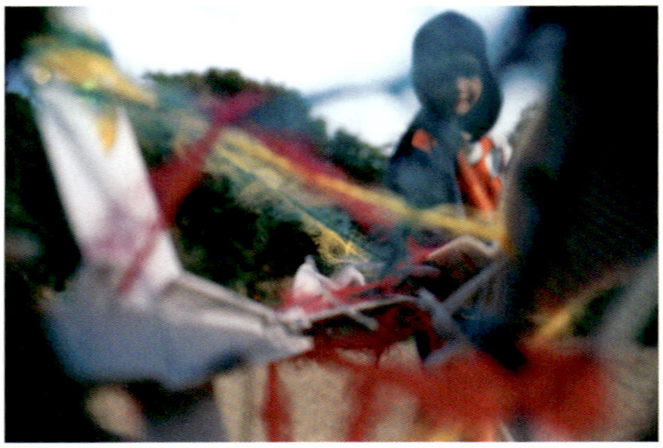

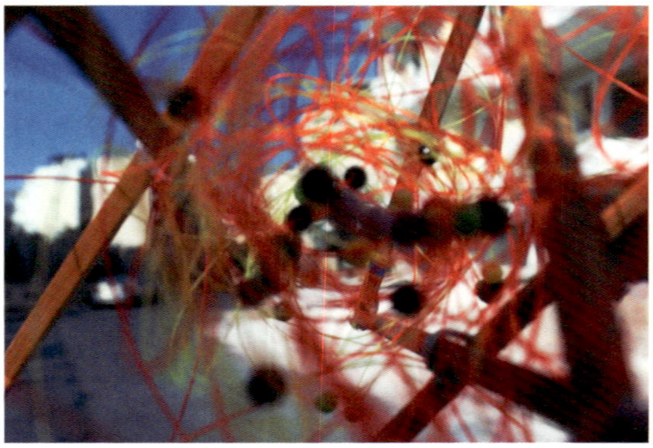

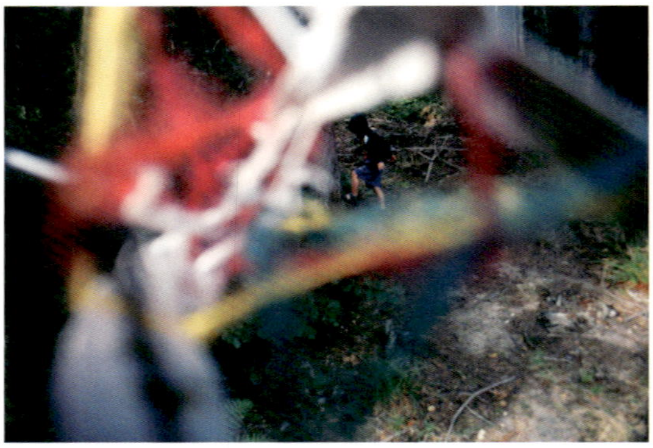

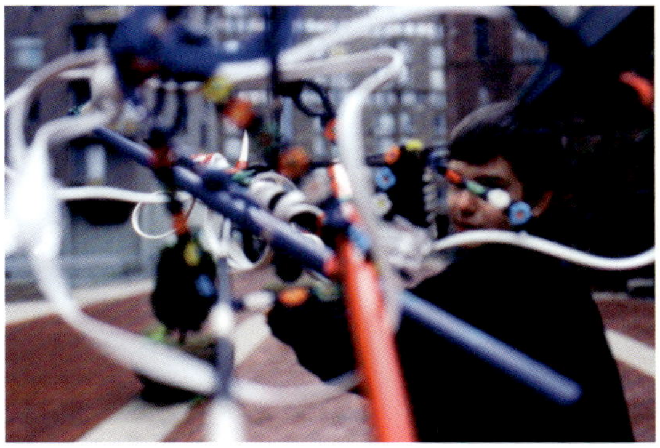

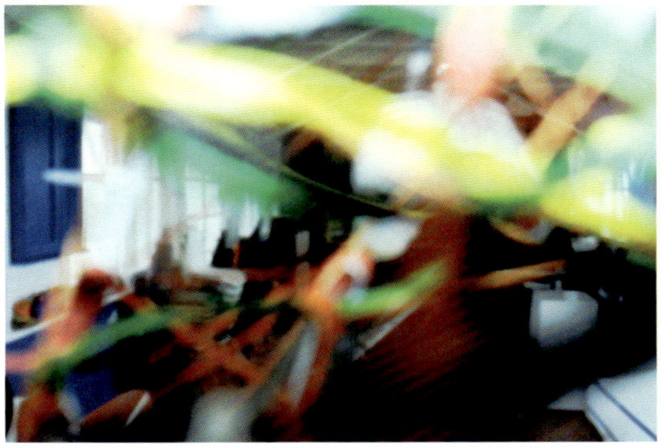

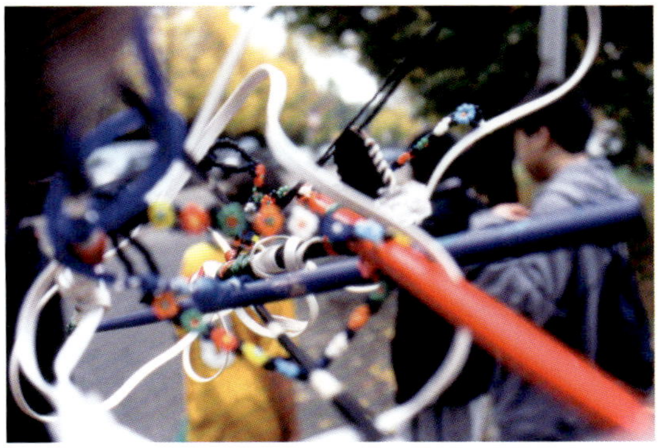

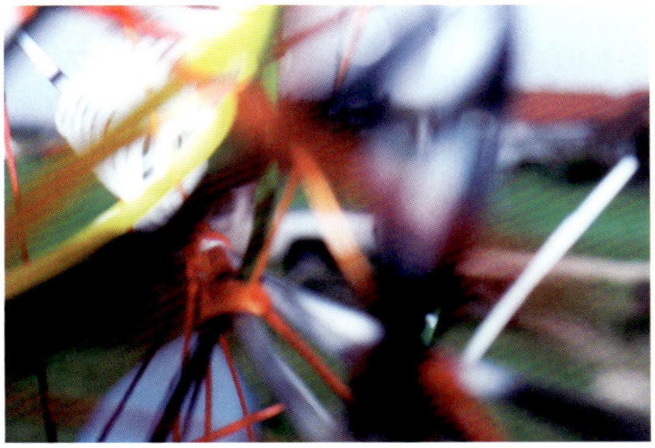

# 40

**Pattern for a Procession with Two Masks** 2007

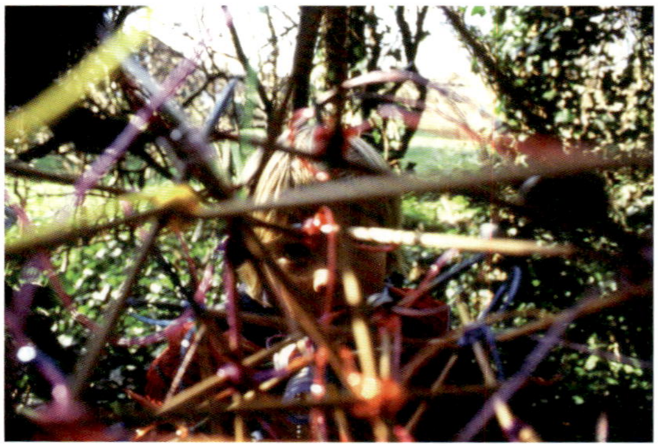

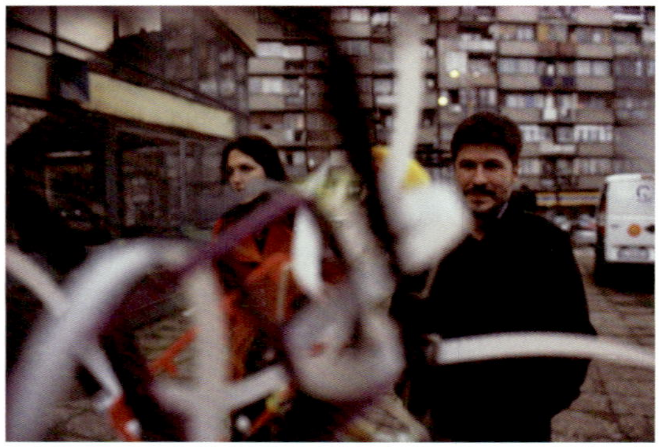

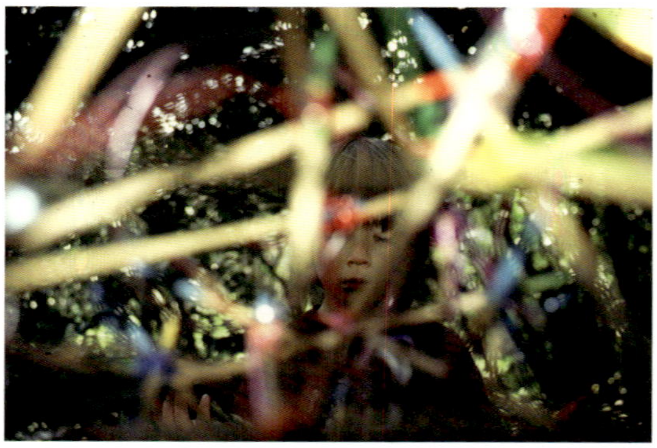

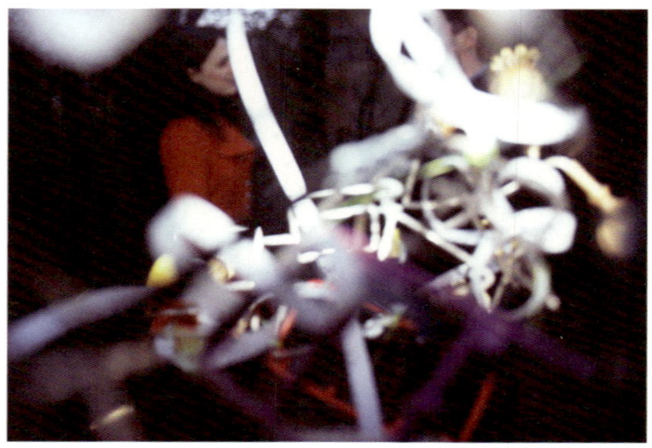

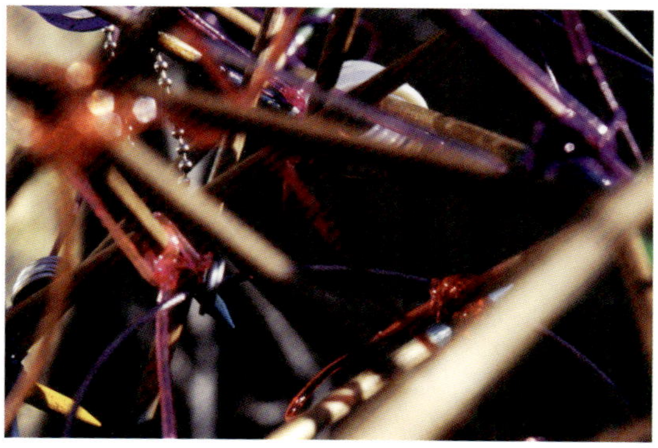
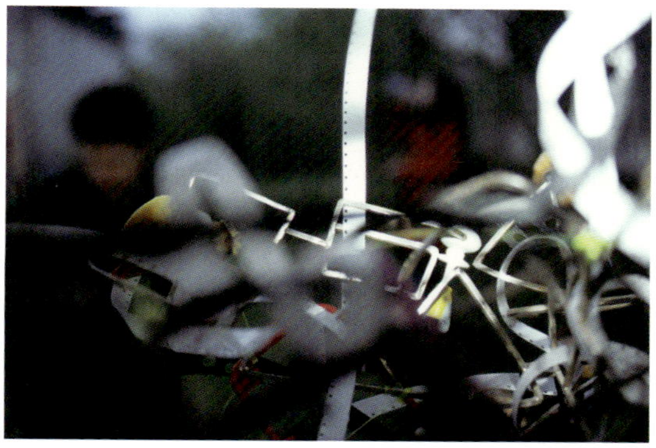
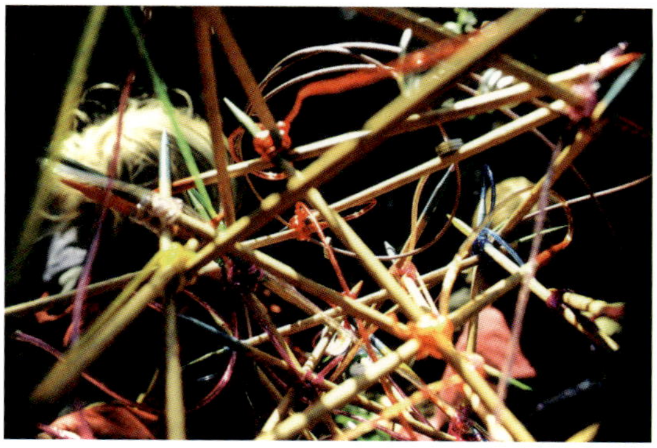
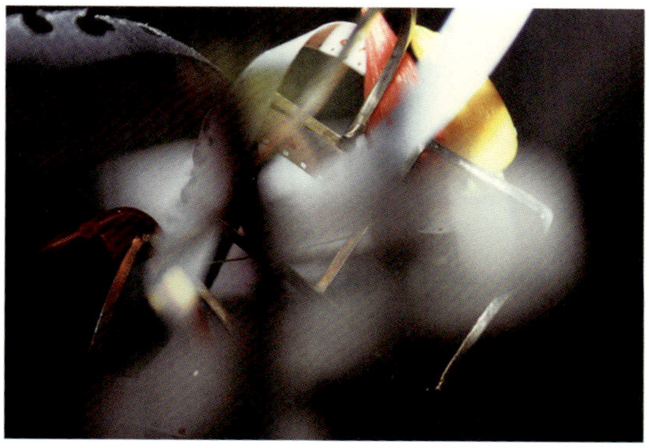

# 42

**Cleaner (a story)** 1999

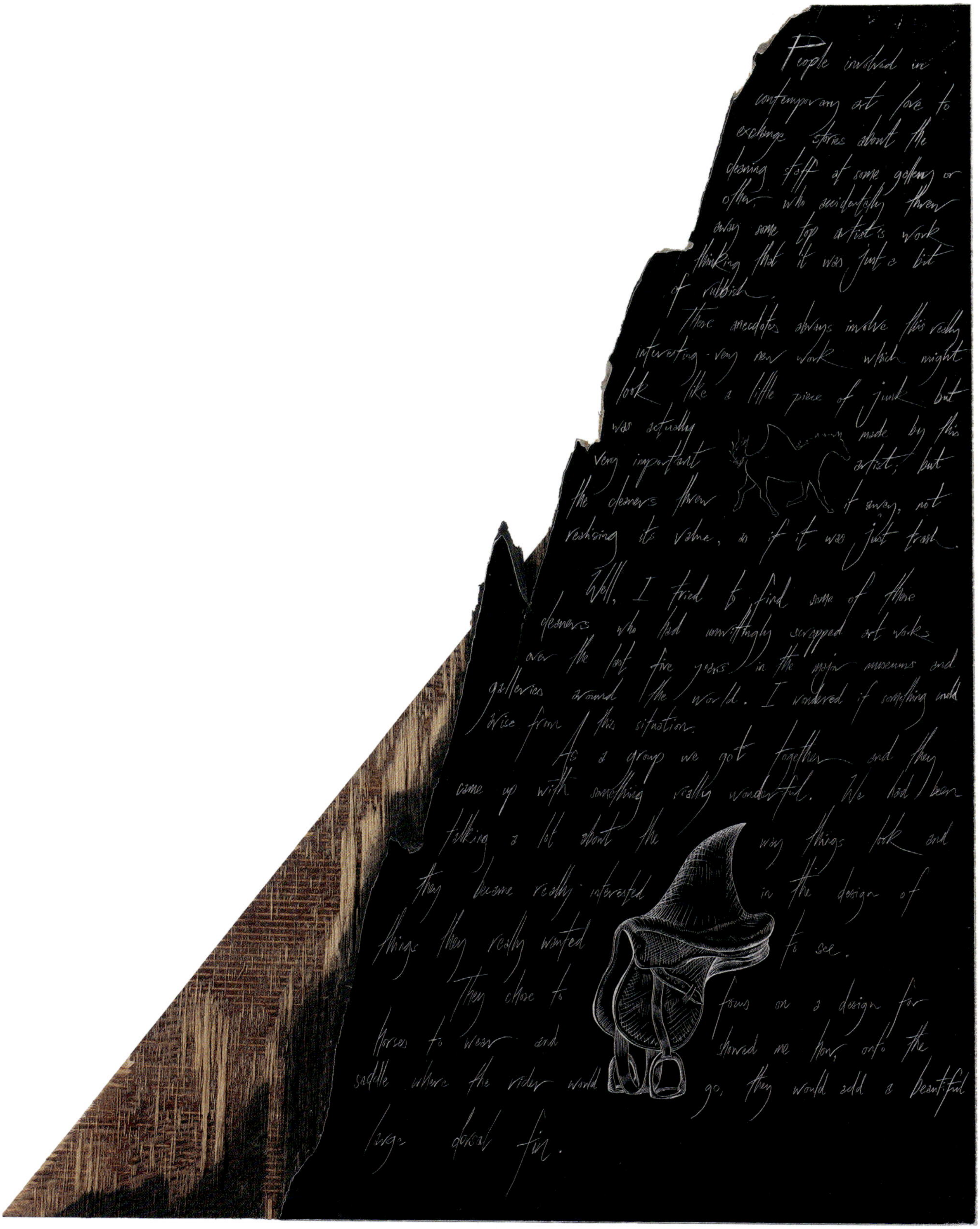

People involved in contemporary art love to exchange stories about the cleaning staff at some gallery or other who accidentally threw away some top artist's work thinking that it was just a bit of rubbish.
These anecdotes always involve this really interesting very new work which might look like a little piece of junk but was actually made by this very important artist, but the cleaners threw it away, not realising its value, as if it was just trash.
Well, I tried to find some of these cleaners who had unwittingly scrapped art works over the last five years in the major museums and galleries around the world. I wondered if something could arise from this situation.
As a group we got together and they came up with something really wonderful. We had been talking a lot about the way things look and they became really interested in the design of things they really wanted to see.
They chose to focus on a design for horses to wear and showed me how, onto the saddle where the rider would go, they would add a beautiful large dorsal fin.

# 44

**White Magic** 2005

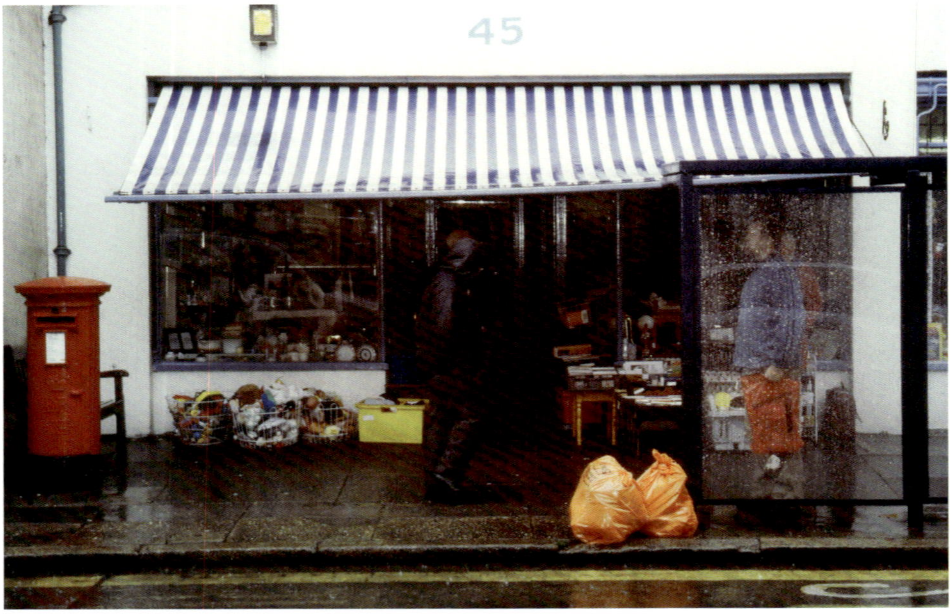

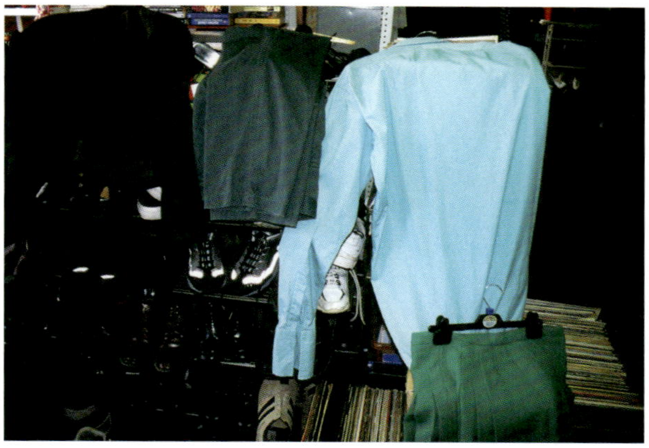
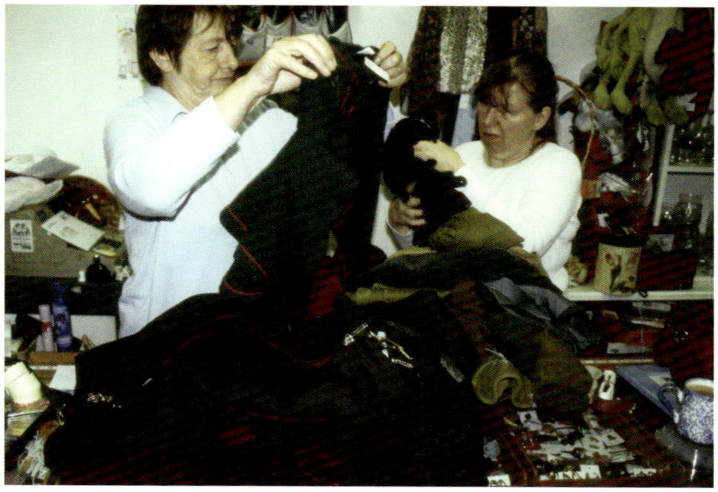
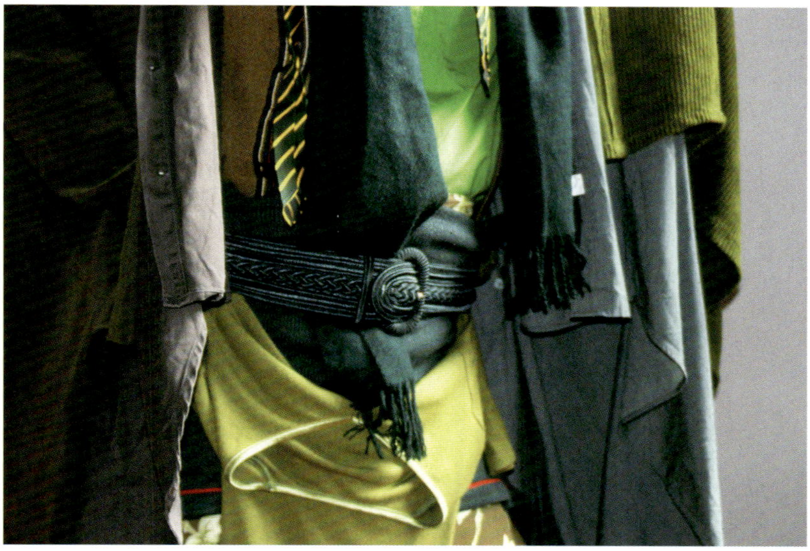
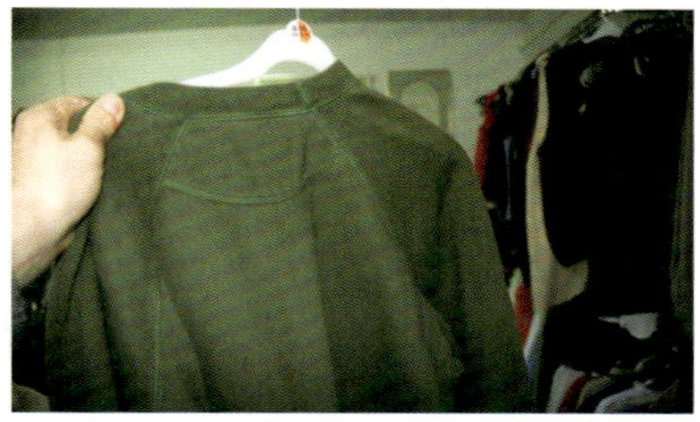
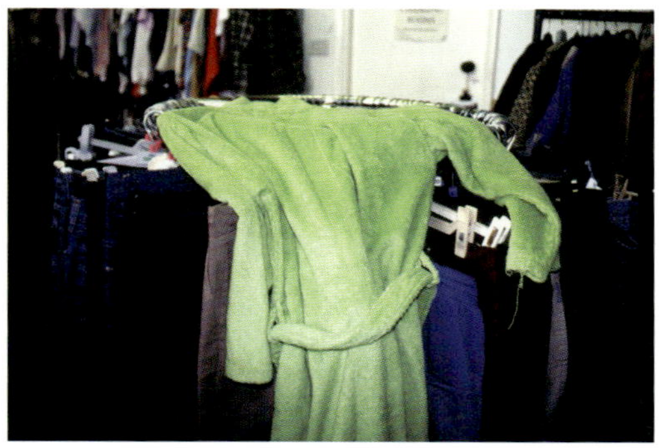
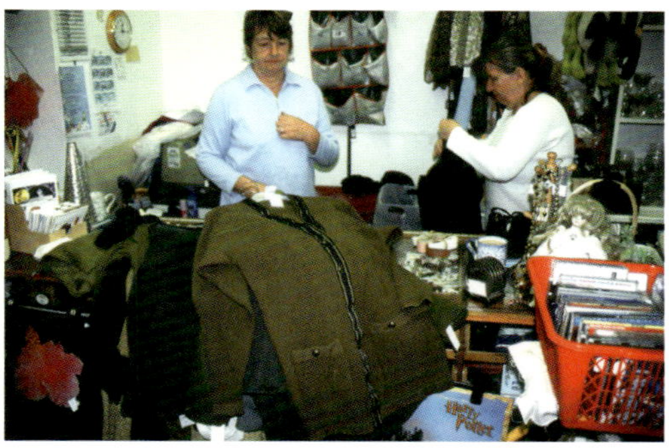
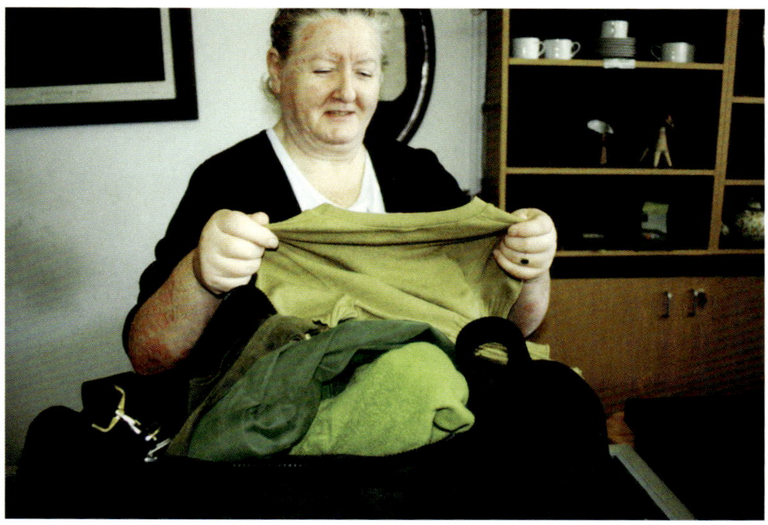

**White Magic** 2005

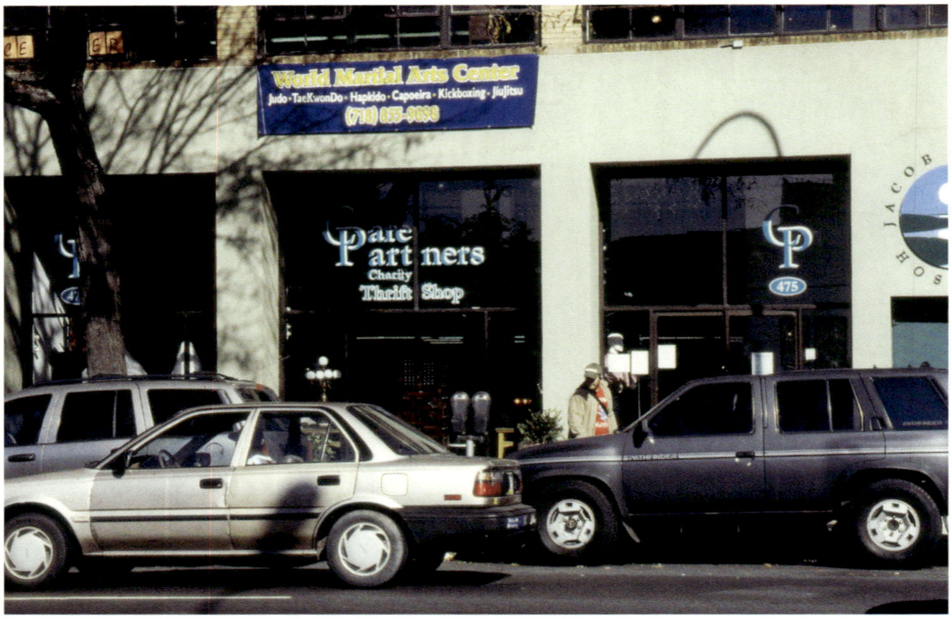

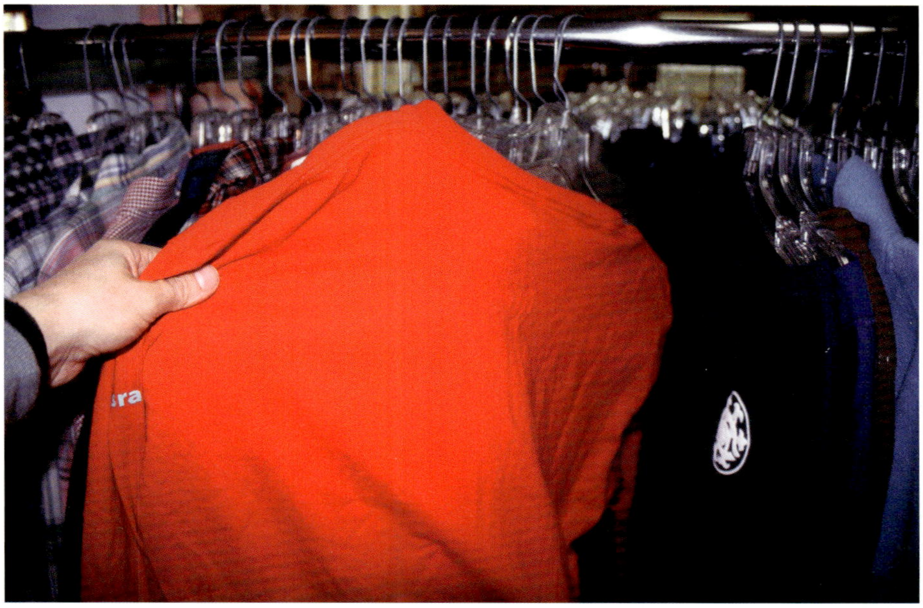
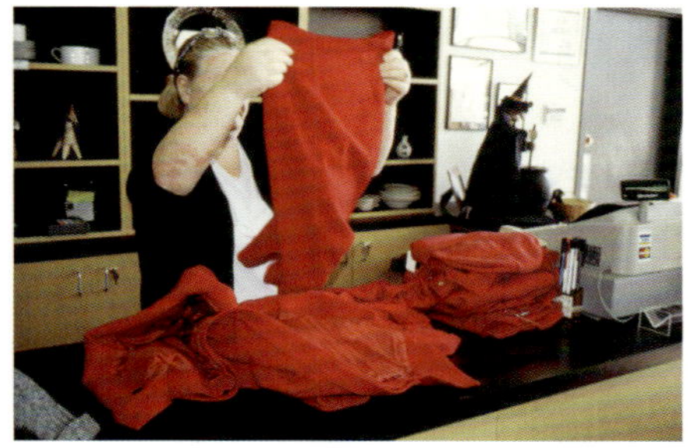
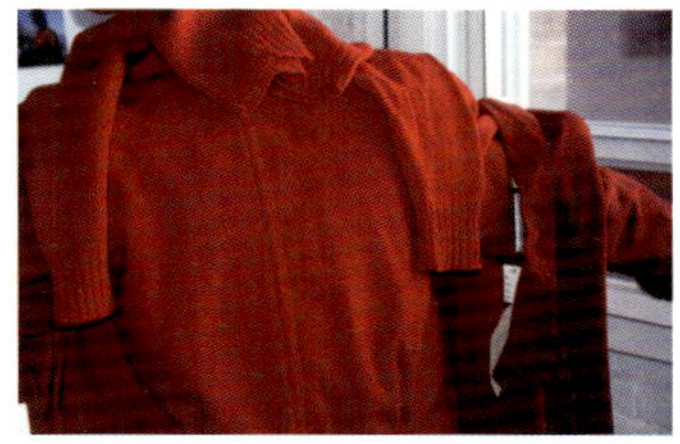
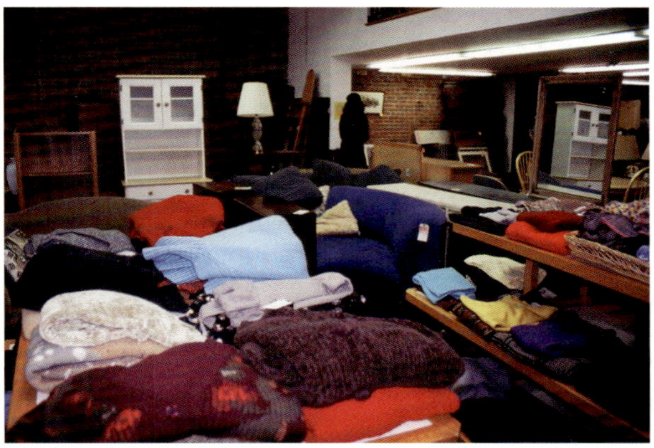
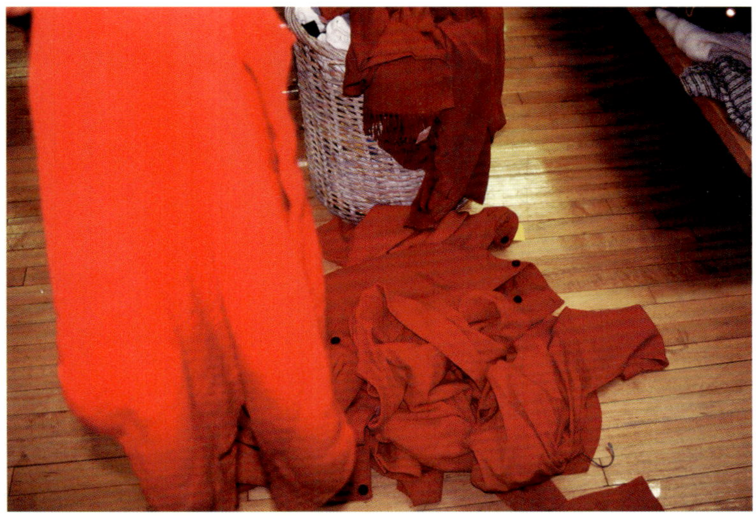
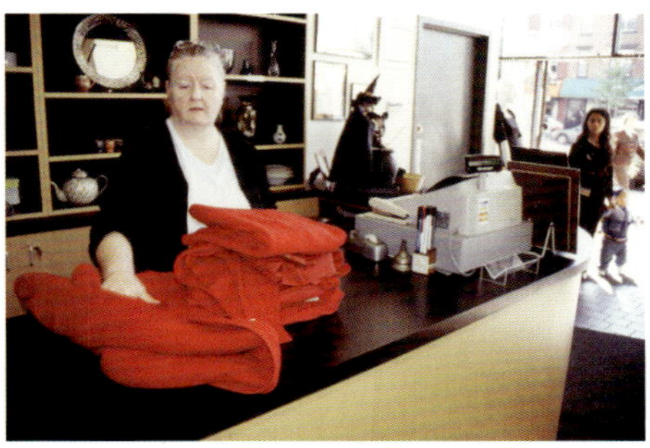
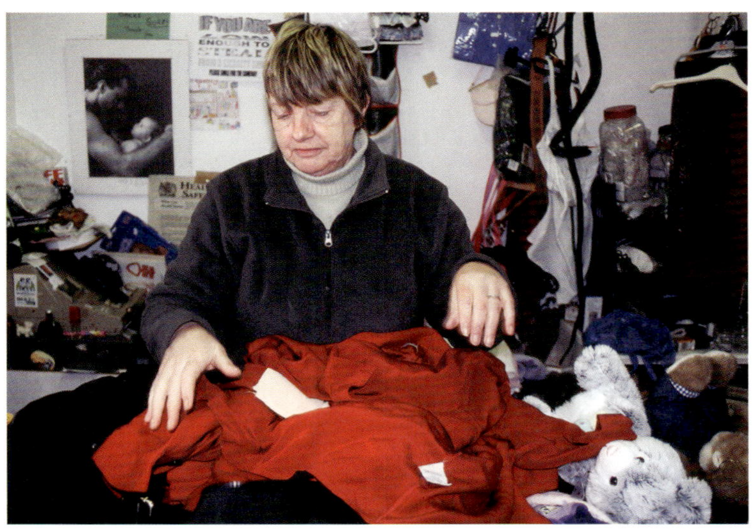

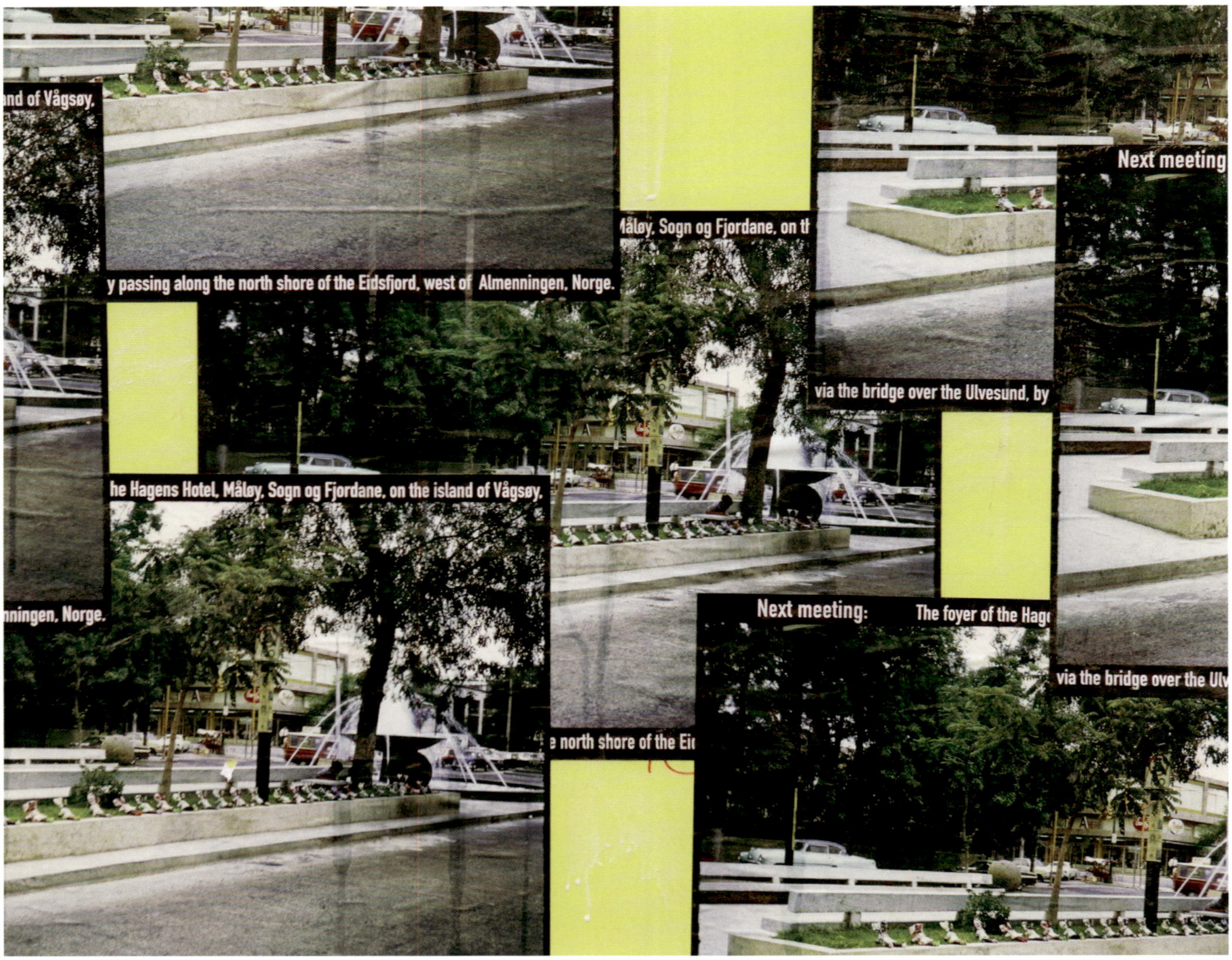


Meeting: The foyer of the Hagens Hotel, Måløy, Sogn og Fjordane, on the island of Vågsøy... 2007

## Not Failing

Lisa Le Feuvre

I have very little (perhaps nothing) to show you. To put this another way: My work is without authority. You will learn nothing from it; you will gain no moral profit from it; it will not even enhance your life with that delight or superior pleasure which, you have been led to believe, artists have the obligation to provide you.[1]

What happens when art is divorced from a redemptive position, when it really cannot save, entertain or educate? What is left? The statement above by Leo Bersani and Ulysse Dutoit proposes that art released from the assumption of edifying value offers a subversive possibility to resist cultural authority and open productive forms of engagement. Using the work of Samuel Beckett, Mark Rothko and Alain Resnais, the authors suggest that such a break can occur when an artwork refuses truth, defies description and becomes paradoxically concerned with both failing and not failing.

In 1949 the journal Transition published 'Three Dialogues', ostensibly a discussion between Samuel Beckett and Georges Duthuit on the painterly practices of Tal Coat, Andre Masson and Bram van Velde. Although published as a conversation, with notes on the participants variously exiting in tears and reminiscing warmly, the text was primarily written by Beckett – many Beckett scholars regard 'Three Dialogues' as the closest the writer came to a statement of his own position. Emphatically stating that failure is the inevitable outcome of artistic behaviour, Beckett argues that engaging with failure offers a possibility for art to refuse expression: a concept he proposes is a misperception at the core of reception of artwork. This, he claims, can be achieved by adopting a stance where 'there is nothing to express, nothing with which to express, nothing from which to express, no power to express, no desire to express, together with the obligation to express.'[2] He continues to assert that 'to be an artist is to fail as no other dare fail' and that 'this submission, this admission, this fidelity to failure, [is] a new occasion, a new term of relation.'[3] Setting out to succeed-to-fail and to fail-to-fail steps aside from the orthodox order to enter instead a realm of doubt and not-knowing in a refusal to give or take authority.

Paying attention to the inevitable gap in an artwork between intention – presumably predicated on success – and realisation allows the production of a generative space through the abstract possibility of failure. Claiming this space opens opportunities for an engaged participation of those who encounter the artwork. The concept of irony can be useful here for thinking through failures of intention – the ironist deals with the how of something said rather than the what, making miscommunication productive. While speculative thought strives for ever-deepening levels of understanding in the search for content, irony asks questions not to receive an answer but to draw out content and form yet more questions. Søren Kierkegaard announced, 'Just as scientists claim that there is no true science without doubt, so it may be maintained with the same right that no genuinely human life is possible without irony.'[4] Kierkegaard's writings are suffused with paradox, choosing a series of endlessly unfurling contradictions over definitive truth.

Adam Chodzko's practice circulates within this ambiguous realm, stepping aside from authority and truth, claiming a space between documentary and fiction and staging equal claims to fictive and factual bases of knowledge. Bersani and Dutoit propose that if a work does not demand to be understood, it has the potential to avoid dogma and remain open and mobile in the face of contingencies. The paradox of

1 Leo Bersani and Ulysse Dutoit, Arts of Impoverishment: Beckett, Rothko, Resnais, Harvard University Press, 1993, p.3

2 Samuel Beckett, 'Three Dialogues with George Duthuit' in Proust and Three Dialogues with George Duthuit, John Calder Publishers, 1999, p.103

3 Samuel Beckett, op cit, p.125

4 Søren Kierkegaard, The Concept of Irony with continual reference to Socrates, Princeton University Press, 1989

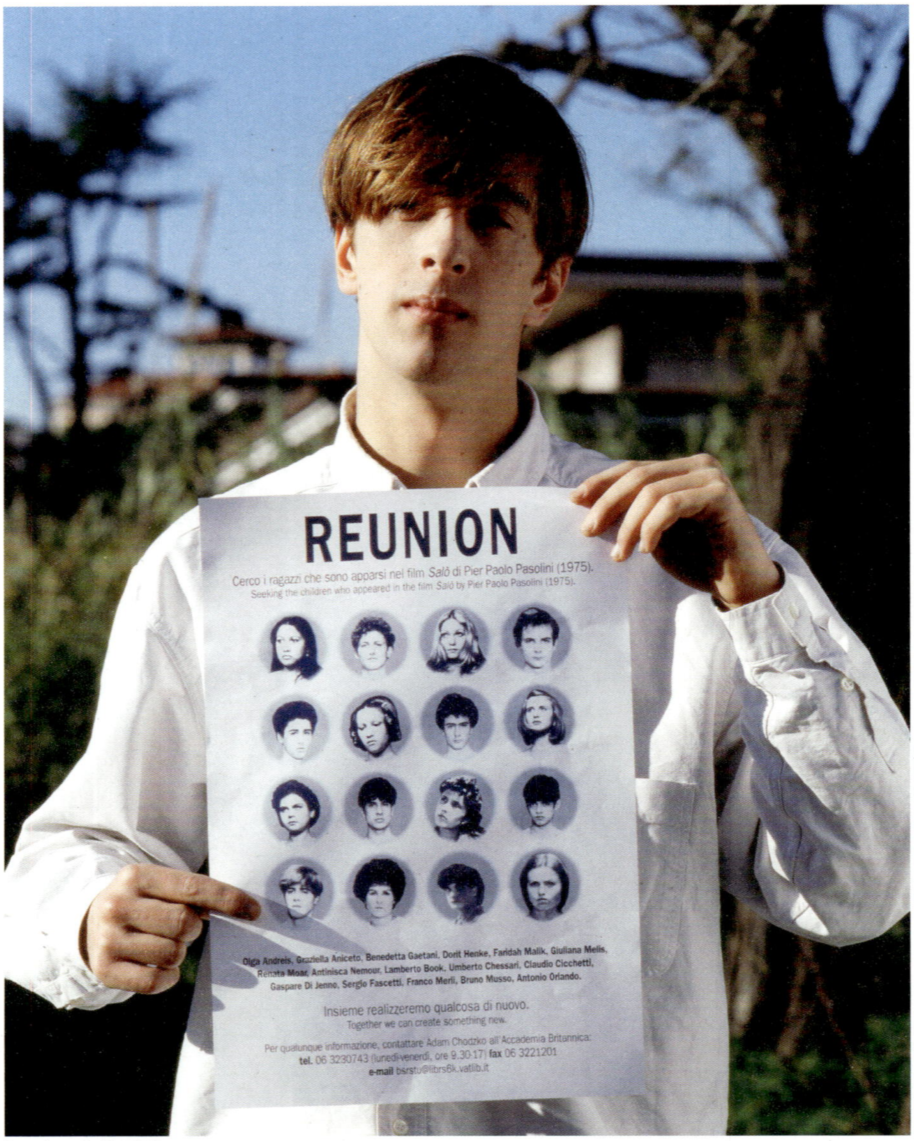


Reunion: Salò 1998

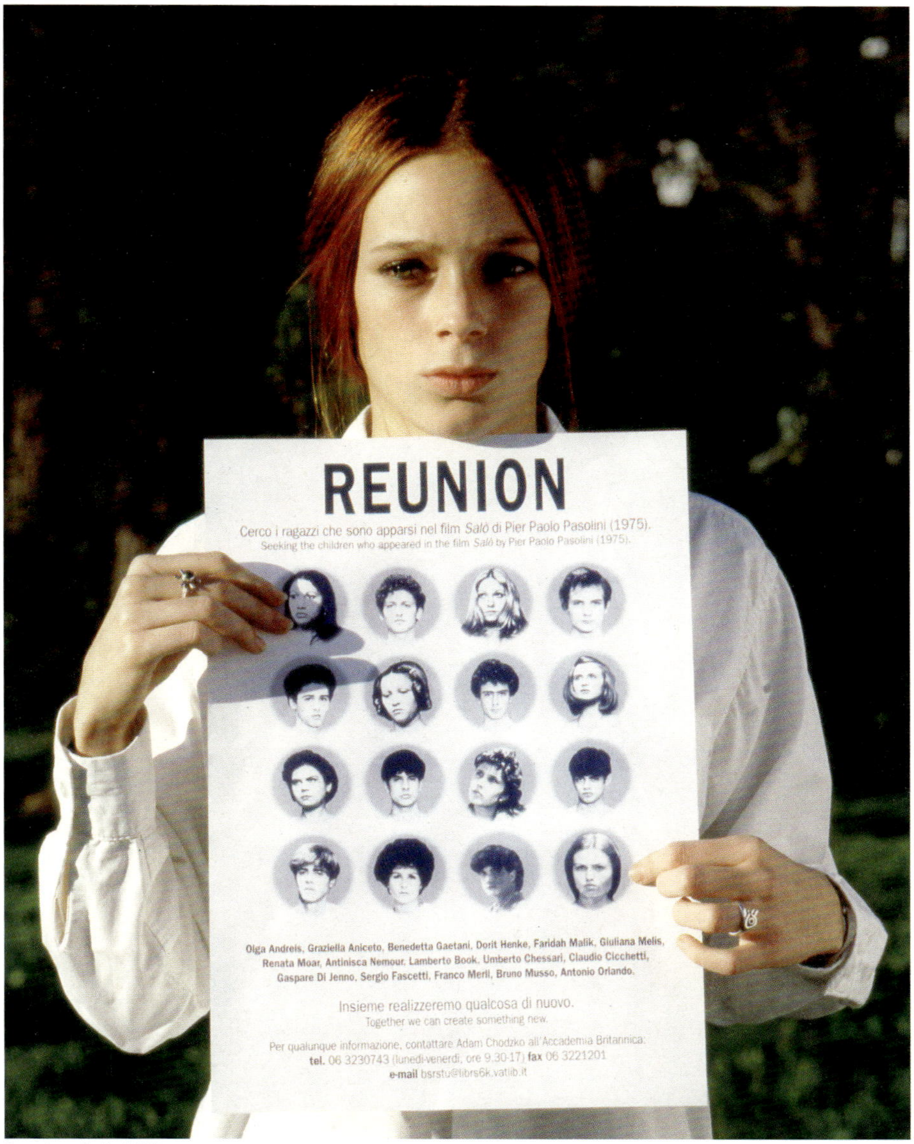


Reunion: Salò 1998

failure is that one cannot set out to fail because the evaluation process of success, measured by failure, becomes irrelevant. For Beckett, failure is to fail to represent. Chodzko engages with and exposes the myths, impossibilities and resistances of representation, taking an attitude that is mindful of the failures inherent in the very operations of attempting to show experience. Using observation and experiment Chodzko interrogates relationships between documentary and fantasy, referring to and refuting both. Whether object, moving image, event or poster, his works are neither puzzles to be solved nor purveyors of information: rather they are demands for an engaged participation through thought and, at times, action. Throughout his practice he presents a fractured notion of experience primed to be rearticulated by those who receive it.

Chodzko's is an artistic practice that suggests distinctions between actual fact and factual fact in a paradoxical network that never assumes a public: the works rather produce publics by initiating engagement and dialogue with uncertainties. Importantly, Chodzko is not demanding participation, he is tendering an invitation to act. To simply encounter one of his interventions, in a gallery or elsewhere, is to be a part of the work. Facts are built on fiction and metaphor as much as they are on incontrovertible truths. Consider maps, for example: these, by definition, cannot accurately represent or duplicate any place. A 'truthful description' would require an impossible 1:1 scale model: maps are fictions constructed through historical contingencies requiring interpretation. Chodzko's representations of locations, be it textual or image based, are used to lose, rather than find, direction – in the process questioning the very assumptions used to understand one's place in the world.

Chodzko initiates conversations between material and non-material components, moving across groups of people, sites and codes of conduct that rarely, if ever, brush up against each other. Yet the use of this term 'conversation' absolutely does not suggest polite articulation – productive conversation is predicated here on questions, interrogations, observations and a desire to avoid consensus. Such conversation initiates the creation of something extraneous to a basic positioning of ideas or material forms in proximity to each other, a generative process operating across space and time. Mary Jane Pratt's notion of the 'contact zone' is relevant here. She uses this term to describe 'social spaces where cultures meet, clash and grapple with each other, often in contexts of highly asymmetrical relations of domination and subordination'.[5] Predicated by the past, the specifics of a present and desires for a future past, such interactions have long-term ramifications extending beyond the moment of contact. The filmmaker Jean Rouch was likewise concerned with the effect and affect of contact and called for an acknowledgement of the influence of the apparatus of film on documentary. Film is a central reference to Chodzko: he says that 'in order to make my work I turn my back on art and look elsewhere, to get close to articulating something, to connect with it, it is important for me to also gain some distance from it.'[6] The experience of cinema easily seduces through the image in a fictionalised reality consumed passively. In film the camera is doubly culpable; it captures and influences reality – a concern looping through Chodzko's work. His works present an activity that can often bring conflicting positions into contact, all the while concerned with the question of how to honour the reality of another.[7] Here dignity prevails.

5 Mary Jane Pratt, Imperial Eyes: Travel Writing and Transcultration, Routledge 1992, p.4

6 'Describing A Fire: A Conversation between Adam Chodzko and Mark Godfrey', in Adam Chodzko, MAMbo 2007, p. 84

7 'Describing A Fire: A Conversation between Adam Chodzko and Mark Godfrey', in Adam Chodzko, MAMbo 2007, p.79

Posters that initiate conversation have been a consistent mode of address in Chodzko's practice: Reunion: Salò (1998), for example, called for actors who had been killed in the execution scenes of Pier Paolo Pasolini's 1975 film Salò to assemble in response to the proposition that 'together we can create something new'; Product Recall (1994) urged owners of 'Vivienne Westwood's Worlds End "Clint Eastwood" Jacket' to get in touch as 'it has been discovered that this design was based on an early scheme for a memory jacket.' In 2003 Chodzko presented the work Looper, a billboard-sized poster in central Turin that is relocated and re-presented in a gallery in the exhibition at Tate St Ives. Looper initiated a series of 'meeting' works, combining text and image and collapsing unlikely locations into each other. Running along the top and bottom of the image a text declares: 'Reunion of the most perceptive: meet in the bar of the Foyer Cultural, a hotel in Jérémie, in the southern peninsula, 12 hours from Port au Prince, Haiti.' Describing this as a 'reunion' intimates that this is a call to gather people who have been estranged for some time; 'the most perceptive' that these individuals are unusually understanding. The meeting point is in a bar of a hotel with – given its name, it is implied – cultural leanings; and the hotel itself, a 12-hour drive from the capital city, is located in a remote spot associated with poets and dissension. The image is from an obsolete 1960s travel guide that has been manipulated through mirroring and inversion, but it shows neither Jérémie nor Port au Prince. Both text and image are ambiguous, yet the authority of this declaration is strong enough to encourage doubt in the reader's own knowledge.

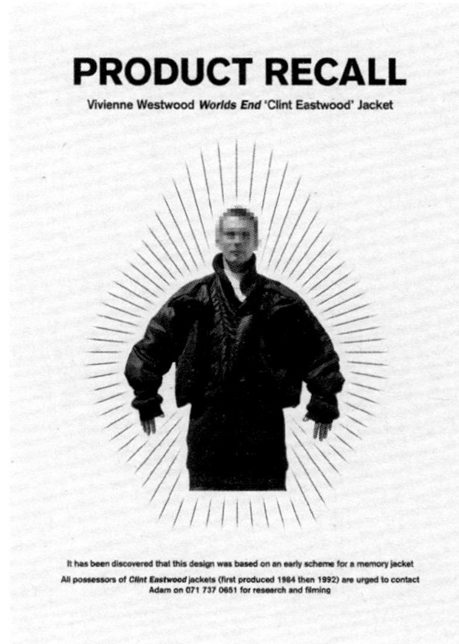

Product Recall 1994

In 2003 Chodzko called another meeting via a poster – this time a 'meeting of people with stammers to describe a fire'. A note that 'Here Everyone Welcome' follows a listing of the particularities of the meeting, indicating that people can attend whether or not they have a stammer. As with Looper, there is no indication as to whether attending this meeting is by choice or invitation. The posters have the impression of being mass-produced, yet each one is hand-drawn, showing a fire centred on the page. Here the very articulation of description becomes its subject: stammering injects intermittent repetition into language. The artist has said 'stammering could be the perfect poetic description of a movement of flames.'[8] Poetics, or even description, may well not be the best response in calling attention to a fire.

Chodzko's artworks operate in a continuous present where imagined futures and remembered pasts intertwine. His is a constantly unfolding practice, with each work opening up into others – and in this process of time travel both the understanding of the history and future of his practice is informed by imagination and projection. Each work is constructed with an eye to the future – indeed some are dated after their making, such as the 2002 work Cell-a, which originally carried the date 2006 in its title. Others imagine a future, as with Hole, commissioned by the Museo d'Arte Morderna di Bologna in 2007, that discussed the museum's future popularity before it had even opened.

In 2007 Chodzko inserted two further meeting proclamations into the arena of advertising, in both cases leaving posters to deteriorate and become consumed by others. On building site hoardings around the Ballymun estate in Dublin a declaration appeared: 'Next meeting: the foyer of the Hagans Hotel, Måloy, Sogn og Fjordame, on the island of Vågsoy, via the bridge over the Ulvesund, by passing along the north shore off the Eidsfjord, west of Almenningen, Norge.' So the instructions state

8 Op cit, p.83

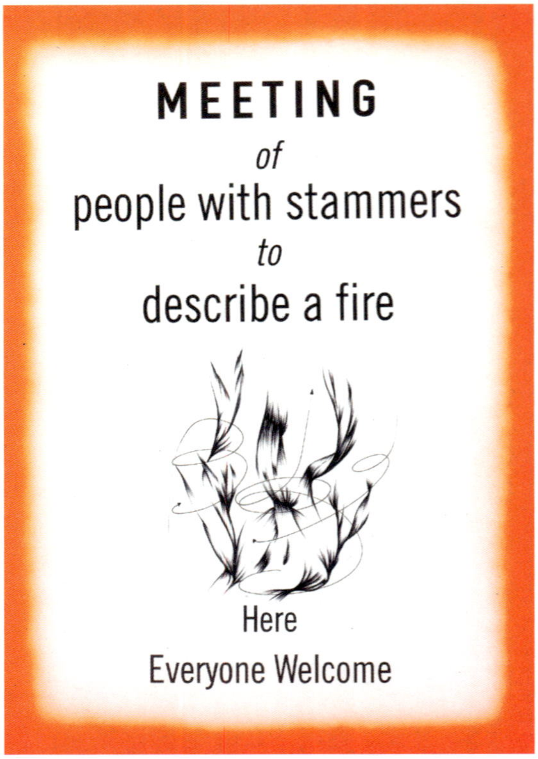


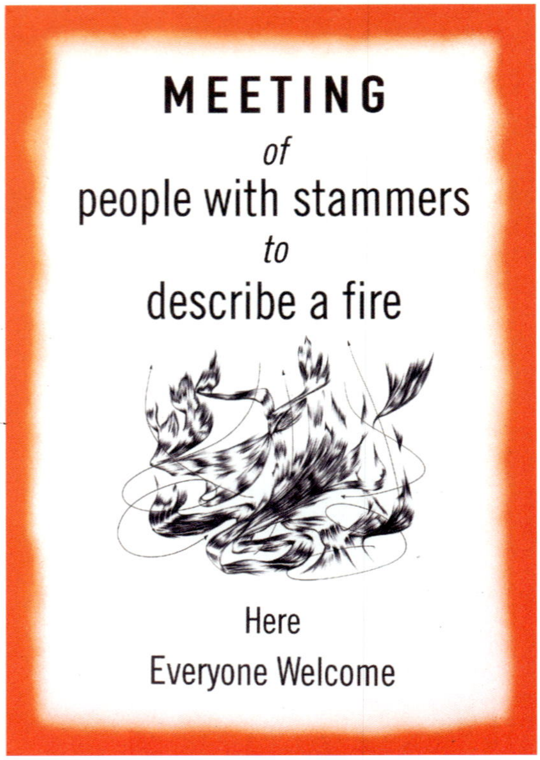


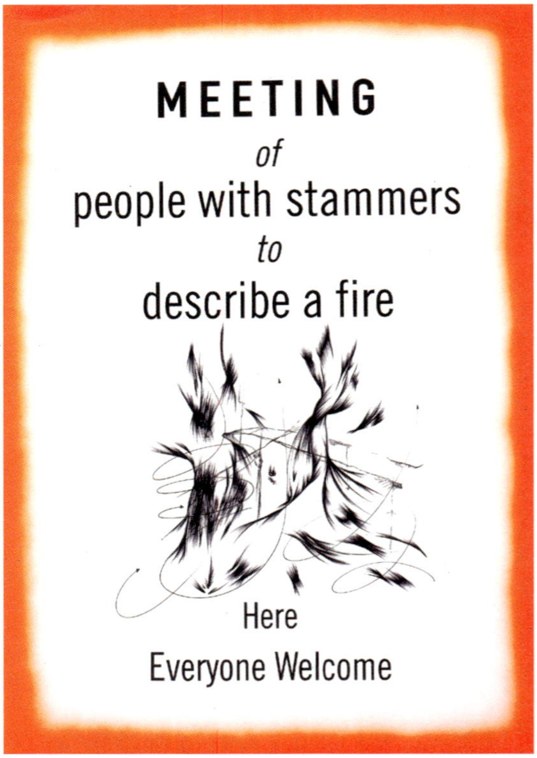


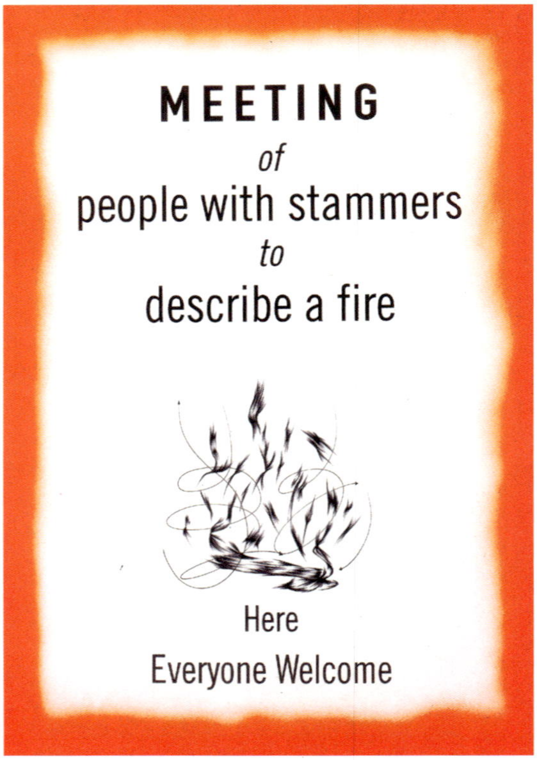


Meeting 2007

that the meeting point is in a port town in Norway, yet the information is being promoted in Dublin without indication of hour, day, month or year – perversely undermining and underlining the authority. And it is not just any old meeting: this is the 'next' meeting, indicating that meetings have been held before, there will be meetings in the future and that the initiated know exactly what this message means. The image shows a street intersection, with a street stall on one corner in front of a glass-windowed boutique. Cars from another, earlier, era crawl along streets lit with a warm southern light. In the centre of the image is an urban square populated with trees, a fountain and a seat looking over to the road. Behind the seat is a patch of grass bordered by a low concrete wall along which a series of variously costumed dolls are perched, and to the far end of the grass a child sits reading. This description of the image, though, is partial and a fiction. Every image-anecdote is influenced by the speaker or writer's own projection that distributes the artwork through a description that is mired with inadequacy.

In Toronto a poster declaring 'Next meeting: opposite the main entrance to the Ordzhonikidze Health Centre, the Sochi-Matzesta Resort between Sochi and Khosta, along the Black Sea coast, Krasodat Krai, Russia' was fly-posted on to hoardings. The image shows a street of brightly coloured buildings with hand-painted Arabic signage. They sit against a backdrop of mountains while in the foreground, on a washed-down road, people go about their daily business. When first distributed around Toronto in 2007 a local blog site, shedoesthecity.com, pondered over this poster's reference, assuming it to be either an information or advertising flyer. The correspondent, Lizzie McNeely, followed a sleuth-like trail via Google and Wikipedia only to be led nowhere. The circulation and reception of these artworks are direct and indirect, experienced and rumoured, approached as artwork and as consumer information. Advertising tells us what to think; and providing we are the target consumer profile, will seduce us into feeling some kind of comforting sense of belonging. Such communication strategies are overburdened with content producing passive reception. Advertising sets up an expectation of satisfaction. Chodzko is not concerned with constructing the closed, complete and expressive set of answers this approach creates. His practice is directed towards discomfort, interrogation and making things difficult. Speaking of other works, Chodzko has said: 'Within each work that I make there are certain anchoring points; places that seamlessly combine the world as it was before the artwork and the artwork that now exists. I cannot unpick this because I am as unsure as the viewer as to what is real and what is not.'[9]

At every turn Chodzko's artworks feed out from and into the museum as a site of cultural authority, with each gesture pointing away from expectations of either entertainment or education. These poster works, which are initially distributed through specific locations, in the future find themselves in a museum context. During Chodzko's exhibition at Tate St Ives, on the coastal path that will take you from St Ives to Zennor, a billboard incongruously collides with museumgoers, dog walkers, ramblers, tourists and locals – identities that can be held simultaneously by one person. The image shows a group of school children gathering together with two teachers – the weather looks warm, there is a shade of optimism from a past moment, maybe even a past ideology. Two banners are lifted high – one shows an image of a man, proudly patriotic, rendered in socialist realist perfection; the other shows writing that might be Cyrillic. The text

9 Cell-a in Adam Chodzko, Peter Fillingham, Jeremy Millar, Terry Perk, Artracks 2004, p.15

again gives a set of instructions for a meeting: 'next meeting: the car park of the plywood factory, just north of the new town of Tolhóin, on the western edge of the Lago Fagna, after taking the Rura 3 southwards along the Río Ewan, Tierra Del Fuego.' The source of the image and text of this poster, in common with the other meeting announcements, are actually from the artist's collection of other people's tourist slides and his archive of obsolete tourist guides. Each pronouncement, be it in text or image, has a specific location that can be cited: this one, for example, is at a pioneer camp in Tashkent in 1964, in a park dedicated to an astronaut. When juxtaposed with an instruction that alludes to deforestation, road travel and industrial production, meaning becomes veiled. Just like the blogger Lizzie McNeely found, it really is of very little help to have such information. Nothing definitive is being shown or said; there is no authority, only proposals for engaged thought.

Lisa Le Feuvre is Curator of Contemporary Art at the National Maritime Museum, Greenwich and Lecturer on the Curatorial programme in the Department of Art, Goldsmiths, University of London.

## 58

**Turning Point**
**(A performance for**
**drivers on a bridge)**
2007

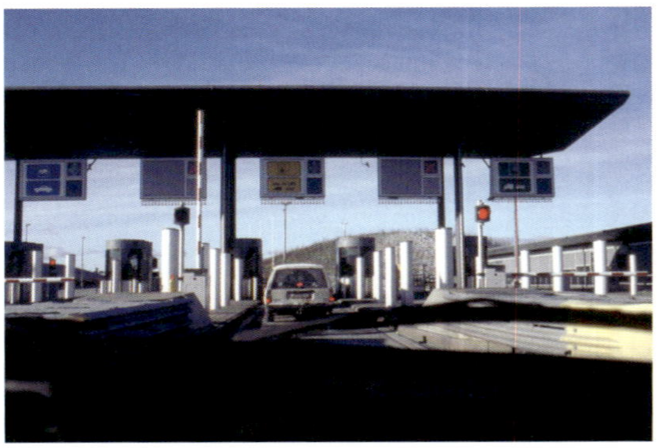

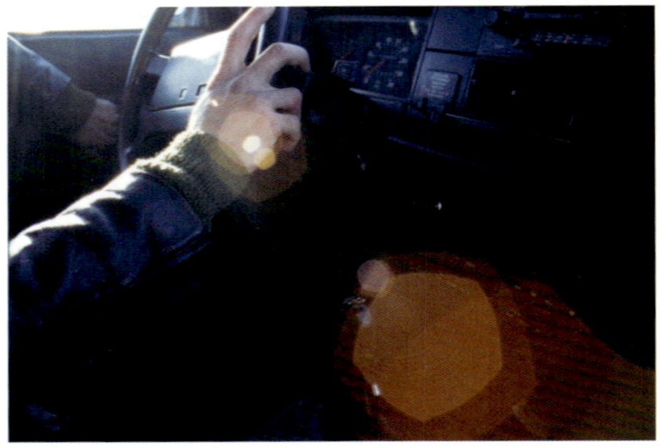

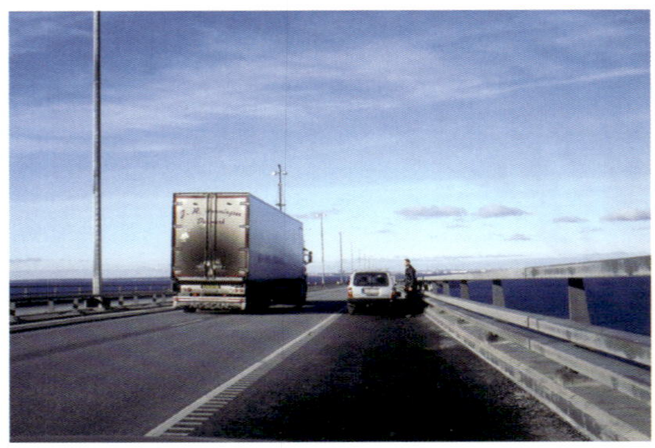

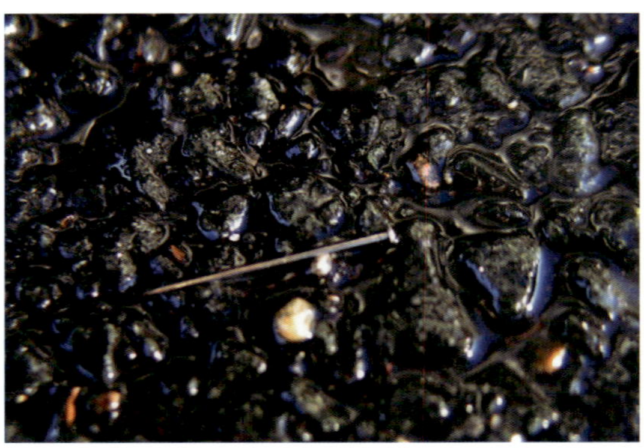

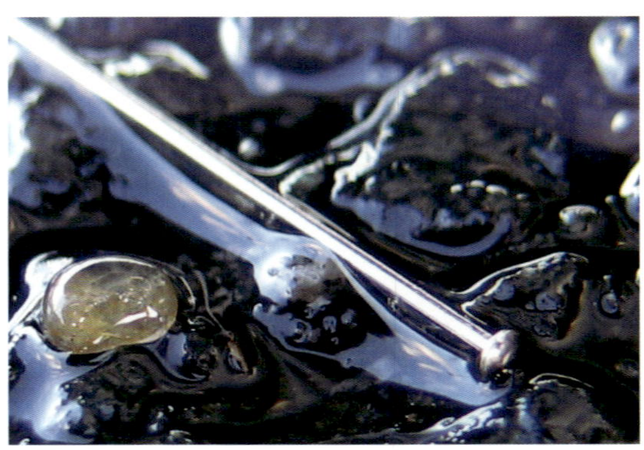

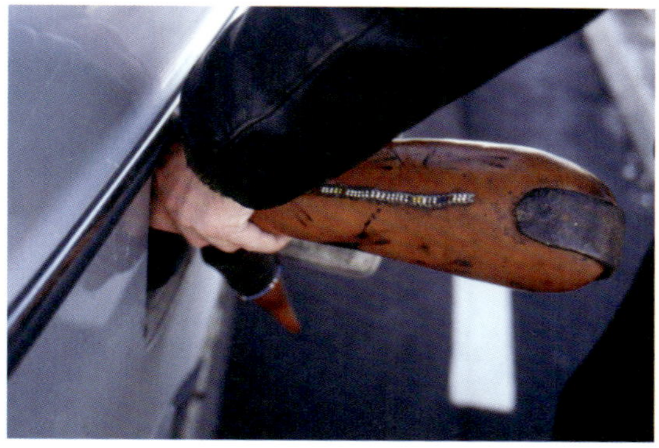

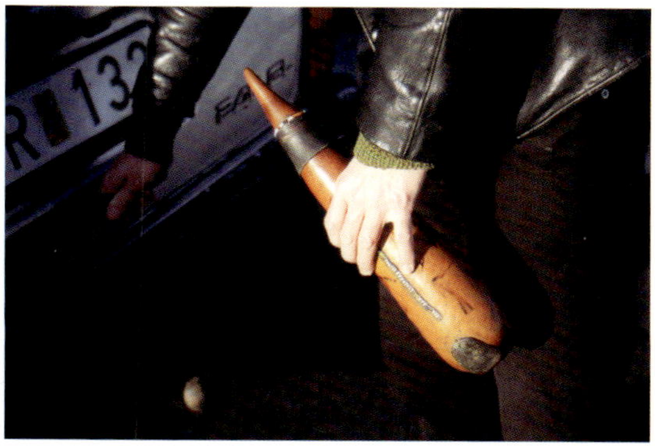

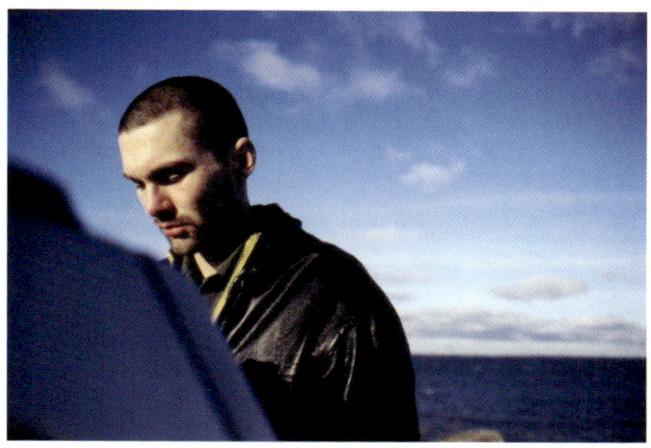

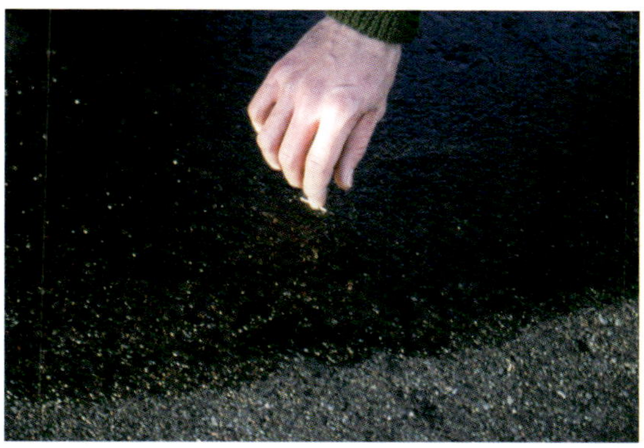

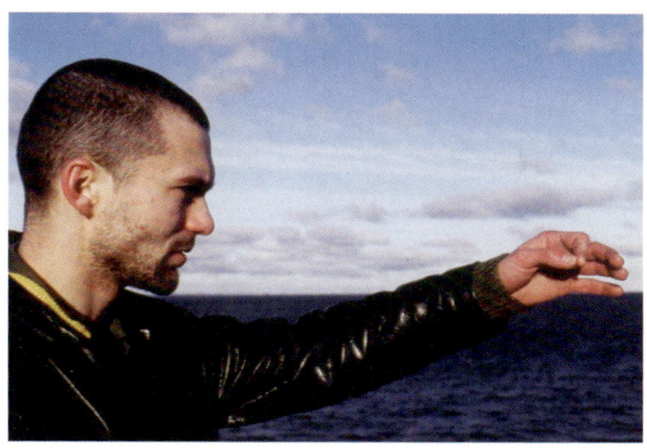

# 60

**Settlement** 2004

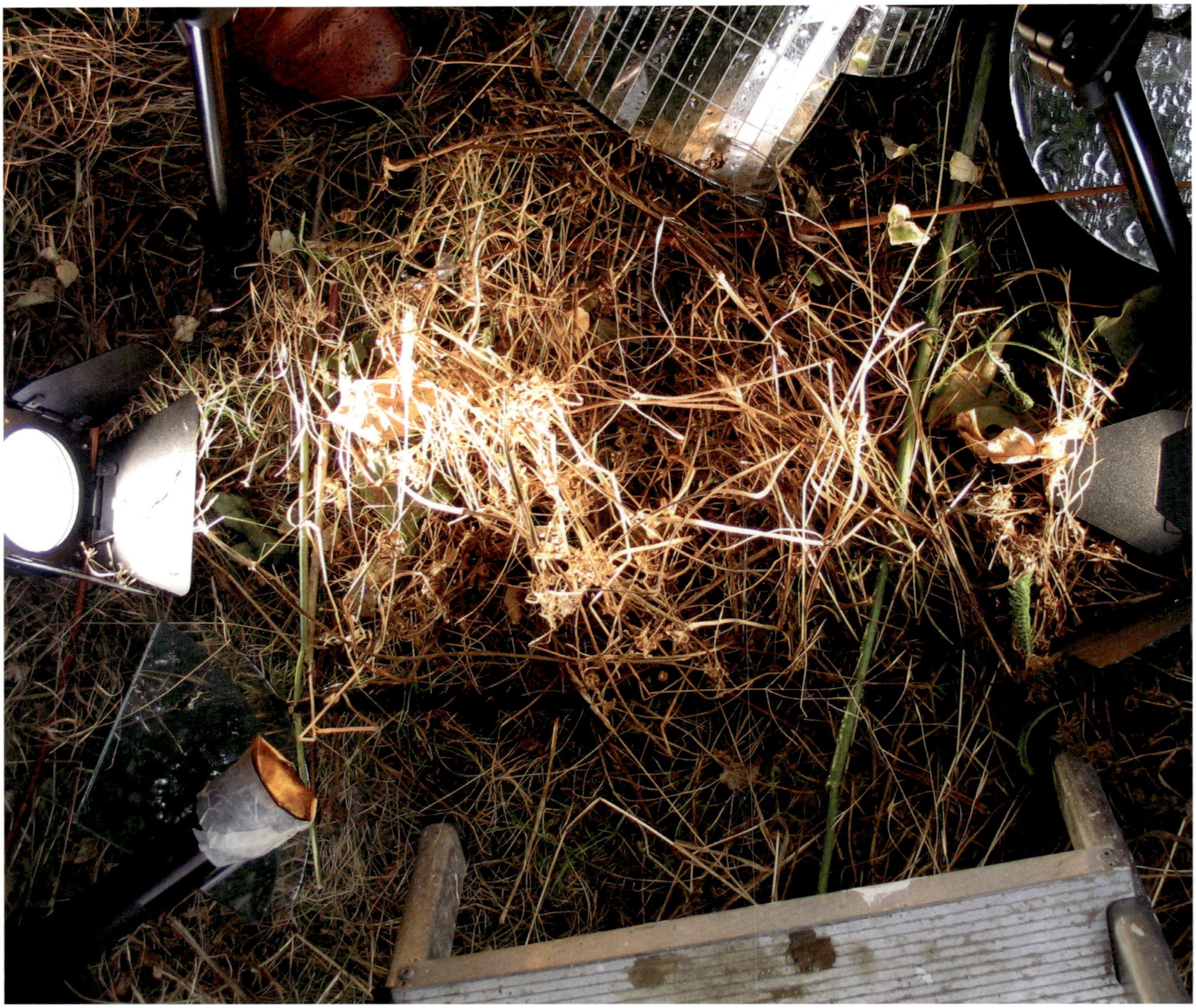

## Part 1 – Restrictive Covenants

The Buyer and its successors in title shall not:

1. Sell the Property or any part thereof, grant any lease or licence, charge or hold on trust for any third party or otherwise dispose of or part with possession of the Property or any part thereof without first obtaining the consent in writing of the Seller which the Seller may in its absolute discretion withhold.

2. Not to use or permit the use of the Property otherwise than for any purposes than as part of a public park or such other use as the Seller may in its absolute discretion designate for Burgess Park or any part thereof (which may for the avoidance of doubt include the Property if the Seller so decides) and at all times to comply with the rules and regulations of the Buyer in relation to the use of the Seller's Land, the Retained Land and Burgess Park

3. Build on or over the Property or erect any structure of any nature whatsoever on the Property which shall include cementing over the Property or covering it with any hard surface provided that the Buyer shall be entitled to place a removable plaque on the Property identifying himself as the Property's owner

4. Dig up the soil or grass forming part of the Property or excavate any part of the Property

5. Not to use or permit to be used the Property or any part thereof for any purpose or in any way which shall cause a nuisance to the Seller and the owners or occupiers from time to time of the Retained Land (which shall for the avoidance of doubt include the general public) or any part thereof or so as to permit or suffer the emission from any part of the Property any noise vibration smell fumes smoke soot ash dust grit radio interference or noxious or deleterious substances effluvia or effluent

6. Not to park or permit its visitors to park vehicles on the Property and not to cause any obstruction of the Accessway or any part of the Retained Land

7. Not to cause any damage to or park vehicles on or otherwise obstruct or deposit mud or any other substance on any of the Accessway

8. Not to alter in any material way or to redevelop the Property or any part thereof

9. Not to bring onto or park on the Property any vehicles whether motorised or otherwise

10. Not to fence off or in any other way to physically segregate the Property from the Retained Land

# 62

**Ants Choose Position for Sequins – 2 Seconds Intervals** 2003

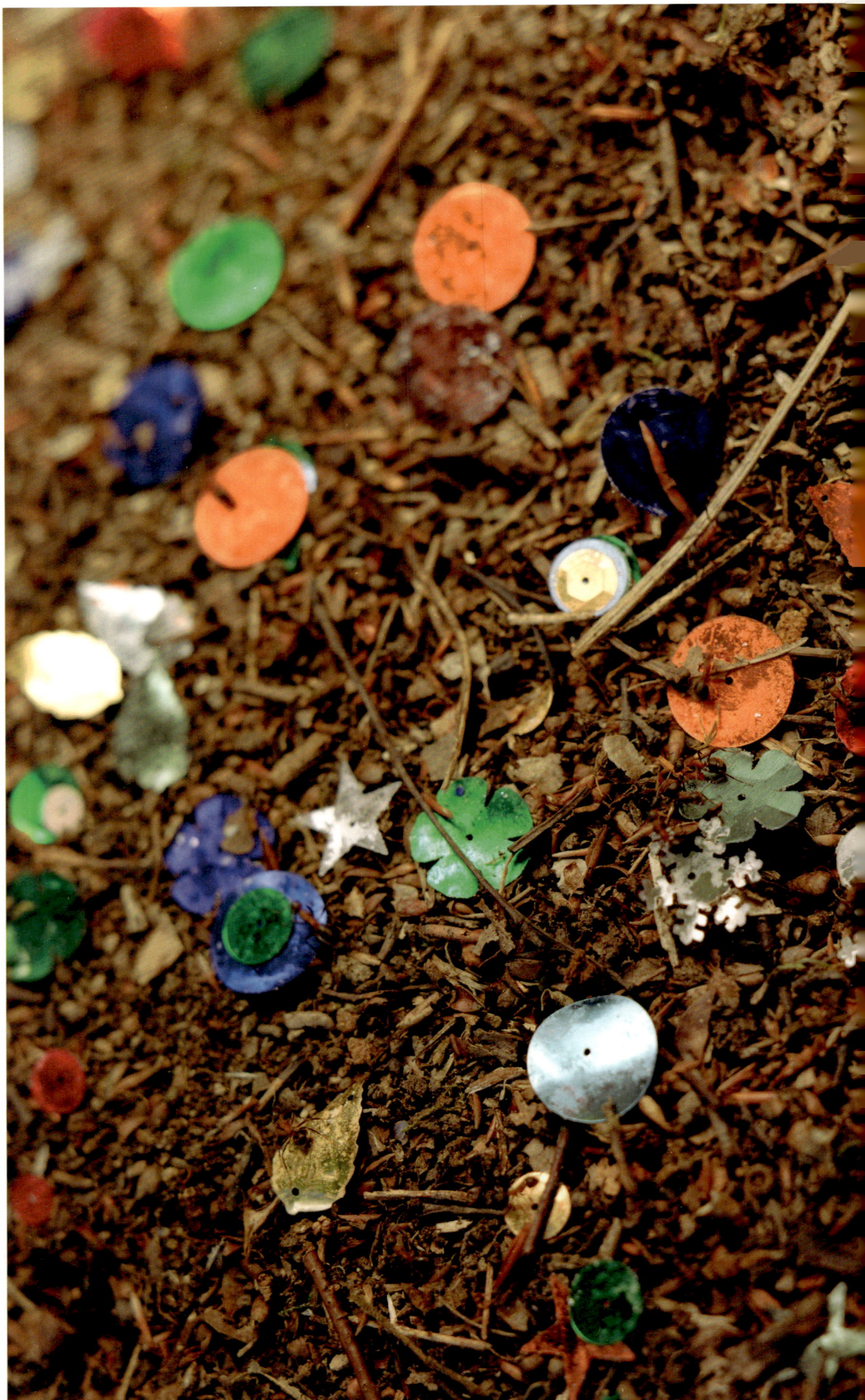

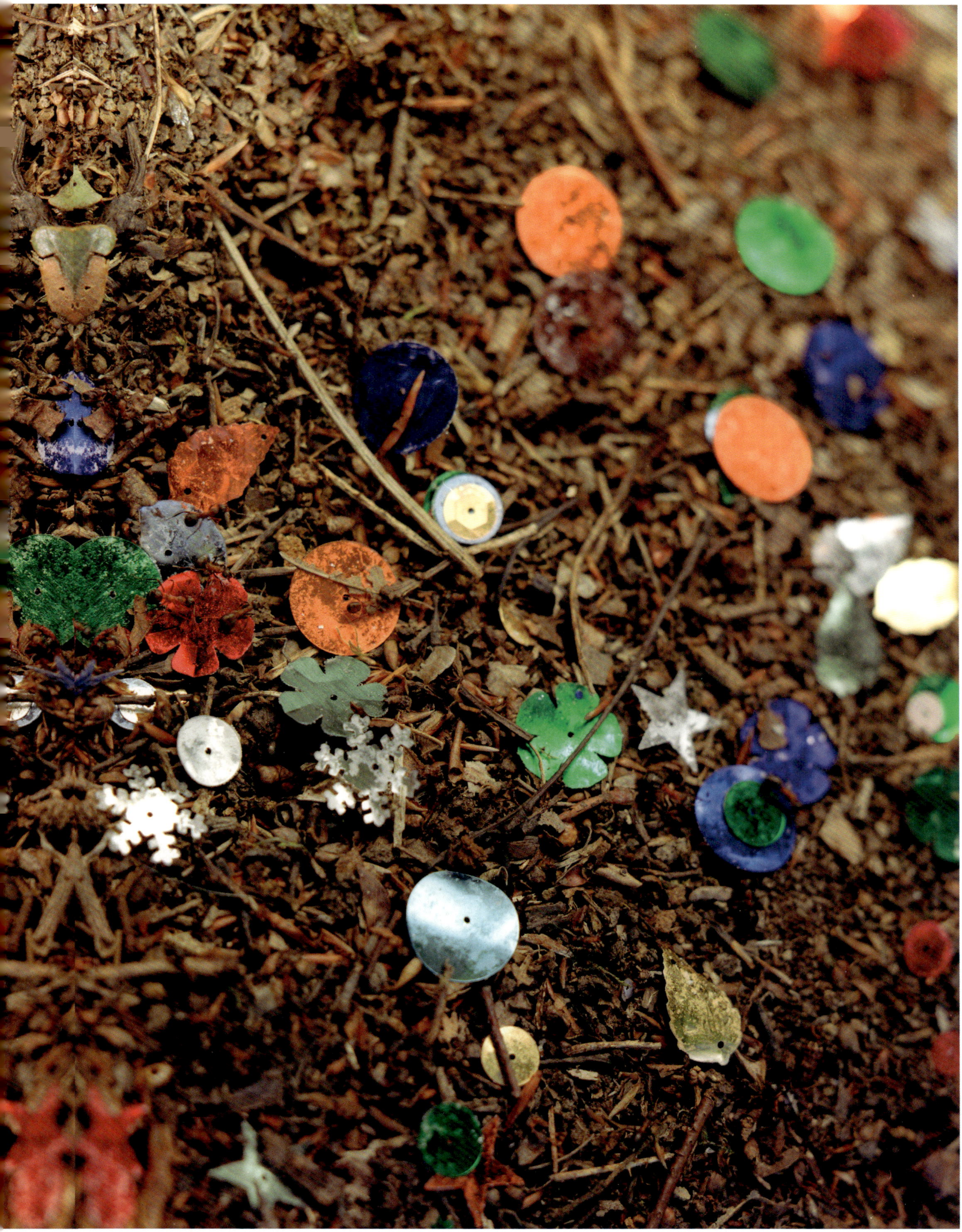

**Plan for a Spell** 2001

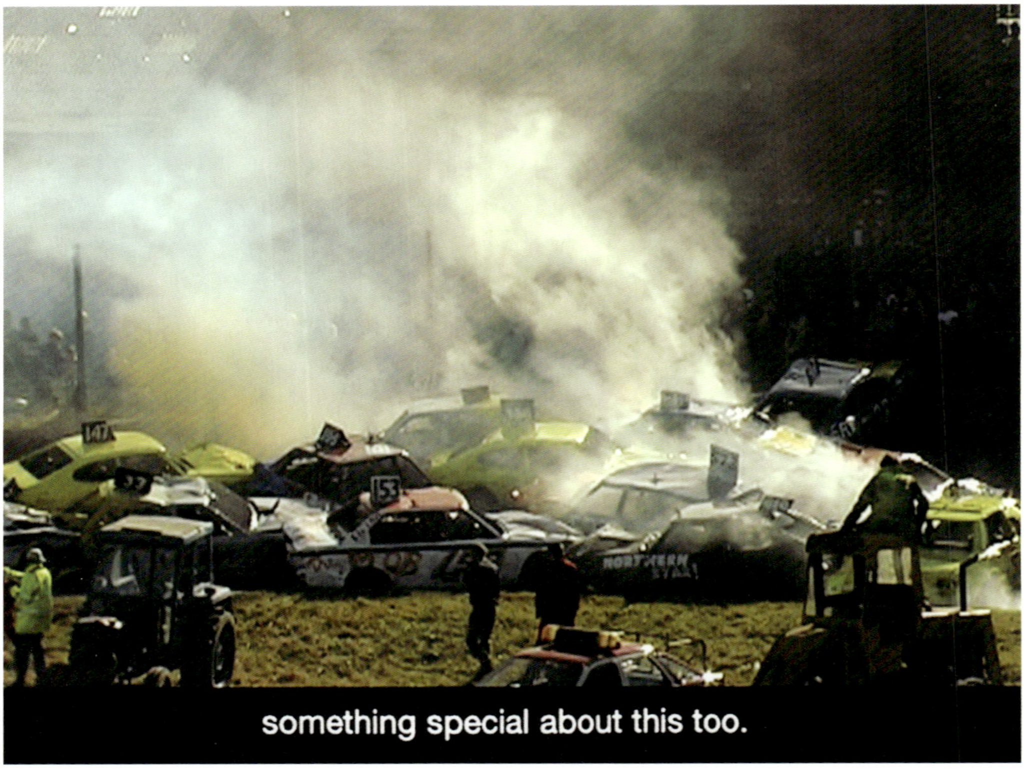

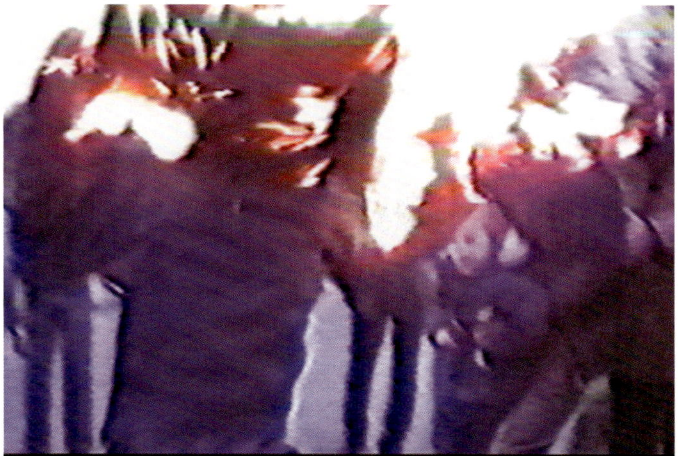

In comes another.

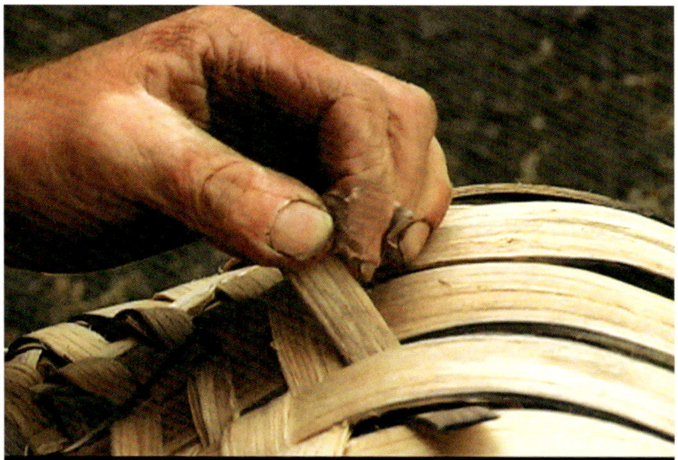

I mean, the energy needed for this system to work

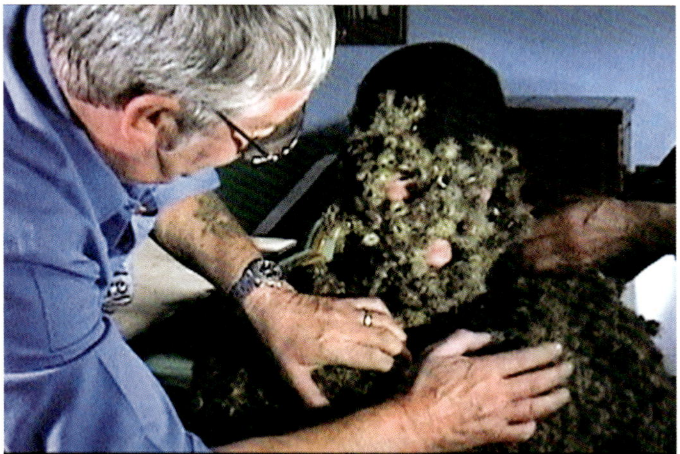

This motion is really good.

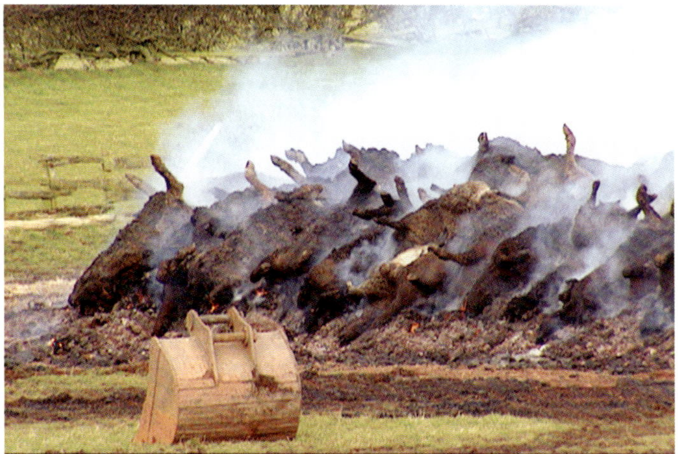

So, I can see there must be

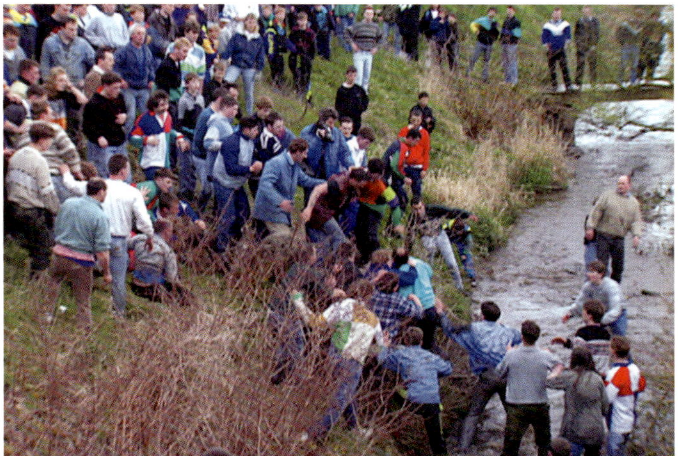

Is it too chaotic?

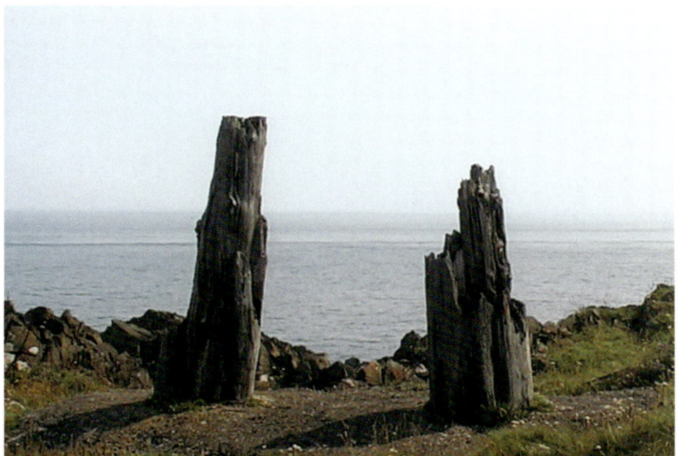

Now that everything seems out of alignment?

# 66

**Transmitter – (Tiny princes)** 2002

chairs, fiddle back, £350. tel. Maidstone ) 968877.
ery old, 2ft 8 wide x 5ft high, stand up back el. Meopham (01474)

at u nit antique pine 0 ono. Tel. Herne Bay

Tel. Chatham (01634) 2.
binet with doors, 30" ondition, £65. Tel. West 7.
ser waxed, 2 piece, th 3ft 1.5 inches, depth quality, very good Maidstone (01622) 7.
igh, in solid mahogany, tre column, £40 Tel. 852.
8ft x 4ft table top, will er collects, £25. Tel. 933.
Beige Velour winged excellent condition, ) 719547.
r beige, very comfor- n, £75. Tel. Canterbury

er armchair, very good ring (01233) 713057.
cabinet in mahogany, storage for CD's and (01634) 221029.
hogany CD/Cassette 0 cassettes, W 24 H 24 front, £15, Tel. Medway

hogany Hi-Fi unit W 18 ition, £15, Tel. Medway

hogany Tv/Video unit 33 H 17 D 18, good dway (01634) 201885.
st of tables, round, leather inlay, perfect e (01634) 221029.
her in laid pedestool oks good, £90 ono. Tel. 93.
wall unit, 4ft 6 wide glass display cabinet, niture, in very good seen £350 ono. Tel. 688860, (07732)

cushions, teak, as new, 34) 375302.
ique, pine colour, ideal ntory, £99 new, bargain 1634) 579762.
ined mahogany, from 40. Tel. Ditton (01732)

ght wood, pine, needs Lordswood (01634)

top rectangular coffee length 127 cms x width cost £199 will accept 634) 300638.
abinet good condition, 1622) 676065.
able plus 4 chairs, ntique pine, £50. Tel. 2949.
s style, good condition, lity, £30. Tel. Sheerness 37) 826053.
offee table, £15. Tel. ) 873882, (07811) obile first)
ding, dark wood, very t, very good condition, 34) 864058.
kcases, black, 33 1/2 x 35. Tel. London (0208) 3994.
ogany legs, with brass st £70, will accept, £35. 25130.

● **Small mahogany** colour floor standing shelf unit, £5. Tel. Strood (01634) 719547.

● **Small pine coffee table** offers. Tel. Chatham (01634) 401407, (07767) 886512.

● **Solid Mahogany** wall unit, three arched bevelled glass doors, mirrors inside plus spotlights and glass shelves, 3 cupboards and one drawer in base, immaculate condition like new, one year old, £275. Tel. West Malling (01732) 848979.

● **Solid Pine Coffee Table** with paper rack, £40. Tel. Herne Hill (01227) 366186.

● **Solid teak desk** full size with drawers and cupboard and shelving on one side £25 Tel. Rainham (01634) 366112.

● **Solid Wood Desk** 2ft x 4ft 6" £40. Tel. Ashford (01233) 740783.

● **Solid wood** dining room unit, approx 10ft wide x 6.5ft high, hand finished, £200. Tel. Sittingbourne (01795) 841018.

● **Solid Wood** grandfather style, rocking chair, high back, ideal for nursing, £55 ono. Te;. Ashford (01233) 643997.

● **Stag Minstrel** pair of book shelves, £260 for the pair. Tel. Maidstone (01622) 817879.

● **Stereo Cabinet** dark oak, long glass door, very good condition, £25. Tel. Maidstone (01622) 831267.

● **Storage Cupboard** 6ft 6, x 19 1/2, x 22inch deep, £40. Tel. London (0208) 402 5619, (07957) 293994.

● **Storage Unit** With tiers, white, square, £4. Tel. Chatham (01634) 321696.

● **Table occasional** round with heavy navy blue cloth, lined and interlined with rolled edge £40 Tel. Ashford (01233) 625130.

● **Tea trolley** solid wood frame with two heavy plastic green trays forming shelves, removeable, 30" x 18", £25. Tel. West Malling (01732) 822083.

● **Tea Trolley** £5. Tel. Maidstone (01622) 729792.

● **Teak Display Units** 58" width x 70" height, sliding glass and wooden doors £60 ono, corner unit 70" high to match included. Tel. Gravesend (01474) 358567.

● **Teak effect dining room** wall unit £25. Tel. Herne Bay (01227) 741637.

● **Teak Effect Writing Bureau** Drop top, 1 drawer, two sliding bottom doors, 30 years old, short legs £30, can deliver. Tel. Croydon. (01689) 845629.

● **Telephone table** and seat, combined plus storage cupboard, £10. Tel. Sittingbourne (01795) 422874.

● **Telephone table** and seat, mahogany, pink draylon seat, £10. Tel. Thanet (01843) 296376.

● **Telephone table** with one drawer and beige velour seat, good condition, £20, Tel Chatham. (07092) 713867.

● **Telvision Cabinet** With video section, £25. Tel. Broadstairs (01843) 842393, (07753) 265387.

● **Thacket coffee table** solid wood, 44x24 inches, brand new unwanted gift, unused, £90 ovno. Tel. Chatham (01634) 844750.

● **Toshiba** Video cabinet, MV2987, for use with models 2987, 2988, 3387, 3388, unused, unwanted gift, brand new still in box, £35 ono. Tel. Gillingham (01634) 570311.

● **Tow fairly old** small wooden chairs, need seats, £2 each, one similar Ercol, £3, one old kitchen chair with curved back, £3. Tel. Whitstable (01227) 261915.

● **TV & Video Unit** In yew, drop leaf, glass panelled front with sliding shelf, £75. Tel. Sittingbourne (01795) 471944.

● **TV And Video** Unit plus matching nest of three tables with glass inlet tops, honey beech 2 months old cost £100 sell for £50Tel. Medway (01634) 711780, (07769) 902386.

● **TV cabinet** mahogany, by Multiyork, includingTV and video needing attention, £80. Tel Hornchurch (01708) 440570.

● **TV Cabinet** with smoked glass doors, tape drawer, £40. Tel. Rochester (01634) 829623.

● **TV Chair** fully upholstered in brown draylon, unused thus immaculate condition, only £40 Tel. Hove (01273) 422657.

● **TV display unit** and matching hifi unit, in dark oak effect with leaded windows, £60 the pair ono, bargain, Tel Rochester (01634) 720534.

● **TV unit** cupboard, 6ft x 3ft, dark wood, Indian style, £75. Tel. Medway (01634) 864058.

● **TV Unit** very long, and unusual, reddy-brown in colour, £5. Tel. Faversham (01795)

(01227) 261915.

● **Winged armchair** in sage green draylon, very heavy frame, very good condition £20. Tel. Faversham (01795) 537417.

● **Wooden rack** suitable for magazines, £5, Tel Paddock Wood (01892) 837465.

● **Wooden Sideboard** very good condition, £20 ono. Tel. Gillingham (01634) 570311, (570311).

● **Wot Not mahogany** £60. Tel. Newington (01795) 844057.

● **Yew furniture** 4ft wide x 6ft high wall unit, base 3 doors and 3 drawers, top 3 glass and wood beaded doors, enclosed stereo unit, large oval coffee table, small lamp table, good quality and in excellent condition, £300. Tel. Bexley (0208) 303 3997, (07779) 487114.

● **Yew Octagonal** occasional table x2, with green leather inlaid top £75 each, also brass ornate firescreen, £30. Tel. Maidstone (01622) 719523, (07751) 566365.

● **Yew pedestal desk** green leather top, 4ft 6 x 2ft 6, 8 drawers, very good condition, £275, Tel Benenden (01580) 240346.

● **Yew Repro TV Cabinet** A1 condition, very attractive piece of furniture, £110. Tel. Ashford (01233) 625130.

● **Yew reproduction unit** with 4 drawers, width 20 inches x height 28 x depth 15, excellent condition £90 Tel. Ashford (01233) 625130.

● **Yew** Corner cabinet, £100 ono, writing bureau £60 ono, 2 sets drawers £65 and £45. Tel. Strood (01634) 725924, (07960) 302137.

## Furniture Misc
## 092 Wanted

● **Any Contemporary** or named designer table or chairs etc wanted. Tel. Benenden (01580) 240346.

● **Chaise Lounge** must be in good condition, cash waiting. Tel. Chilham (01227) 731845, (07796) 165289.

● **Free standing** hat and coat stand, preferably with umbrella rail at bottom, any colour considered. Tel. Maidstone (01622) 744660.

● **Ikea Storage** lounge furniture required and cabinet suitable for videos and DVDs. Tel. Maidstone (01622) 812476. 07941 412444

● **Leather Red** Chesterfield armchair wanted, wingback, Queen Anne style please. Tel. Medway (01634) 864058.

● **Pine glazed** Georgian style unit required, cash waiting. Tel. Maidstone (01622) 812476.

● **Stag Minstral** corner unit, must be dark wood, in good condition. Tel. West Malling. (07092) 472084.

● **Welsh Dresser** in solid pine wanted, approx 4ft6" wide. Tel. Maidstone (01622) 817125.

● **Winged leather** fireside chair in red wanted. Tel. Medway (01634) 864058.

## General Household
## 094 Offered

● **ARE YOU MOVING HOUSE? We sell boxes and bubblewrap for removals. Maximum prices: Tea chest size box £2.34 (three other sizes), Box Tape £1.24, Bubblewrap £9.49, White Paper Wrap £8.49 (500 sheets). Discounts for buying 10, 20 boxes, etc. You collect or we can deliver. Phone (01634) 373736. Actionpoint, Gillingham.** *(T)47758*

● **House Clearence** all furniture is as new, 3 piece suite with 2 recliners, wall unit, dining room extending table with 4 chairs and 2 carvers, 5 drawer chest of drawers, Ercol table and chairs, china, curtains, glassware, carpet. Please call Ashford (01233) 627979.

● **Household Items** reasonable prices, e.g. beds, tv. cooker etc, house move forces sale. Tel. Ashford (01233) 660125, (07950) 411998 try mobile first.

limited edition of 50 prints, local artist, purchased for several private collectors, presented to HRH Prince of Whales, £50. Tel. Thanet (01843) 863073.

● **Hosemade**

● **Hosemade Fantasy pictures** Good price and previews are available! These pictures can be framed but it will take the price up to £6.00, entirely up to you! It suits any room of your house to add that extra mystical touch! Price for pictures £3.75 each. Tel. Gillingham. (07092) 409296.

● **Hurricane by Robert Taylor** First Edition print, 1979, signed by Bob Stanford-Tuck, framed, mint condition, sole owner, very collectable, £550. cash Tel. Dartford (01322) 528921.

● **Large Georgian** Style mirror, dark oak, £20. Tel. Chatham (01634) 321696.

● **Large mahogany mirror** brand new, 4ft x 4ft 4" £20 ono. Tel. Thanet (01843) 599174.

● **Large mirror** with flower surround, £25. Tel. Chatham (01634) 827782.

● **Large Painting** Picturesque Kentish village, gold frame, 42" x 32" £85. Tel. Strood (01634) 725924, (07960) 302137.

● **Large picture** framed, lady in long white dress and hat standing on a moor, in very good condition, £10, Tel Whitstable (01227) 261915.

● **Limited Edition Modern** Maritime Print, Ships at Harbour at East Coast Falkland Islands, by D Lincoln Rowe, £7.50 Tel. Broadstairs (01843) 862630.

● **Mahogany Georgian bow window style mirror** made up of 9 panes of bevelled edge mirrors, 31in high x 37in wide, very attractive, very good condition, £95. Tel Chatham (01634) 684657.

● **Mahogany mirrors** x 2 matching, 100cm wide, 70cm long, both in very good condition, £80. Tel. Gillingham (01634) 324811.

● **Mirror glass** 19 1/4" x 46 3/4" heavy with bevelled edges and supports, also suitable for a feature project, £8. Tel. Medway (01634) 250766.

● **Mirror** 4ft x 3ft, very large, pine frame, £35. Tel. Medway (01634) 864058.

● **Oil paintings** complete with 12" x 10" antique gold frames, floral designs, set of 2, £30. Tel. London (0208) 886 7690.

● **One long pine standing mirror** £20, and one pine dressing mirror, large with 2 sides, £10 or both for £25, Tel Maidstone (01622) 200052, (07759) 085477 please phone mobile first

● **Painting on Pure** Silk by Wei Tseng Yang, the awakening of spring, colourful peacock and mountain background, size 40x16 approx £85. Tel. Gravesend (01474) 564894.

● **Pair of Stags** two pictures of, in Scottish Highlands, Victorian prints, £20 the pair. Tel. Dartford (01322) 272780.

● **Picture of Chilham** square, by George Hawkins, mounted in gilt frame, A1 condition, £30. Tel. Ashford (01233) 625130.

● **Pictures of dogs** playing pool, ideal for pool/snooker room, x 2 £10. Tel. Ashford (01233) 621741.

● **Pine mirror** 4ft 4 inches x 3ft 4 inches, very good condition, £45. Tel. Maidstone (01622) 661186, (07770) 968877.

● **Series of 4 drawings** of tiny princes in battle, large pastel drawing of earlier computer, 2 small oil paintings of red clouds, slightly scratched, 6 lithographic prints of utopian canal systems, 1 beautiful pencil sketch of thighs, 1 small clay figurine on dying girl solider, unglazed, £150 ono the lot. Tel. Whitstable (01227) 275429.

● **Set of 8** fish pictures, about 40 years ago, from Angling Times, £80 the set. Tel. Dartford (01322) 272780.

● **Square mirror** with pretty picture of flowers in the centre, hangs on a chain, quite old, £10. Tel. Whitstable (01227) 261915.

● **Two water colours** by Mable Lucy Attwell, best offer over £700 for the pair. Tel. Dartford (01322) 272780.

● **Various Pictures** including country scenes, all in quality frames, open to offers. Tel. Medway (01634) 250766.

● **Very large pine mirror** 52" x 40" £30 ono Tel. Gravesend (01474) 533897.

## Paintings/Pictures/ Mirrors

(01227) 780015.
● **3 piece suite** Medway (01634)
● **3 piece suite** and 2 armchairs a very good conditi (01634) 310146.
● **3 piece suit** condition, £120 Te will deliver locally.
● **3 piece suite** seen, multi colour (01634) 727284.
● **3 piece su** background, pink covers for cleanin Tel. Rainham (016
● **3 Piece Suit** deliver, £80, Tel. R
● **3 Piece suite** settee and 2 arr excellent conditi (01227) 832264.
● **3 Piece Suite** multi beige, goo Gillingham (01634
● **3 Piece sui** armchairs and condition, £40 o 283572.
● **3 Piece Suite** seater, one year pink and blue st piping at front, £1,400, will acc please. Tel. Walde timewasters.
● **3 piece suite** seater settee ar damage on fron, £45. Tel. Folkesto
● **3 plus two S** navy blue, eleve condition, £150 7366, (07984) 5
● **3 seater s** traditional style, cushions brown very good condi Rainham (01634)
● **3 seater set** settee, fair condit Tel. Maidstone (0
● **3 seater set** settee, new, exc Northfleet (01474
● **3 Seater Set** and cushions, £ 1636, (07930) 9
● **3 Seater S** x31inches wide, (0208) 402 5619
● **3 seater sofa** recliner, mink an draylon, £200 o 890547.
● **3 seater sofa** very good condi Tel. Medway 948850.
● **3 Seater Sofa** 'Oxford' cottage background, ve filled, £150. Tel. B
● **3 Seater Set** style, superior £95. Tel. Canterbu
● **3 X 2 seater** cushions, cost £ £350. Tel. Orping
● **A Sofa** with exclusive Cub immaculate aqua cushions, Scotch depth x 2.4 metr £2,500 new, contemporary s Balcombe, Hayw
● **Antique Bro** and studs, 3 sea Anne style, very Orpington (0168
● **Aquamarine** cushions, as new 241693.
● **Armchair** w lumbar support material, only £4

# 68

**Transmitter – (Swing seat)** 1991

ick.
tball Shirt, England, blue, brand new, d, Umbro official shirt, unwanted pre- ize 92-102cm. 081-518 7311 Ilford.
uine Tottenham Hotspur football, new, and signed by all their team, £50. 73595 Essex.
man backswing made by Ketler brand new, cost new £200, sell for £100 784 244543 Ashford & Staines.
f club, ladies, Wilson Patty Berg, 8 2 woods, 8in rigid bag, iron head covers, condition, £80 ono. 081-681 1430 Croy-
f clubs, brand new, unused, precision in England, set of 9 cavity backed irons metal woods, will deliver, £150. 081-204 Kingsbury.
f clubs, full set of Wilson X31, in excel- ndition, complete with professional size mbrella and wide wheel trolley, first to ll buy, amazing bargain at £165. David 59 3277 Deptford.
f clubs, full set, Tour model 2, 9 irons, , 2 putters, 3 Ally drivers, leather bag etachable hood, £110 ono. 081-688 8666 on.
f clubs, left handed, irons numbers 3, , 9, putter, woods number 1 and 4, large ag, very good condition, £75. 081-698 Catford / Bellingham.
f clubs, woods 1,3,4, irons 2,4,5,7,8,9, nd putter, gold bag, some irons need re- ng hence £55 ono. 0322 521623 Kent.
f clubs, Craigton / Neil Coles, full set of 11 clubs), rigid shafts, good condition, 81-674 4264 Tulse Hill / Brixton Hill.
f clubs, Dunlop, irons, 3,4,5,6,7,8 and ods, 1,3 and 5, putter, Dunlop bag and olf trolley, £150. 081-592 5944 Dagen-
f clubs, Hogan Metal, Thru - Bore , new ex USA, graphite shafts, driver and d, £150 ono each. Robert 081-458 5607 's Green.
f clubs, TP11 irons, 2 sand irons, 2 tay- de metal woods, putter and bag, £375 Sunderland Gortex waterproof rainsuit, 81-398 9395 Thames Ditton.
f clubs, 7 irons, putter, wood, bag, lla, £80 ono. 081-698 0097 Catford / gham.
f trolley, £15. 081-460 0628 Bromley.
f Clubs, full set, 9 irons, 4 woods, putter, rolley and umbrella, £200 ono. 081-804 Ponders End.
f Clubs, American Dynamic, almost irons, 1 metal wood, 1 Regal putter, plus ag, excellent condition, paid £225 3 s ago, will accept £95. 081-360 4451 more Hill.
vity boots, and frame, £50. Robert 58 5607 Golders Green.
n, multi-purpose, Leisurewise Body- with added leg and arm butterfly attach- , folds for easy storage, cost £210, as will accept £100. 0322 336143 evenings

**LF CLUBS, cheapest in town. Full new irons, £75. Set of woods, £45. from £15. Putters from £5. Trolleys ndividual irons £8 each. Also lots her sets of good quality irons, all 0 per set. Call 081-330 5807 any-**

**LF CLUBS, we are the trade-in spe- t. Buying, selling or exchanging, paid for all your surplus equip- Trade one for one. Balls for £4.99 , leather gloves £2.50 each, all her £1.95, Woods, irons, putters £5.99 etc. The Golf Centre, 24B ch Lane, East Finchley, N2. 081- 096.**

ne Multigym, York 2001, with leg curl g mate, excellent condition, £280. 0707 Herts.
hockey boots, Bauer, very good con- size 6, with blade guards, £30. 071-237 Bermondsey.
hockey kit, complete, fit 10-14 year 30 ono, also hockey boots, size 6, £30 71-241 5395 Dalston.
skates, black leather, as new, size 6.5 71-370 0563 Earls Court.
skates, black, leather, size 7, £15. 071- 753 Clapham.
skates, leather boots, white, size 6, 81-398 0602 Thames Ditton.
skates, white, for women, size 5, £10. ating pants, size 12, £10. 071-930 6641 1 769 6815 evenings and weekends



new, bargain at £75. New golf clubs, half set and bag, unwanted gift, serious realistic offers only. 081-520 7795 Walthamstow.
- **Nike leather baseball** boots, white, size 7, £15. 071-727 0896 Bayswater / Notting Hill.
- **Nordic skis,** Sundei Zebra sport with Rottesella bindings, 200cm, used once, excellent condition, ski poles, £75. 081-767 0138 Tooting.
- **Nordica ski boots,** for men, size 6.5-7, can deliver West London, £25. 0494 721274 Bucks.
- **Outbound rucksack,** 2, colour green, brand new, £80 each. 081-983 0279 East Poplar.
- **Pair skis,** please call for details. Ray 071-927 0019.
- **Power Glide 1,** computerised rowing machine, cost £125 new, will accept £45. 081-651 2256 Sanderstead / Selsdon.
- **Prinz expander** squash racquet, unused, £21. Prinz squash racquet, £12. louisville Slugger softball bats, £12.50. Softball net, very expensive leather, £20. Phil 081-894 6104 Twickenham.
- **Riding hat** for child, blue with peak and strap, size 6.5 (53), hardly used, £8 ono. 0895 630136 Uxbridge / Ruislip.
- **Riding jacket,** brown, and jodphurs, size 12, £15 each. Black riding boots, size 5, £10. 071-930 6641 Westminster.
- **Roller blades,** Bauer, size 7, bought Christmas, too small, hardly used, cost new £80 sell half price. 081-367 2268 Enfield.
- **Roller skates,** mens, size 8, leather boots, with skate board style tracks and wheels, hardly used, £15. 081-659 9442 Sydenham / Penge.
- **Roller skates,** size 8/9, leather soles, suede uppers and front stoppers, made in USA, as new, £35. 0689 842612 Orpington.
- **Rossignol Eagle skis,** 190cm, used for 2 weeks, excellent condition, £70. 0442 215472 Hertfordshire.
- **Rossignol Zephyr skis,** with Salomon bindings, 180cm, brand new, never used, in bag, with ski poles, £150. 081-767 0138 Tooting.
- **Rowing boat machine,** very good condition, £30. 081-346 3182 Finchley.
- **Rowing machine,** £10 ono. 071-635 0287 Peckham / New Cross.
- **Rowing machine,** Kettler GS Fitness, very good condition, £45. 0920 462800 or 0992 469929 Hertfordshire.
- **Rowing machine,** Tunturi TRGL, gym standard, padded seat, adjustable hydraulic oars, very good condition, £75. 081-520 1380 Walthamstow.
- **Rucksack,** Karrimor Lynx II, detachable pouche, £25 ono. 081-989 0702 after 1pm Wanstead.
- **Saddle,** firm leather, 17in, general purpose, Lovett and Ricketts, 3 years old, £100 ono. 081-592 0571 Dagenham.
- **Salopettes,** black, small size, as new, £10. 081-291 9576 Forest Hill.
- **Salopettes,** ladies, black, size 12-14, £15. 071-930 6641 Westminster.
- **Ski boot,** Nordica, size 5.5, grey / white, £25. 081-958 6946 Edgware.
- **Ski boots,** adult, size 8, as new, £30. 0708 727916 Essex.
- **Ski boots,** size 3, Nordica, pale grey. Also, ski suit, 5ft 2in, one piece, C & A, both very good condition, £20 the lot or £15 each. 071-735 8554 Kennington / Oval.
- **Ski boots,** size 6, ideal for beginners, plus ski boot bag, £55 ono. 081-977 6917 Teddington.
- **Skis,** Kastle FX Penta, 190cm, suit wide range from beginner to high intermediate, with Tyrolia 290D bindings, £50. Salomon FX61 ski boots, size 8, suit beginner to intermediate, £25. 081-671 5358 evenings or answerphone Tulse Hill / Brixton Hill.
- **Skis,** 180's with bindings, £50. 081-904 8806 or 0836-272764 after 6pm North Wembley.
- **Slazenger squash balls,** individually boxed, brand new, yellow dot, 50p each. 081-429 2964 Pinner / Eastcote.
- **Speedboat,** 17ft, 3 litre, OMC cobra inboard, galvanised trailer, £6,500. 0992 440771 evenings Waltham Cross.
- **Squash racket,** head, graphite, brand new, extended strings, also aluminium, £15. 081-959 1302 Mill Hill.
- **Sunbed,** 6ft, 6 tube, as new, £100. 081-518 2430 Ilford.
- **Super exerciser,** chrome black, for shoulders and chest development, 2 strengths available, £5 each. 081-688 3986 Croydon.
- **Swing seat,** lemon-yellow fibreglass, surf board style, with dorsal fin and stabilisers, excellent condition except small scratch, minus ropes, unwanted present, £100. 071-407 3101 Southwark.

**◆ SKI CLOTHING, and a variety of sports clothing available. Sport services include ski clothing hire, racket restringing, repair of footballs and cricket pads, regripping all golf clubs and engraving trophies. SQUARE DEAL SPORT, 460 Chiswick High Rd, London, W4. Tel 081-995 6870.**

- **Table tennis bats,** 2, £1. Jokari bats, 2, £2. Nordika skiboots, size 10, £6. Caver ski boots, size 8, £5. San Marco ski mountaineering boots, £5. Rock boots, EB, size 11, £5. 2 cork dartboards, £4 each. 081-449 7957 Barnet.
- **Tennis racket,** Donnay Athena, top of range, powerful, comfortable, 85 per cent

6282 Streatham.
- **Tennis racket,** Prince JR Tour, good co dition, £10. Wimbledon Junior, aluminiu good condition, £15. 081-890 9558 Feltham East Bedfont.
- **Tennis rackets,** 2, small head Slazenger, £20. Wooden Dunlop, £20. Wilso large head, £35. 071-930 6641 Westminste
- **Tennis racquet,** Advantage, mens g size, £8 no offers. 071-371 6741 Earls Cou
- **Top tennis,** squash, badmington, rack string maching, all sensible offers considere 081-942 1217 New Malden.
- **Top Stringing machine** for tennis, squa and badminton racket, any senislbe offer co sidered. 081-942 1217 New Malden.
- **Tunturi EL400** exercise bike, wo £1,700, offers around £300 considered. 08 983 0859 Bethnal Green.
- **Two tennis rackets,** in frames, £5 eac 081-767 0138 Tooting.
- **Wave ski,** raider, complete outfit and w suit, £150 ovno. 081-886 1441 Palmers Gree
- **Weider XR140 Club** class rowi machine with hydraulic cylinders and electro counter, hardly used, cost £100 new, w accept £50. 0474 509506 Graves End.
- **Weight bench** with butterfly press, l extensions, weights with bar and 2 ha weights, Weider. 081-671 4190 Tulse Hill / Br ton Hill.
- **Weight bench** with leg lifts and sit bench, plus weights and barbells, very go condition, £65 ono. 081-533 5636 Hackney.
- **Wilder weights,** and chest expander, £ Tony 071-372 0720 West Hampstead.
- **Workout bench and** weights, never use brand new, £65. 081-524 2050 Chingford.
- **York multi-gym 2001,** £250 ono. 08 15066 Gorebridge.
- **York sit-up bench,** £10. 081-688 39 Croydon.
- **York vinyl weight** lifting set, big bar / dum bells, also Incline Inch, nearly new, £45 or 081-888 8940 Wood Green.
- **York Multigym 101,** with pec deck and s of dumb bells, only 5 months old, only used times, £220 ono. 081-788 9905 Putney.

***For Winter Holidays/Skiing see 858***

## Sports equipment general

**211B** **wanted**

- **Aerobic bouncer / trampoline,** sturdy and in good condition, will collect from northwest London, cash paid. 071-794 9510 West Hampstead.
- **ABSOLUTELY ALL SPORTS equipment wanted for cash or exchange. All accepted in any condition, positively none refused! (Plus all electrical and general goods wanted). Also large selection on sale. GENERAL GOODS EXCHANGE, 64 Notting Hill Gate, London W11 (open 7 days, 10am-8pm). Enquiries, 071-221 1075. (1 minute from Notting Hill Gate Tube).**
- **Boxing gloves,** 2 pairs for adults and also a large punchbag, the type that hangs from ceilings, for martial arts training, cannot pay cash but will swap large ghetto blaster and collect anywhere in SE London. Alan 081-694 2485 after 5pm, Deptford.
- **Dumbells or Barbells,** x 2, approximately 10lbs each, wanted. 071-794 4879 Hampstead.
- **Exercise bike,** second hand, in good condition, will collect. Rao 071-241 4270 Dalst
- **Golf clubs,** left handed, and 1 set ri handed clubs, practice or second hand g balls also wanted. 071-928 8111 Kenningto
- **Golf shoes,** ladies size 5 and men's si 11. Will pay up to £20 each for as new sho 081-542 9606 evenings Merton / South Wi bledon.
- **Hang glider harness,** suitable for Go marque Gyr 188, also any other accessori cash waiting for decent equipment. 081-9 7113 Wanstead.
- **Mens ski boots,** size 8.5, skis, bindin and poles, also ski suit or jacket and salopett to suit 38in chest, 32in waist, good quality, go condition and reasonably priced. 071-277 67 New Cross.
- **PT Bouncer,** trampolet, achieve aro exercise indoors safely and easily, £30. 07 724 8518 Paddington.
- **Ski suit,** must be red and in good conditi size 12 - 14. Also boots required, size 7. 07 486 7921 days 081-566 1590 eves Ealing.

## Craft products, tools & equipment

**215A** **offered**

- **Clarke professional mechanic** stacking tall chest and cabinet, red, fully locking and secure, brand new, never used, unwanted gift, cost £400 brand new, will accept £275. 081-888 8940 Palmers Green.
- **Dress maker's stand,** Kent and Lindsale, child size 4 years, brand new, £150. 081-951 0769 Edgware.
- **Gravelgraff motorised engraving** machine, set of brass copies, cutters, approximately 1,000 engraving plates and over 55 3in x 1in laminated plastic badges for engra ing, £550 ono. 0372 377724 Surrey.
- **PHOTOGRAPHS ON PLATES. A wo derful way of having your favouri photo on display. We have a good ran of gift plates and trays for every eve So why not give it a try and see for you self? Contact M.D. PHOTOGLAZI 081-965 9275**

**Inverter (Clearance Sale)**
**(No. 2)** 1999

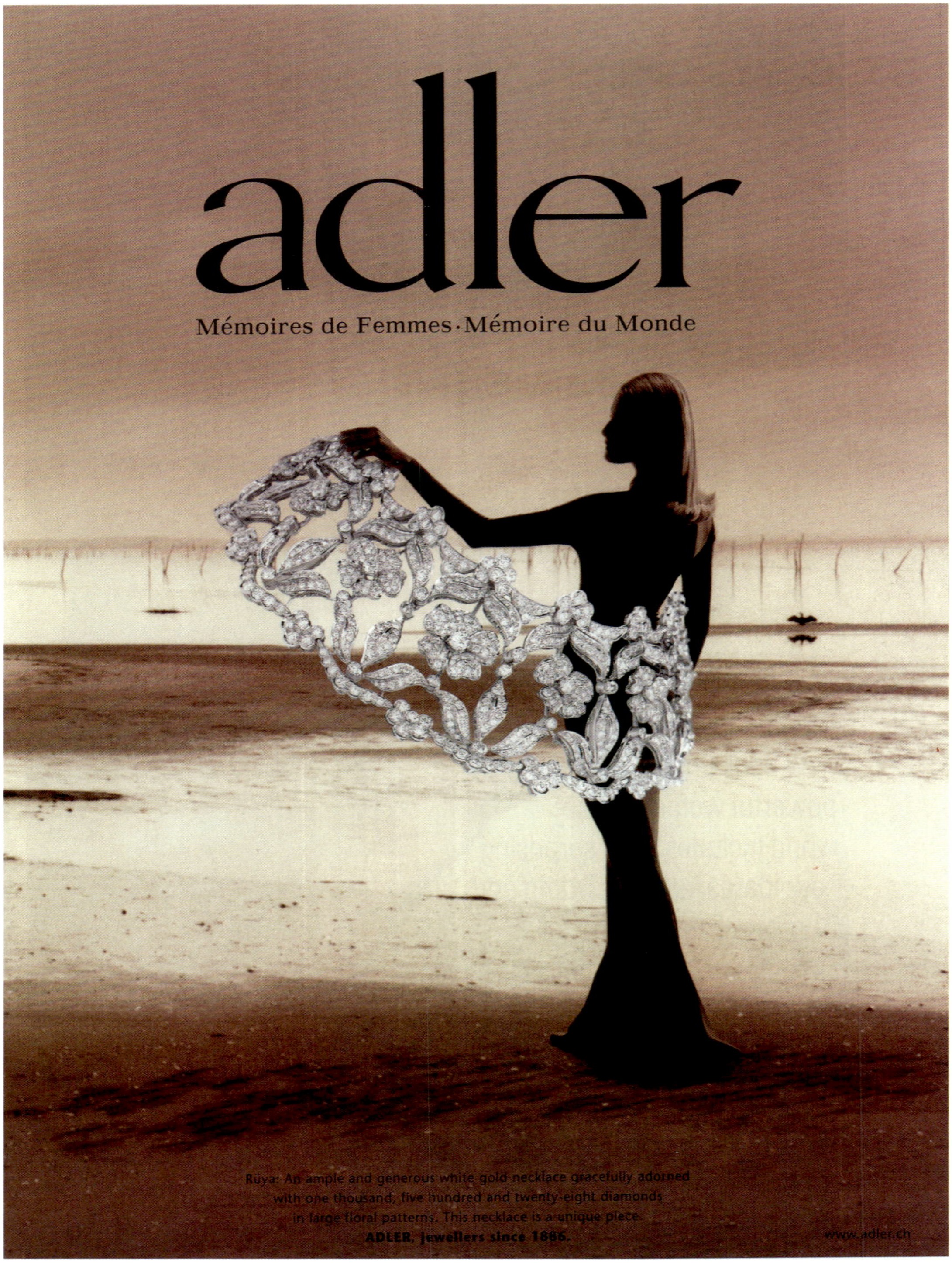

ı, Askedal model, 2 blue
s, 236 x 80cm, never used,
1353 after 4pm. .

ngle, antique, pine, excel-
) new, will accept £400.
ıssex.

solid pine, 180cm high,
deep, with cornice & extra
ost new, quick sale, £230.

cm wide, £150 ono. 0170

g size, wooden surround,
£800 ono. 0181-451 4447

**ıest quality, lowest pri-
eds from £350, superb
ecialized service, fully
ıcts, low prices include
lation, Tel 01542 409076.**

**HIGHEST QUALITY, lo-**

0181-908 6850 NW

● **Diesel Jeans,** zip fly, bootleg, unwanted present, cost £60, will accept £20 no offers. 0181-265 6853 Greenwich

● **Donna Karan** evening jacket, stunning, wild, silk, green, with sash, size 10-12, worn twice, bought £1,500, accept £450 ono. Three cream casual tops, Ralph Lauren, cost over £100 each, accept, £38 each. 0956-248 168 SW.

● **Dress,** slim, long, dark sepia, faded patches, very plain, flat looking, £36. 0171-737 0651 SW.

● **Dresses,** 1950s, floral prints, bright patterns, bag full, £15 ono. 01189 506255 / 0181-561 0297.

● **Four seasons** khaki coat, fur trim hood, size 10/12, warm, vgc, £80. Italian angora wool dress, size 10, £20. Black trouser suit, with lining, polyester / viscose, size 10, £40. 0181-930 5635 Harrow Weald.

● **Girls skirt,** green, pleated, and pinafore dress, girls green school cardigan, whole uniform age 6 to 7, £20. 01992 613666 Herts.

● **Jacket, black leather,** size 12, Sacks & Brendlor, hardly worn, cost £275, accept £90

£200. 0181-993 515

● **Mac,** knee length
good condition, £8.

● **Maternity dres**
and other plain dark
£10 each. 0171-277

● **Mink fur coat,** th
ful, mixture of brown
value, offers please.

● **Mink tail hat** / he
888 9739 North.

● **Numerouas Eva**
18 to 24, shirts, blou
pants, from £1 each

● **Pastal mink co**
as new, with origina
620420 Cheshunt, H

● **Red squirrel** in c
491 3674 .

● **Rifat Ozbek** dres
cellent condition, cos
0181-524 9763 Chir

---

690. North.

**Collector of phonecards** is looking for phonecards from all word. I'll pay for the consigment of your phone cards or change it. V. Brezina, Gorkeho 791, 43601Litvinov, CZ

**Denby storage jars,** original Arabesque, 1970, £45 the lot. Poole plate, 8in, signed, dated 1960, £35. Poole plate, scalloped trought-style, black / brown, £35. Grays jug, Suzie Cooper design, £35. 0181-390 6410 Surbiton.

**Freddie Mercury** autograph, on colour photo on stage, framed, offers. 0181-351 7595.

**Fruit machine,** Belle Fruit, £10 jackpot, many features, modern style, £110 ono. 0181-88 1389 or 0410-494 108 mobile .

**Gollywog badges,** 36 different, first £100 secures, collectors items. Phone Ireland: +353-1321558

**Helicopter,** radio-controlled, F1 Carbon 60, with OS61 engine, tuned pipe & upgrades, only 3 hours use, uncrashed, no radio, £350. 0181-

● **Ty Beanie,** slip on tag protectors, £10 for 100. 01732 359996 Kent.

● **TV Beanies,** Snowball, £32. Glory, £30. Gig, £15. Whisper, £15. Pinchers, zip, £15 each. Teddy 98, £50. 01732 359996 Kent.

● **Warhammer,** Chaos figures, offers. 0181-760 0628 Surrey.

● **Wing,** made of metal, broken glass, 1m long, q pair, strange fancy costume, £30. Double duck, stuffed sepia coloured, tiny, ornamental, reasonable condition, no timewasters, £50. 0171-733 8681 Brixton.

● **X-Files signed comic,** limited edition, signed by Ray Thomas incl authentic certificate, sealed, very rare piece. $500 or ono. email: clippartnership@hotmail.com

● **Zipper Star lighters,** from Saigon, Vietnam, set of 12 engraved with poetry from the war, all original, each item is different, offers. Kevin 0961 156946 mobile NW.

---

for only £14.95
per square yard + VAT
MASSIVE STOCK OF
PRE-FINISHED FLOORING
19 Colindale Ave, NW9 5DS
0181 358 6222
50919

**Doors,** solid pine, 2100 x 900mm & other 100 x 850mm, 5 panels front & back, £75 each. 171-602 0896 West.

**Double glazed window,** 420 x 420mm, obscure glass, opening vent, as new, £35. 0181-50 9601 Bromley

**Electrical earth cable,** 16mm, £20 per 0m drum. Also 77mm, £100 per 50m drum. 20 arth clips, £10. 0181-292 4021.

**EWELL RECLAMATION, reclaimed flooring and timber, 2nd hand stock bricks, RSJ's, York stone pavings, cast iron fire laces & surrounds, pine doors, flooring &**

● **POLESTAR FLOORING LAYING, SANDING, FINISHING. all types of hardwood flooring supplied and fitted to high standard, traditional design to modern laser cut imported panels, existing floors sanded (sand, fill and finish £20-£30 m2) depending on floor and area condition, we import our own hardwoods. Competitive prices. Tel 0171 266 2966 or Fax 0171 266 2984**

● **Quarry tiles, grey,** 170, very good condition, some boxed, £50 ono. 0181-556 9530 / 0961 428689 mobile. East.

● **Radiator,** 60 x 90cm. 0171-221 3041 West.

● **Sand,** sepia coloured, mixed grain, 2 large bags, £25. 40 decorative sticks, useful for gardening / fencing, £20. Paint, estuary water, bright off white matt, water based, 3 gallons £40. 0181-450 5846 NW.

● **Shelving,** plastic coated, metal, adjustable, 1 metre wide sections, 20/10cms deep optional, with pull-out shelves, 1000 metres total, will separate, offers. 01277 372112

# 72

**Flasher** 1996 –

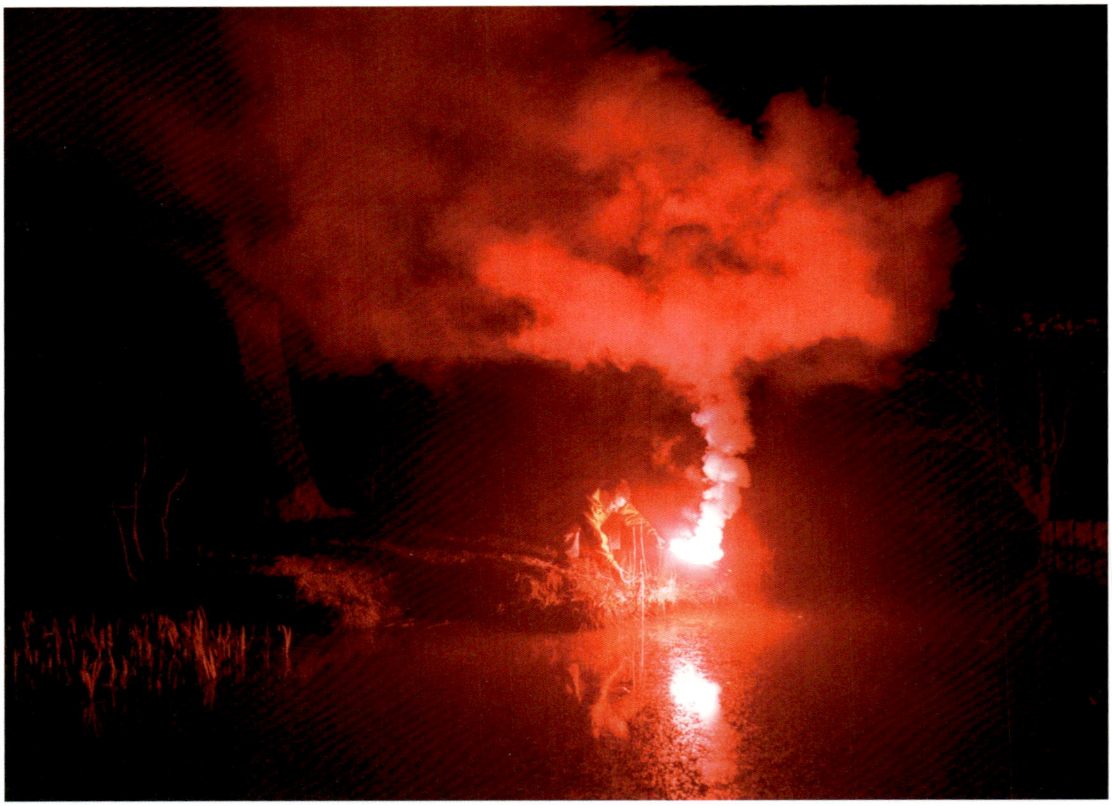

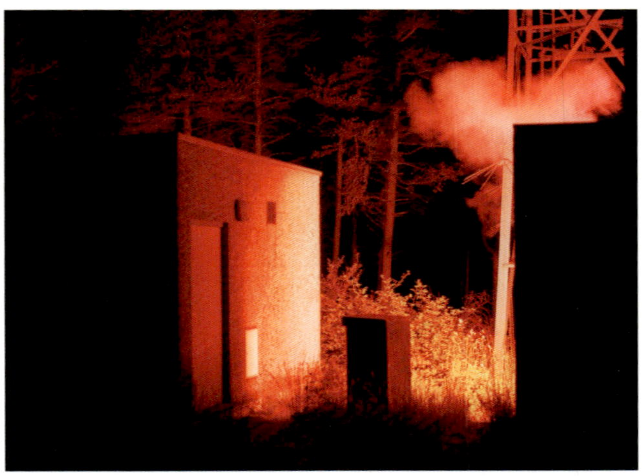

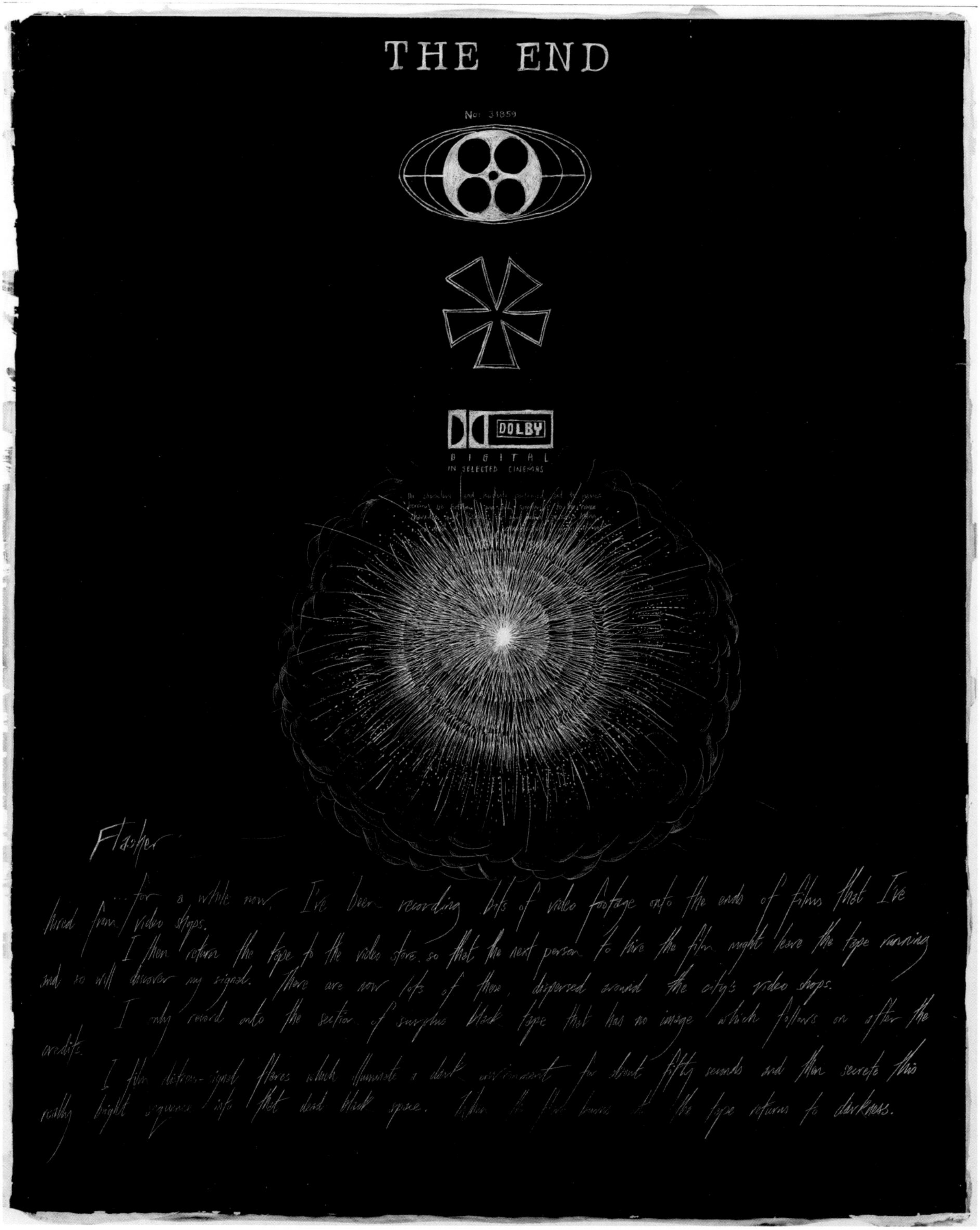
THE END
No: 31859
DOLBY
DIGITAL
IN SELECTED CINEMAS
Flasher
...for a while now, I've been recording bits of video footage onto the ends of films that I've hired from video shops.
I then return the tape to the video store so that the next person to hire the film might leave the tape running and so will discover my signal. There are now lots of these, dispersed around the city's video shops.
I only record onto the section of surplus black tape that has no image which follows on after the credits.
I film distress-signal flares which illuminate a dark environment for about fifty seconds and then secrete this really bright sequence into that dead black space. When the flash burns out the tape returns to darkness.

**Better Scenery** 2000

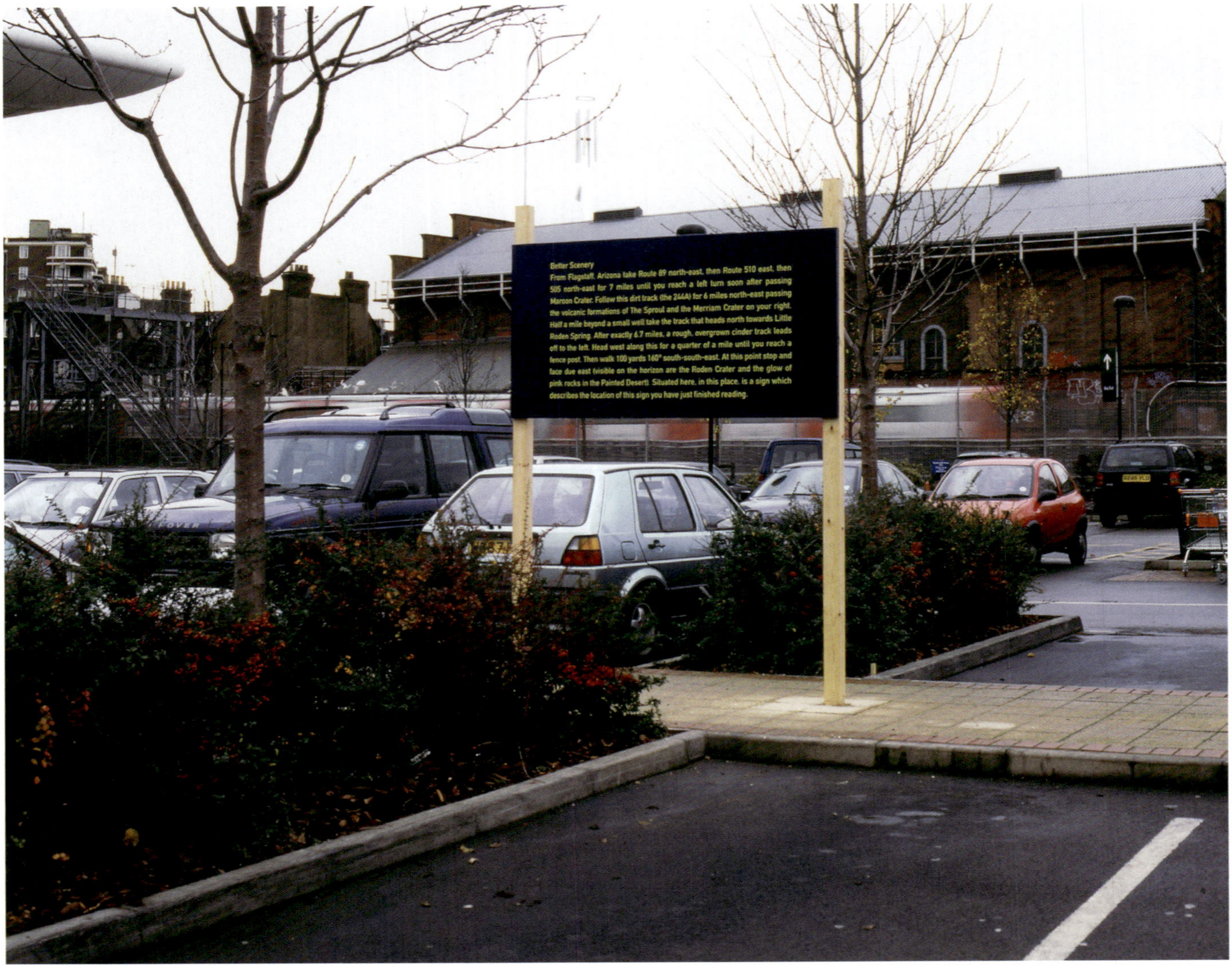

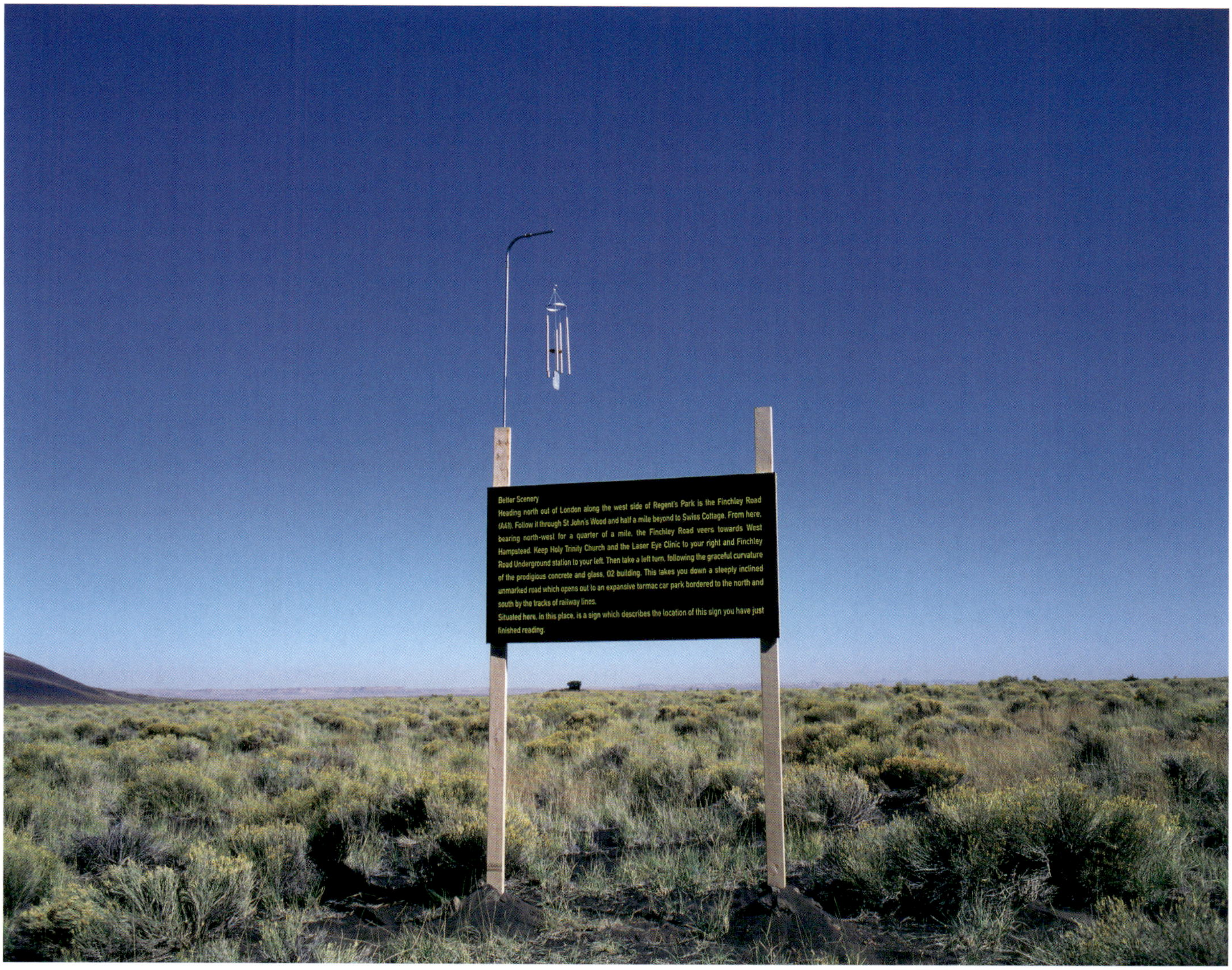
Better Scenery
Heading north out of London along the west side of Regent's Park is the Finchley Road (A41). Follow it through St John's Wood and half a mile beyond to Swiss Cottage. From here, bearing north-west for a quarter of a mile, the Finchley Road veers towards West Hampstead. Keep Holy Trinity Church and the Laser Eye Clinic to your right and Finchley Road Underground station to your left. Then take a left turn, following the graceful curvature of the prodigious concrete and glass, O2 building. This takes you down a steeply inclined unmarked road which opens out to an expansive tarmac car park bordered to the north and south by the tracks of railway lines.
Situated here, in this place, is a sign which describes the location of this sign you have just finished reading.

**Untitled Stile (Teenage Version)** 1991

opposite page:
**Meeting** 1999

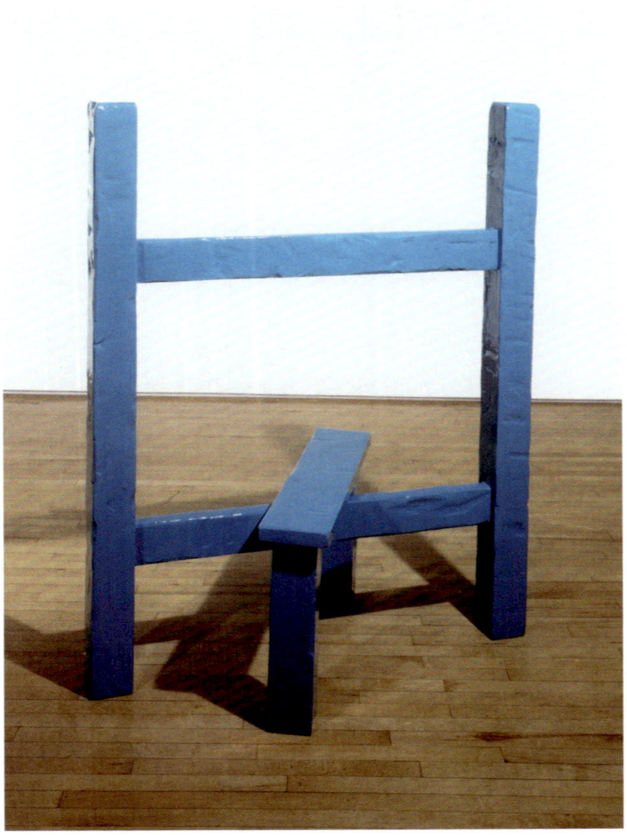

# MEETING

*of*

people with stammers

*to*

describe a fire

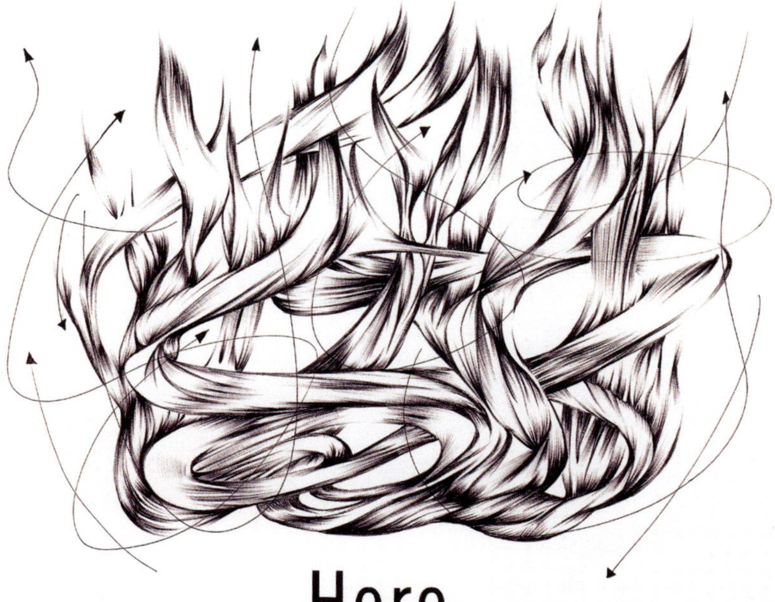

Here

Everyone Welcome

**Night Shift** 2004

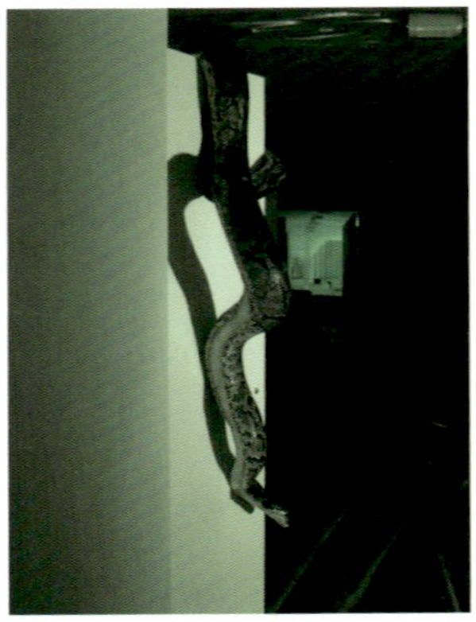

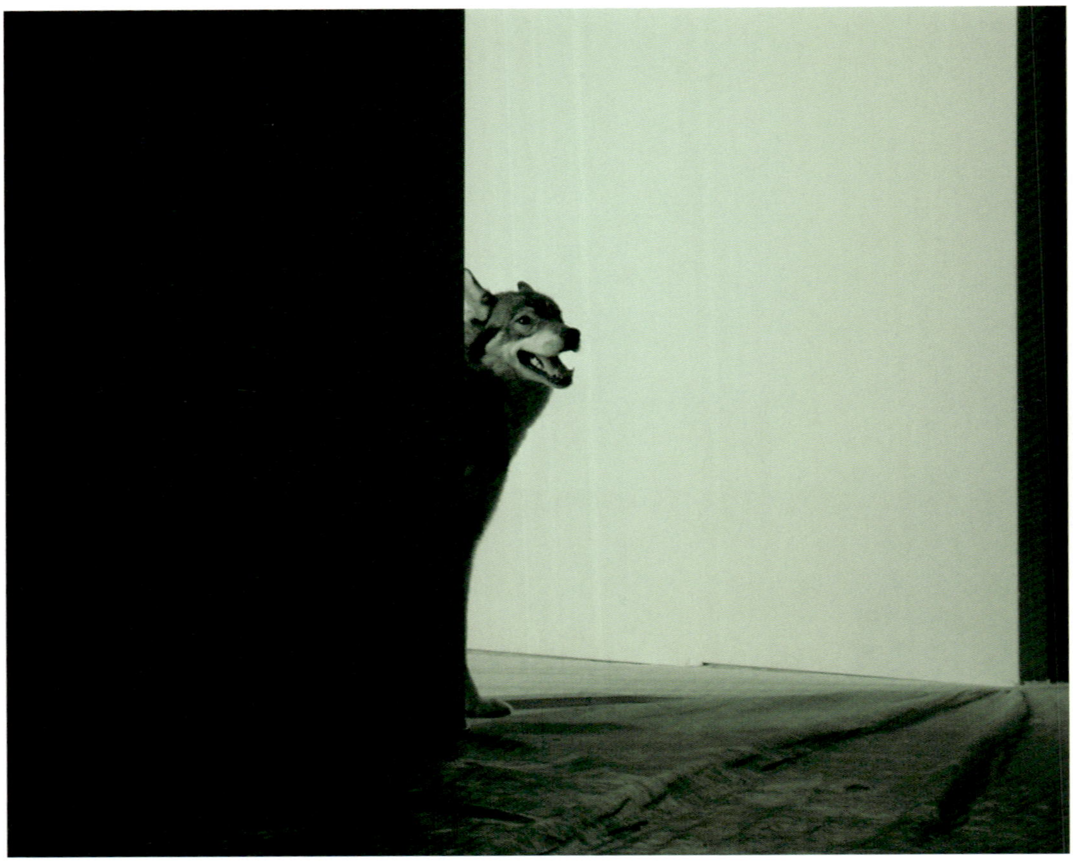

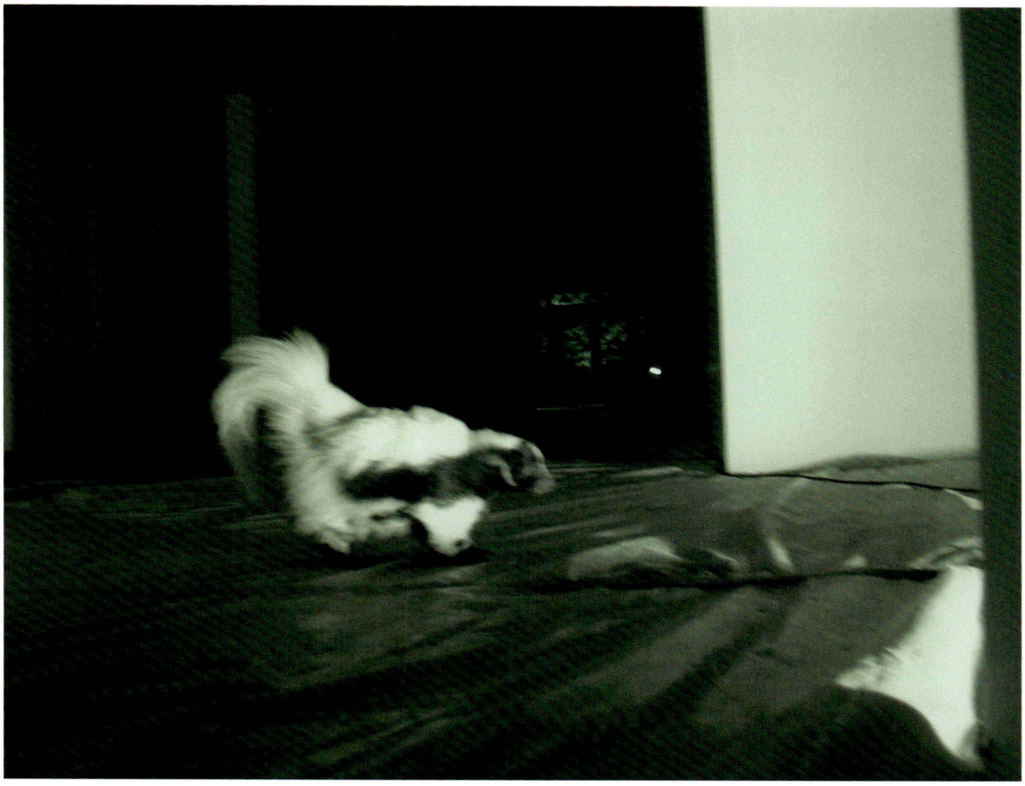
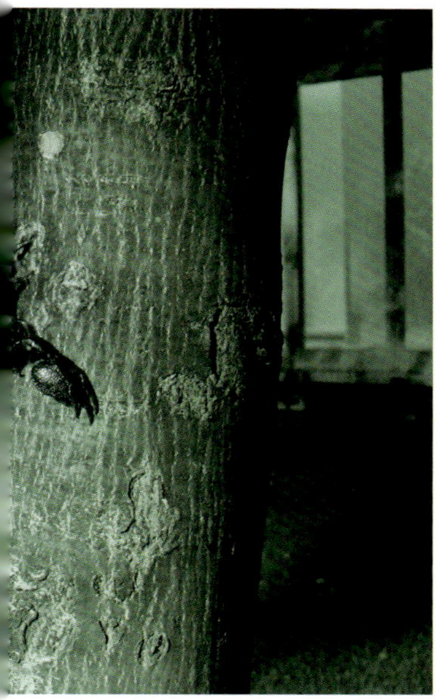
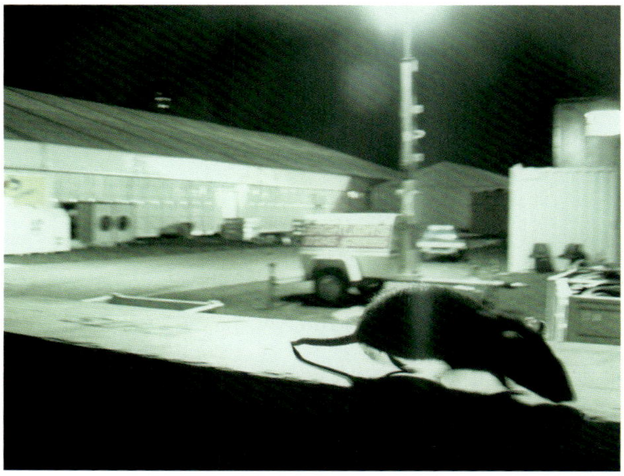

**Night Shift** 2004

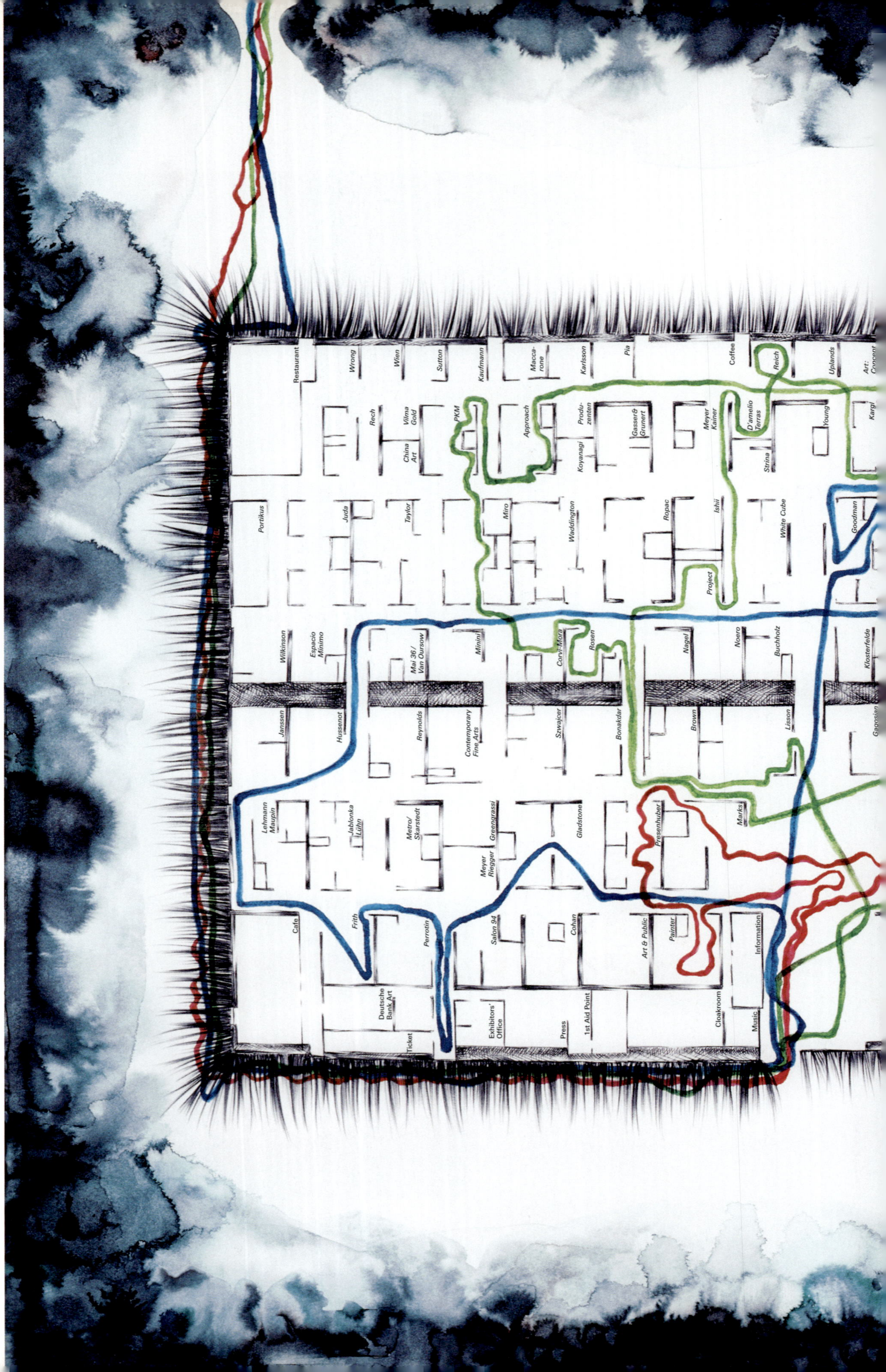

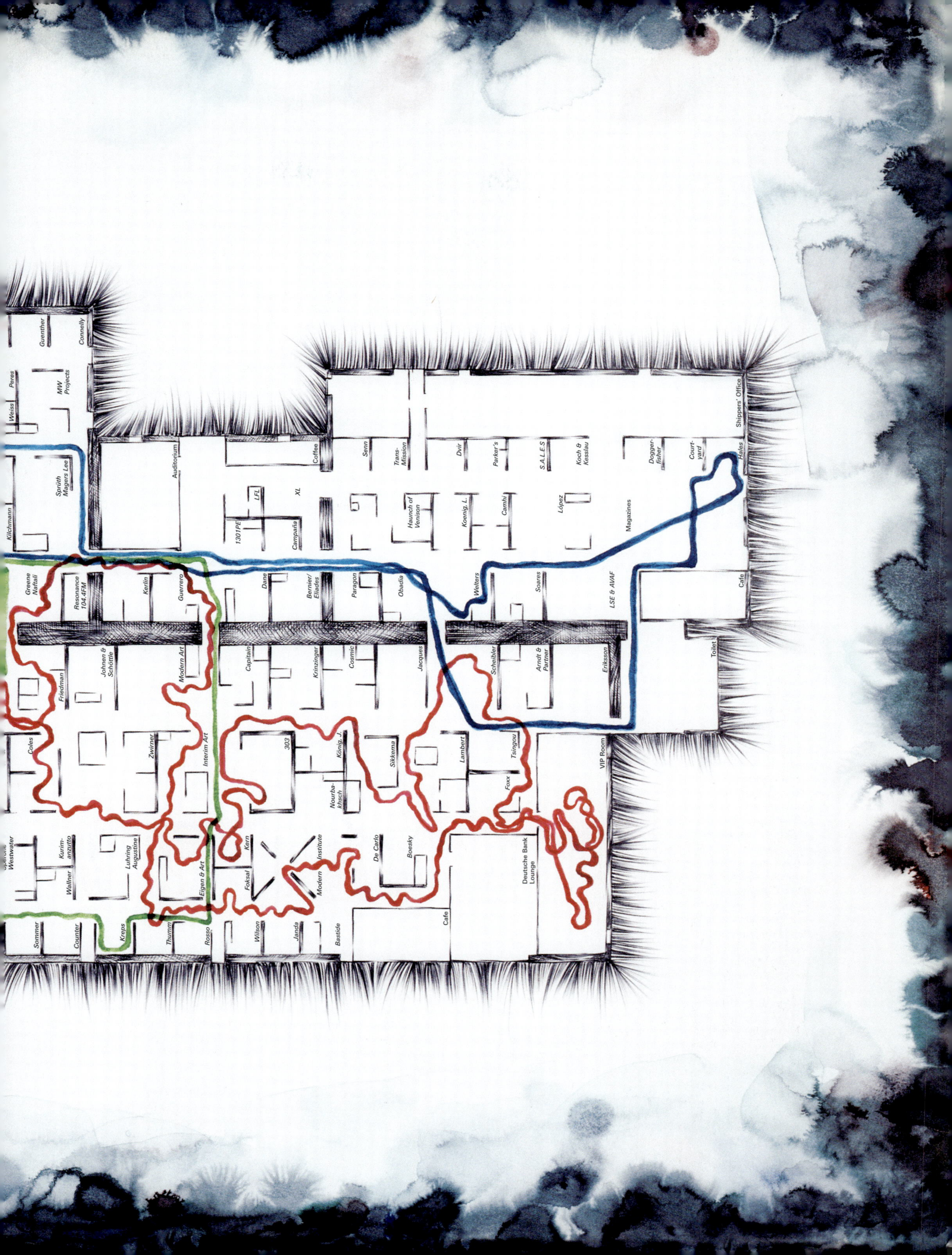
Guenther
Connelly
Peres
MW Projects
Weiss
Sprüth Magers Lee
Kilchmann
Auditorium
Coffee
Senn
Trans-Mission
Dvir
Parker's
S.A.L.E.S
Koch & Kesslau
Dogger-fisher
Court-yard
Hales
Shippers' Office
LFL
XL
1301PE
Campaña
Haunch of Venison
Koenig, L.
Camhi
López
Magazines
Greene Naftali
Resonance 104.4FM
Kerlin
Guerrero
Dane
Bernier/Eliades
Paragon
Obadia
Welters
Soares
LSE & AVAF
Cafe
Toilet
Friedman
Johnen & Schöttle
Modern Art
Capitain
Krinzinger
Cosmic
Jacques
Scheibler
Arndt & Partner
Eriksson
Coles
Zwirner
Interim Art
303
König, J.
Sikkema
Lambert
Tsingou
Foxx
VIP Room
Nourbakhsch
Westwater
Kurimanzutto
Luhring Augustine
Wallner
Kern
Modern Institute
De Carlo
Boesky
Deutsche Bank Lounge
Foksal
Eigen & Art
Sommer
Counter
Kreps
Thumm
Rosso
Wilson
Janda
Bastide
Cafe

**Flasher** 1996 –

opposite page:
**Night Shift** 2004

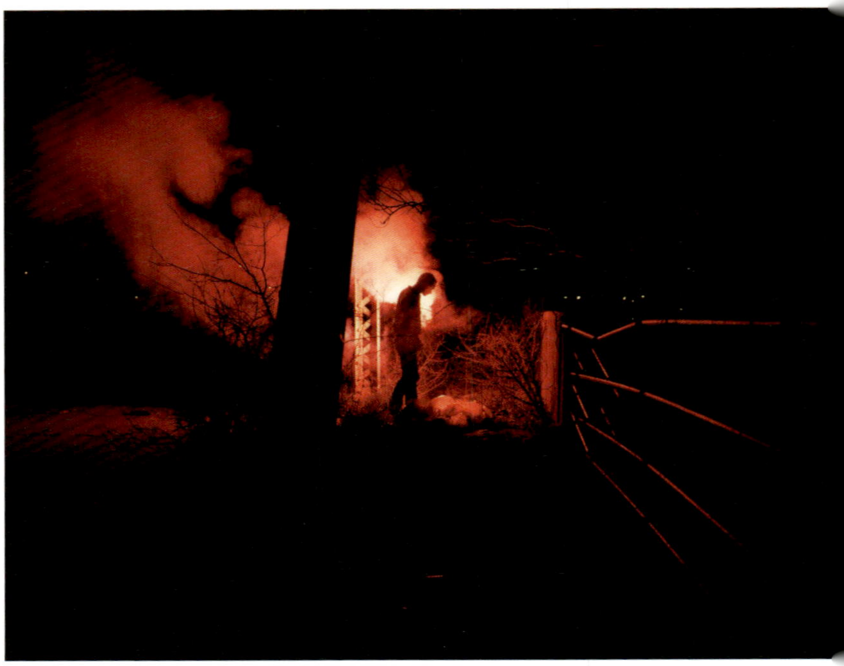

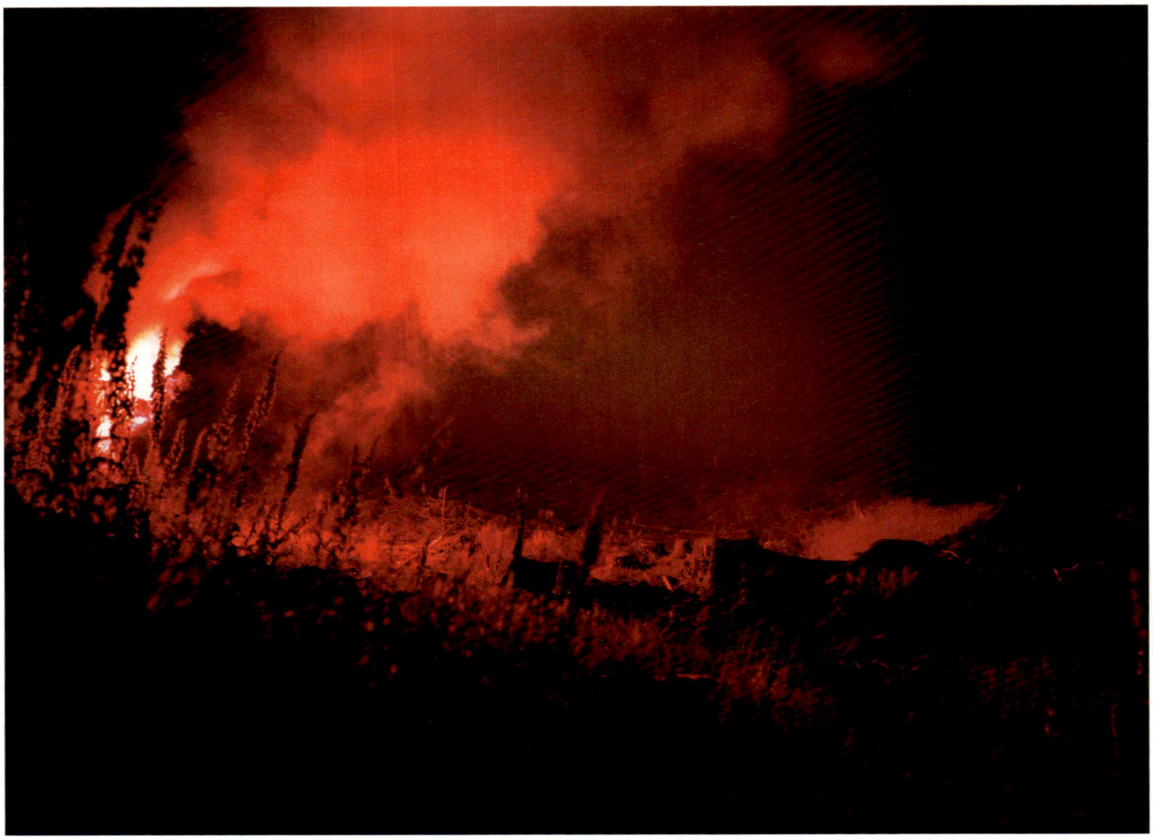

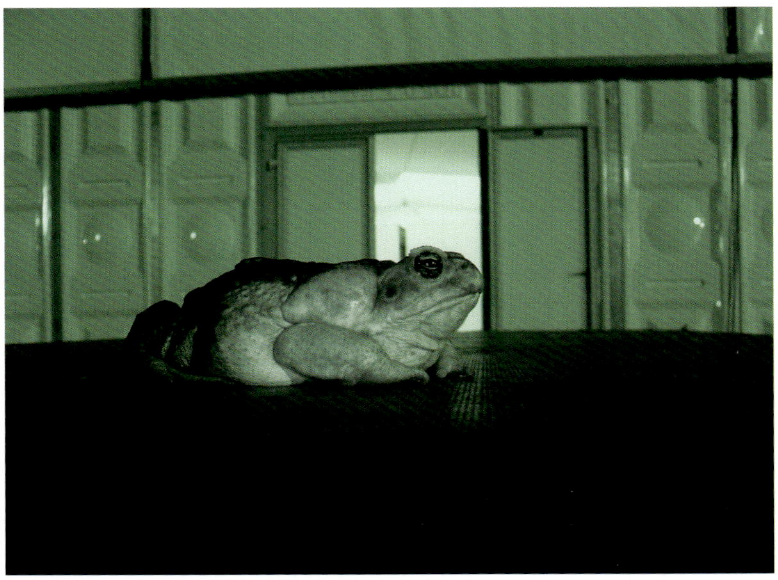

**Looper** 2003

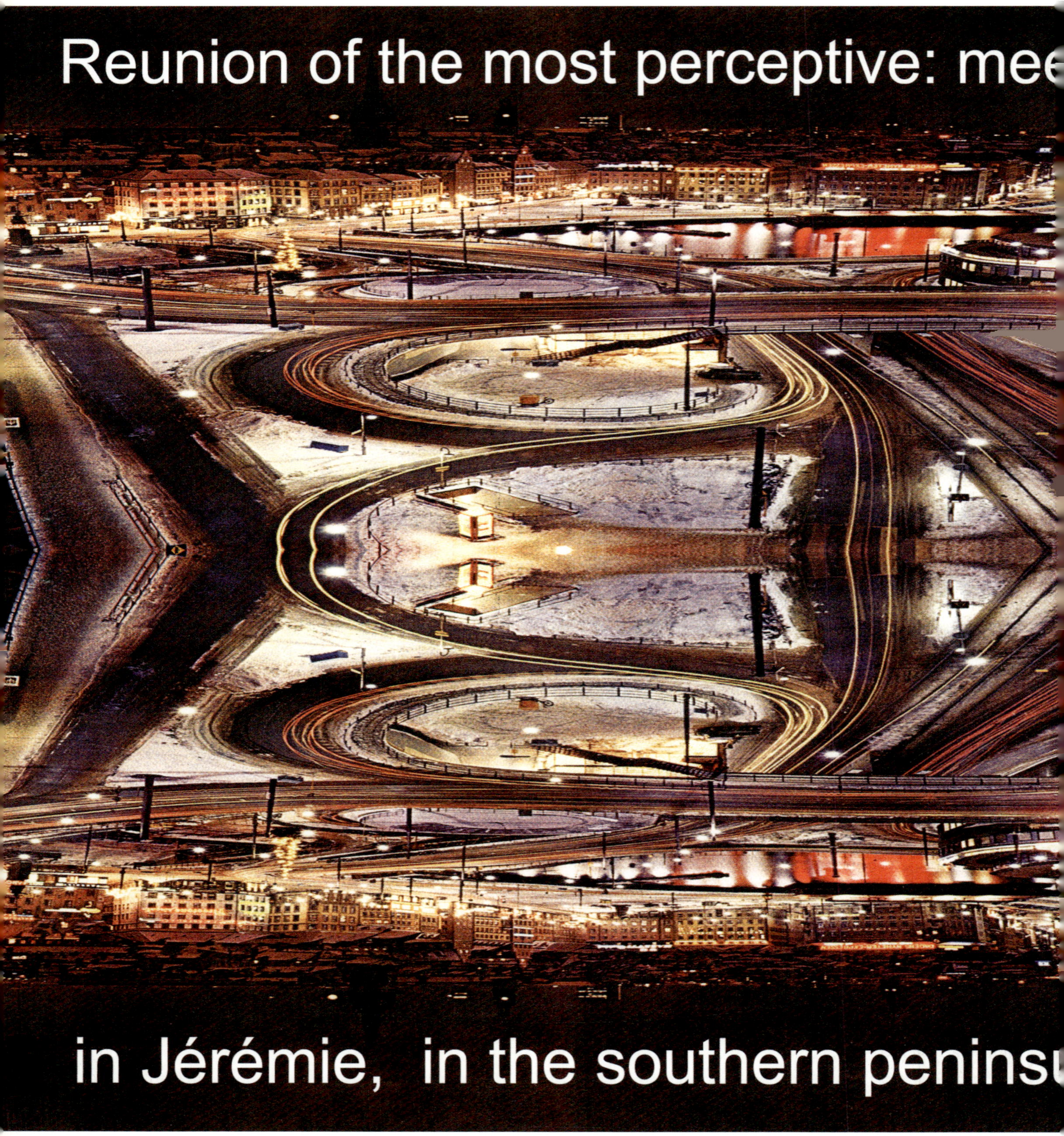
Reunion of the most perceptive: mee
in Jérémie, in the southern peninsu

the bar of the *Foyer Cultural*, a hotel

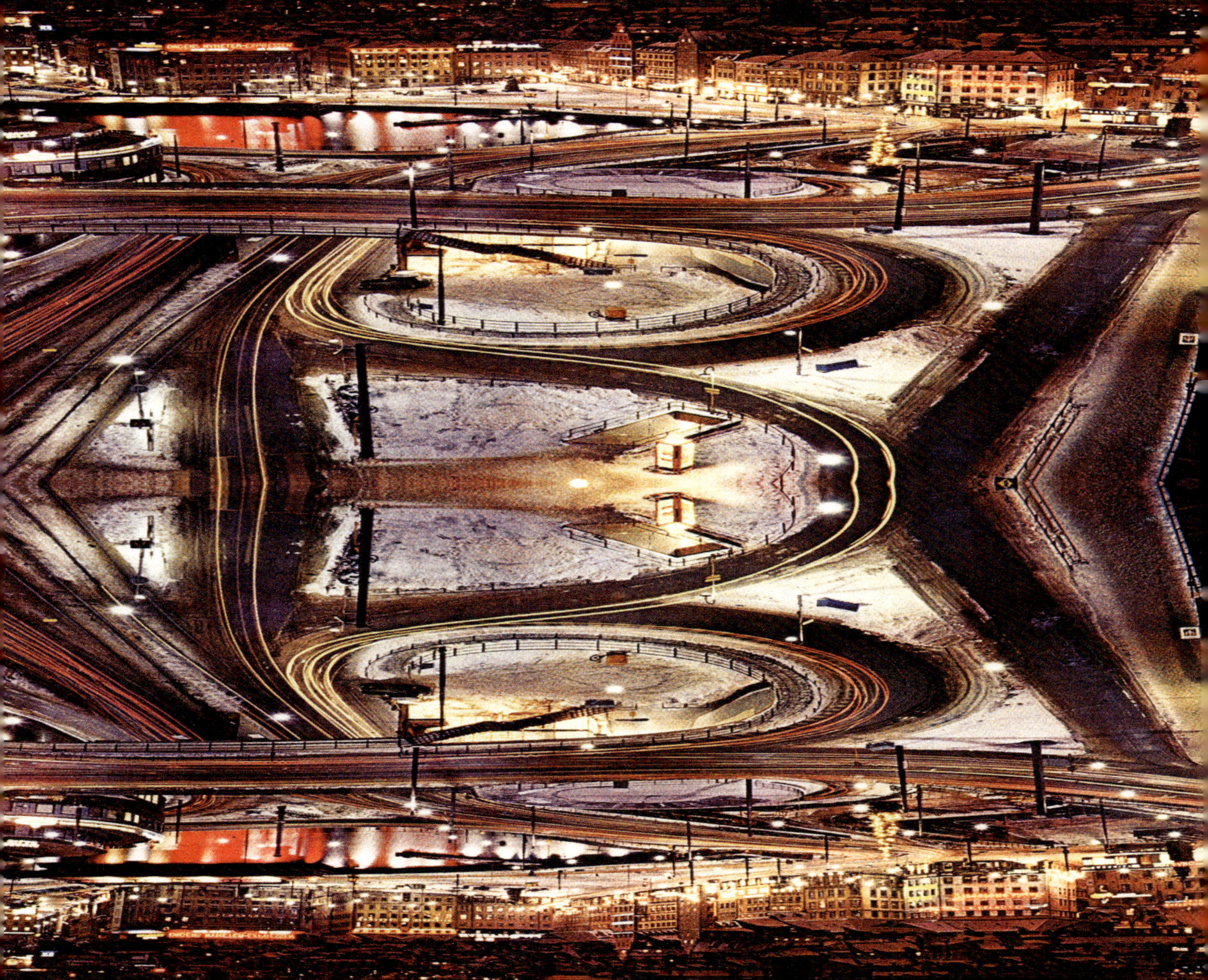

12 hours from Port au Prince, Haiti.

## More Dark

Martin Herbert

When getting on for half a lifetime has been spent in one conception of order, reorientation is no five-minute business.
John Wyndham, The Day of the Triffids (1951)

Countenance this: a world where Ikea employees are in charge of managing important data. They've lost some, attempt to retrieve it from a landfill, but instead discover an archive that – for all that it appears composed of old copies of Artforum and VHS cassettes labelled 'Chodzko' – bespeaks, they feel, some big agricultural disaster. Photographic and Super-8 footage, supposedly extracted from these annals, features withered vines and wind-dried leaves, people scrabbling through dirt in sunshine. 'It was only early summer,' say Finnish and Cantonese speakers (in English), 'but all the plants were already dying. Time had accelerated again.' In order to divine the import of their bleak bounty, the researchers go to an 'Editing Station', a precarious shack perched in a cabbage field; but they fall out and split up, dividing the files. One takes their share of the files to 'The Ark', where this simulacrum of mankind is storing its treasures; another worker, a young boy with striking blonde curls, lowers his bag of information over a cliff-edge towards the mysterious 'Chalk Pit People', in what looks like a gypsy encampment; a third takes his to the 'Comparison Centre', and places it thoughtfully next to some nascent flora. 'Slowly, because of "and yet despite all this",' says the voiceover in the film's closing stages, 'the plants slowly began to recover. And time ... stood ... still.' Finis.

Much of Adam Chodzko's nine-minute film Yet (2006) is voiced by the narrators in their own languages, whose geopolitical disconnect from each other reinforces the film's mood of alienation, its embrace of a parallel present where this consonance of countries makes sense. The musicality of the languages carries the viewer along, just as a dream logic of conundrums and resolutions propels the scant lineaments of narrative. Nevertheless, the whole is eminently collapsible: a solution is found, but the voiceover suggests that the workers might have hindered as much as helped. And actually it's not clear that there was ever a problem. The Ikea data-clerks, so it might appear from the 'archive' material cut into the film (and ominously soundtracked with bursts of BBC Radiophonic Workshop-style static and bleeps), have merely uncovered some vintage footage of an archaeological dig and some photographic documentation of dried plants, and jumped to conclusions. Maybe they simply got the seasons wrong. What they solve, and how, is left tantalisingly unclear in a manner that resonates with the film's title: for 'yet', as a conjunction, implies a persistent, external, conditional aspect to the film, an extra parameter or further qualification. There is often the sense of such a 'yet', or a cluster of them, animating Chodzko's artworks: and, usually, a withholding of precisely what that 'yet' is.

Yet is among several of his recent films ghosted by the approximate atmosphere of earthbound science fiction, hitched thereby to an amorphous tradition in which apparently believable normality is tweaked in order that a fabulist story might be convincingly assayed. This not-quite-pantheon admits of a range of practitioners. Chris Marker, whose economical repurposing of photographic stills in La Jetée (1962) resonates strongly with Yet, is one obvious inclusion. But so are exponents of the dystopian English sci-fi tradition such as John Wyndham and JG Ballard, who use the cloying familiarity of the everyday as a counterpoise to root eruptive strangeness. One might also factor in John Smith's film The Black Tower (1985-7), whose

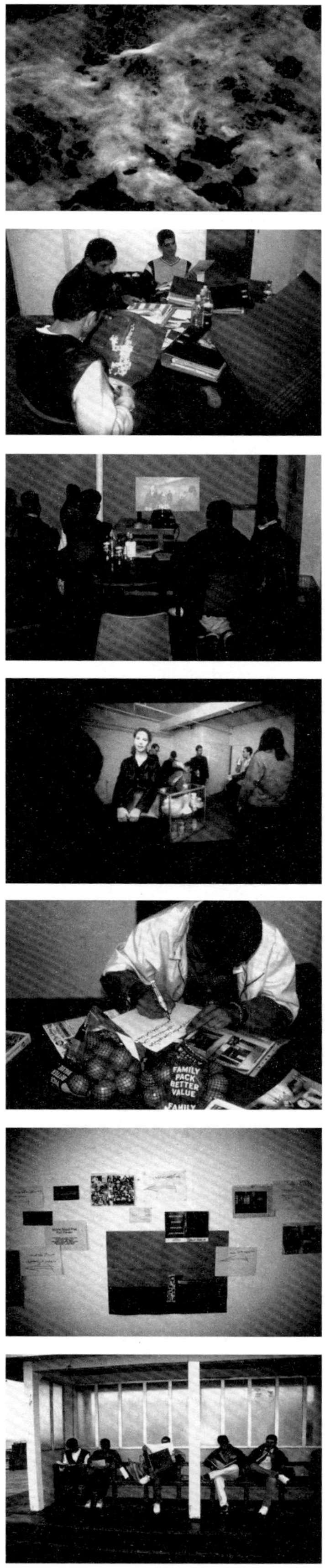


Cell-a (details) 2002

narrator feels himself pursued by a menacing fragment of London's architecture; Patrick Keiller's imposition of semi-fictional narratives upon neutral footage of London and suburban England in London (1994) and Robinson in Space (1997); and even artists such as Stanley Spencer, who envisioned resurrections and crucifixions in his Berkshire hometown of Cookham. Chodzko's filmmaking, of late, has been characterised by a comparable estrangement of environmental familiars: an analogy, perhaps, for the fragile disorder that trembles beneath the supposed solidity and clarity of the social.

And so Around (2007, one of four works for Breaking Ground, Dublin) speaks of a mysterious spectral force enclosing Ballymun, a Dublin housing estate (outside of which, for example, electronic devices such as Tamagotchis temporarily die and kites strike invisible barriers before plummeting from the sky). Meanwhile in Hole (2007, created for the contemporary art gallery MAMbo in Bologna, Italy) a woman agrees to an artist's request to broadcast her daily thoughts and feelings on an LED board in a newly opened museum. This never actually happens, yet five holes bored permanently in the museum's frontage attest to the removal of the board. Chodzko's project-in-progress for the 2008 Folkestone Triennial, Pyramid, involves the elaborate falsification of a history of fateful misfortune connected with the inverted pyramidal supports that allowed a local architectural landmark, Leas Cliff Hall, to be built into the edge of a precipice.

In each case, with tactical modifications in the texture of reality, Chodzko co-opts innocuous details as verisimilitude for a shadowy, half-constructed narrative, one also peppered with enough lacunae to accommodate subjective interpretation. In each case, some kind of superficial rationality begins to misfire midway, leaving the viewer with the task of reconstruction. For Chodzko, though, science fiction is merely a trope in a bigger game, it would appear, a convenient way into his larger project of figuring other potential realities or proposals about what the real might be. In so doing Chodzko employs several of these provisional models: some ideational, some formal, all of them allowing a degree of manoeuvrability on the audience's part. (In a 2007 interview with the art historian and critic Mark Godfrey, he itemised some of them: 'metaphysical spaces . . . cinematic space, the carnivalesque, and beauty . . .'). Around, Hole and the work for Folkestone all explore the possibility of fabricating a false mythology around a place, as do a number of the new works in the show at Tate St Ives.

In Design for a Carnival (2003) – a five-minute film shot, like Yet, close to Chodzko's hometown of Whitstable on the Kentish coast, and part of a larger complex of pageant-related works – three main narratives involving some kind of focused construction intersect in an allusive sketch of the carnivalesque. Red ants in woodland carry away shiny sequins; a group of mud-smeared, 'hoodie'-type local teens are pulling down skinny trees in order to tag and conjoin their branches with brightly coloured plastic strips; and the accoutrements of needlework are viewed in close-up. The latter feeds into the work again in the shape of a lacy doily, which sits on top of and snags a spinning vinyl record that plays A Certain Ratio's Winter Hill (1981), a heavily percussive piece of music that redoubles the tribal, celebratory ambience of Chodzko's video. Beyond this, however, Design for a Carnival is essentially ambiguous. The actions of the youths (and, to an extent, the ants) are carefully pitched between destruction and construction. Furthermore, it is uncertain whether what one is witnessing is the carnival itself, a rehearsal for it, or something else, and whether the film is a complete piece or, as its length suggests, some kind of trailer. The work is suspended, stuttering, on the verge of articulation.

There is a good deal of contemporary art out there that seeks to propose alternative models of reality: such an approach might even be the core of its broad cultural project. Chodzko, though, is for an art that doesn't just pay lip service to such a notion. For him content is a fragile thing, liable to atrophy into a set of wearisome givens if the artist isn't also a tactician, a dealer in surprise. In Design for a Carnival, which, notably, doesn't suggest a template for a festival at all, Chodzko's thoughts on practice are explicitly contextual, revolving around questions of how to maintain mobility and vitality within the reception of art. His response is to espouse a determinedly awkward aesthetics of the not-quite-done and the perpetually-in-play; to problematise and complicate social processes rather than simply enact them, symbolically and safely, in the idealised space of art. As this work's title suggests, he prefers whenever possible to project his art back a stage, to stall it, in the ripe mulch of ambiguity and away from the paralysis of closure.

Plan for a Spell (2001) similarly situates itself in some nebulous region anterior to a never-completed version. Here, a collation of apparently found film images, adding up to a herky-jerky portrait of Britain – burning infected cattle during the foot-and-mouth crisis; digitised footage of city streets and rustic English villages from some violent computer game; a Burry Man being ceremonially walked down a country road; craft traditions such as basket-weaving; clips from the 1973 horror film The Wicker Man; wind farms; stock-car racing; some uninscribed scuffle between groups of figures – is shuffled by complex DVD authoring so that it never plays the same way twice. In subtitles that accompany and comment on the film's contents with the vague specificity of horoscopes, the narrator appears to be searching for something: a set of qualities that one wouldn't normally put together ('hard' and 'unstable' among them). Some combinatory logic is being followed that borders, so the title suggests, on the occult: some convening of images (and, perhaps, of language too), will, it seems, add up to the 'spell' of the title. What that enchantment might be, and upon what it might be operating – a balmy synthesis to somehow 'help' the discontinuous land being surveyed? – is concertedly held in abeyance. As is any certainty about art's therapeutic capacities. For if this endless recombining of imagery can be seen as equivalent to art-making itself, there's a sense here (as there is in Yet, where the perhaps-helpful archive of magazines, videos, etc is metonymic for creativity as a whole) of hopefulness and frustration regarding art's capacity to work on the world.

Plan for a Spell may be one endpoint of Chodzko's unstable approach to filmmaking, but reflexivity and structural irresolution attend his work in the medium at every turn. Among Chodzko's touchstones is the German director Michael Haneke. In films such as Funny Games (1997/ remade 2007) and Caché (Hidden) (2005) Haneke regularly pulls off an unlikely update on the Brechtian mode of shattering the 'fourth wall' of art. Managing to make a fully convincing and immersive naturalism sit side by side with an acidly deconstructive approach to the cinema, it is one that assertively implicates the viewer in their own consumption of the unpalatable. Other filmic influences upon Chodzko's

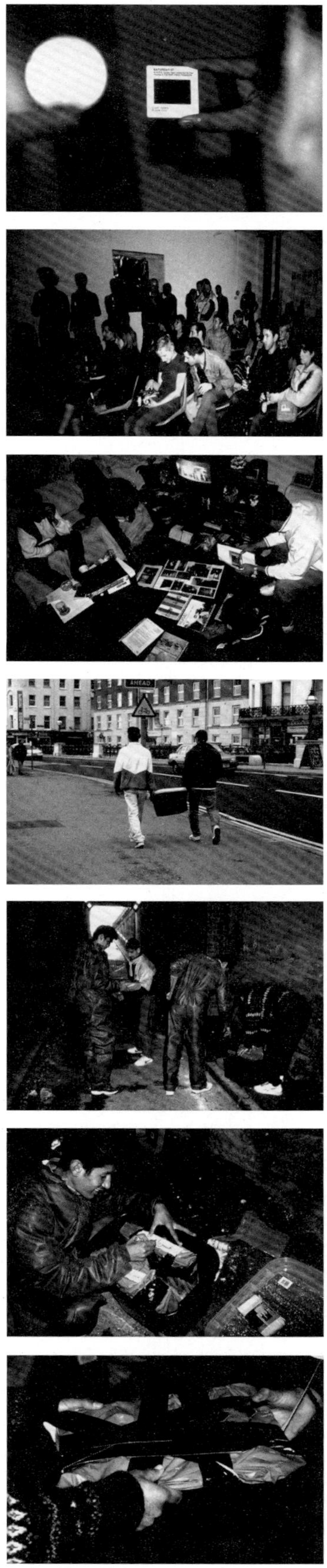

Cell-a (details) 2002

approach, such as the French anthropologist Jean Rouch and English filmmaker Alan Clarke, operate similarly (though in dissimilar fashions) to create an 'unstable' mode of representation in their windows on to cultures and milieus. In all of these cases, a substantial part of the viewing experience lies in confronting our own preconceptions and involuntary prejudices about what is on screen. And Chodzko's work in recorded media (filmic and sonic) takes this on board. But for an artist whose production is attuned to questions of expectation and engagement, and the mental conditioning of audiences by various types of discourse, a larger question arises: how can a materialist, static, linear medium be made fluid, open, insistently incomplete?

Chodzko was considering that question back in 1996 in Flasher – for which he rented VHS tapes from outlets across the UK and in Brooklyn and, before returning them, taped one-minute videos on to the ends, involving figures holding up signs and launching flares in woodland on the edge of town. (In an associated photograph, children hold up placards, bearing the legend 'More Dark' – an inversion of Goethe's famous dying words – which might stand as a slogan for Chodzko's refusal to deal in pat enlightenments, art-as-torch.) He was still reframing and reconsidering it in 2005 in Test Tone for Landscape, the audio work set to harmonise Tate St Ives' Loggia intermittently with a randomised selection of tones (humming fridges, pinged vases, amplifier noise, wine glasses, etc.) recorded by the artist around his house and chancily combining into chords at irregular intervals. For all its ambient serenity, ominous undercurrents prevent this work from feeling pacific. (In this sense, while Test Tone echoes Brian Eno's experimental software-driven generative music, a close cousin in mood is Eno's earlier record On Land (1978), which traces the subtle anxieties of the English landscape.) Chodzko's filmic aesthetic, too, has a deep-seated uncertainty about it. It sits with pointed disquiet between a loose, hand-held, fast-shutter documentary aesthetic and the constructedness of cinema, partaking of the immediacy and truthfulness of one and the artifice and fictional space of the other.

Not that he's a formalist, concerned with hybridising extant languages. At the same time, however, the viewer must take care – as does the artist – to avoid conversely crediting his art with too much inbuilt about-ness, allowing strong suggestions of specific content to lock his work down, turn it inert. Chodzko, as we've seen, doesn't really do 'about' so much as he does process and ramification; he'd much rather set things in motion and let them spin out of control into interesting trouble than proffer a pat conclusion. When he works with film, his open-ended narrative approach serves to avoid easy solutions, that is, the shutdown of thought. And nowhere is this more apparent than when his adoption of possible alternative realities takes the form of collaborations with groups considered to be beyond the velvet rope of the artworld or outside society altogether.

A latter-day biographical pretext may exist for Chodzko's recent collaborations with people of other cultures: the artist's adopted county of Kent is the arrival point for many migrants arriving in England from Europe and beyond, for whom the transition is not always made smooth. Rather than generate bogus social engineering projects or well-meant but ineffectual 'sticking plasters', however, Chodzko has instead dug deeper, seeking to skew the unconsidered hierarchies that attend making art with disenfranchised groups in the first place. The black-and-white slide projection, Cell-a (2002) is among the earliest of Chodzko's works pitched into a possible future: 'the archive of a London gallery was given to a group of Kurdish asylum seekers to edit and protect outside the capital'. It also announces his poetic interest in archives buried like packages of potential, which recurs in Yet and Around. In Cell-a the Kurds inter the archive in the windswept beach at Margate.

Chodzko here conjures a world wherein 'we' are prepared to grant respectful authority to a migrant class, yet his aim is not quite empowerment (it is, in any case, left quite open to question how much in the 81-slide 'documentation' is real, how much fictional). Chodzko is too clear-eyed about art's actual social potential for that. Rather he aims, with deep pragmatism, for something that art can actually achieve: questioning the foundational notion that a British artist has the right to speak for such a group, to shape its ongoing narrative of dispossession and relocation. Cell-a does this in part via an inbuilt self-criticism: it's an awkward and even clunky production, right down to its means of transmission. Why a drab monochrome slide projection, except insofar as it deliberately leaves out a lot of information and is structurally frustrating? (There is, lest it need saying, a bathetically funny side to this incongruousness, this deliberate falling-short; Chodzko's art is studded with such humorously prosaic judgements.) Cell-a, in its conspicuous failings and ambiguities, doesn't so much say, 'this is how one engages other cultures with art' as lay out a set of problems with doing so; to x-ray our preconceptions; and call for an approach that might preserve the autonomy of others rather than clumsily and imperially instrumentalising them.

It's possible to see hints in many of Chodzko's works of a dream of interpenetration between different spheres: from the linking scenes of blue ink infiltrating water in Around (a film which, in dealing with social housing, is explicitly about insides and outsides) to the figures poking their fingers into punctures in concrete in Hole; from the collapsing of distance between the audience and the world of revered cinema in Reunion: Salò (1998) to the commingling of life and death in Limboland (2001) and Nightvision (1998). This is a politics of sorts; though Chodzko, crediting his audience with sufficient intelligence to see what's beneath the surface, is careful not to amplify the idea, lest what has been usefully liquefied should harden into a banal diagram of a stance. (Indeed, even writing about it feels counterproductive.) It's also a future position, which may be reached across a minefield. Chodzko's art may optimistically forward solutions of sorts to situations (a carnival, a handing-over of authority, a gathering of unlikely strangers), but this fictional point is rarely reached without stumbling over a lot of reflexive pitfalls along the way.

Settlement (2004) is exemplary in this regard. A short 'documentary' recording the artist's gift (at a cost to him of £10) of a 34 x 23cm plot of land in Burgess Park, South London, to an individual named Singh, *Settlement* seems at first like an atypical excursion into fixity. The land's boundaries, we're told, are defined by 'the proportions of the camera frame that films it' (although, of course, this is already slightly screwy since it's dependent on the camera's distance from the ground); and a legal document, summarised in the owner's intermittently amused voiceover, is drawn up defining what can and cannot be done on the land. Still, the film manages to renege on its own promise. That very document, with its 'restrictive covenants', engenders a real ambiguity about the purpose of the land itself — possibly, nothing can be done with it; the owner doesn't seem sure; it's not

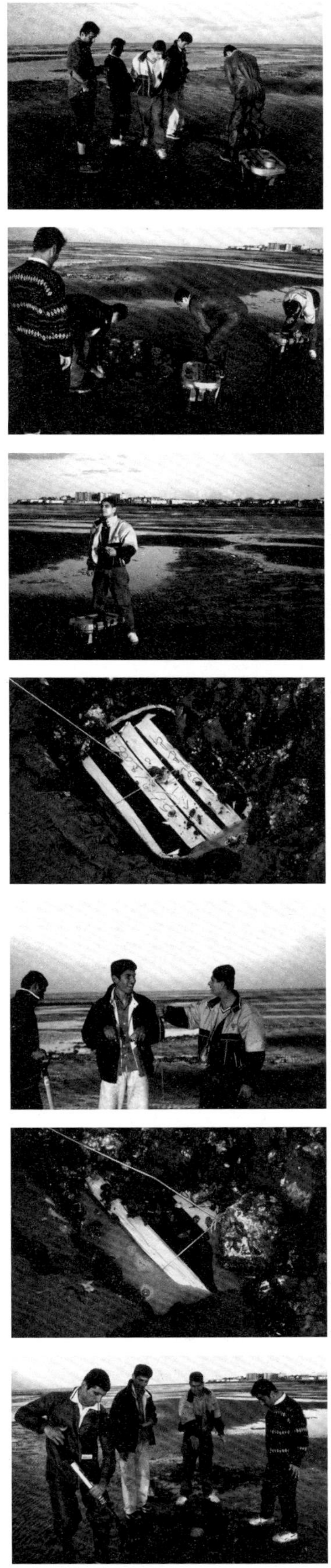

Cell-a (details) 2002

even clear whether it can be built on; the owner has subsoil rights but isn't allowed to dig it up, etc. – and, furthermore, as a film Settlement is a destabilising experience. The more the viewer is forced, in the absence of any other visual stimuli, to look at the apparently static scene of dried, yellowing grasses over the film's nine-minute run (Chodzko has credited the long, slow scenes of Iranian filmmaker Abbas Kiarostami as an inspiration) the more mutable it seems. The land sits in continually changing light and the rumble of traffic, its flora shiver in the wind, it gets rained on, etc. Clearly there is content here: territory and airspace, responsibility, gifting, the moral piety that art can empower and assist. But Settlement, in which so much is snarled up or derailed, doesn't codify these ideas so much as offer a designated zone for them to jostle within, in which inherent difficulties can be made visible and, hopefully, one day, overcome. It's not a meaning-space but, rather, a problem-space, the kind that people need when they won't be told, as Chodzko knows we won't: a space framed by phalanxes of engaging specificity (dimensions, conditions, sub-clauses, etc) but finally as unsettled, and susceptible to cognitive breezes as this changeable arrangement of grasses within the small rectangle of screen. And in those perpetual shifts, it lives.

Martin Herbert is a writer based in Tunbridge Wells, Kent. He contributes regularly to *Artforum*, *frieze* and *Art Monthly*, and is European editor of *Modern Painters*.

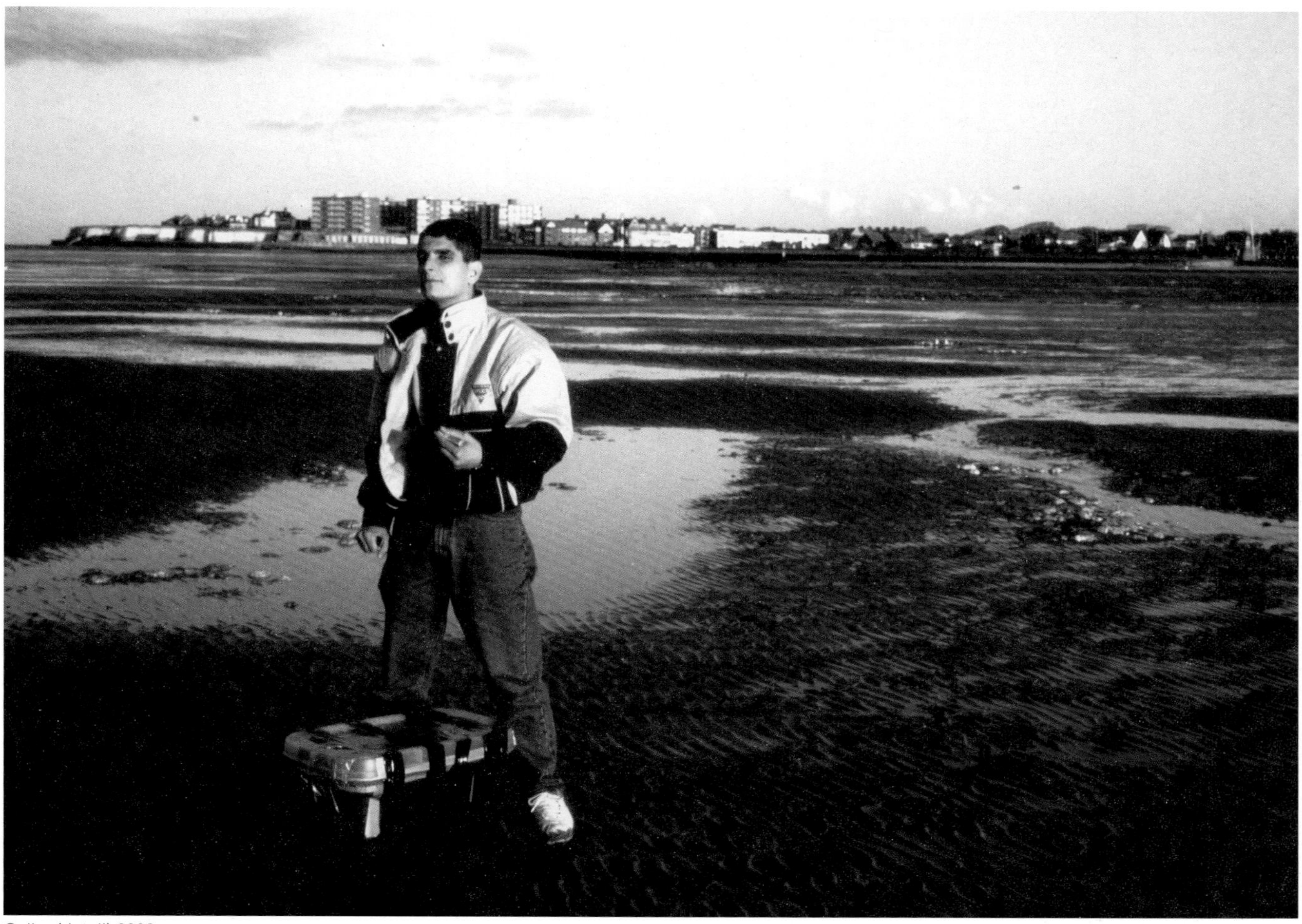

Cell-a (detail) 2002

# 96

**Around** 2007

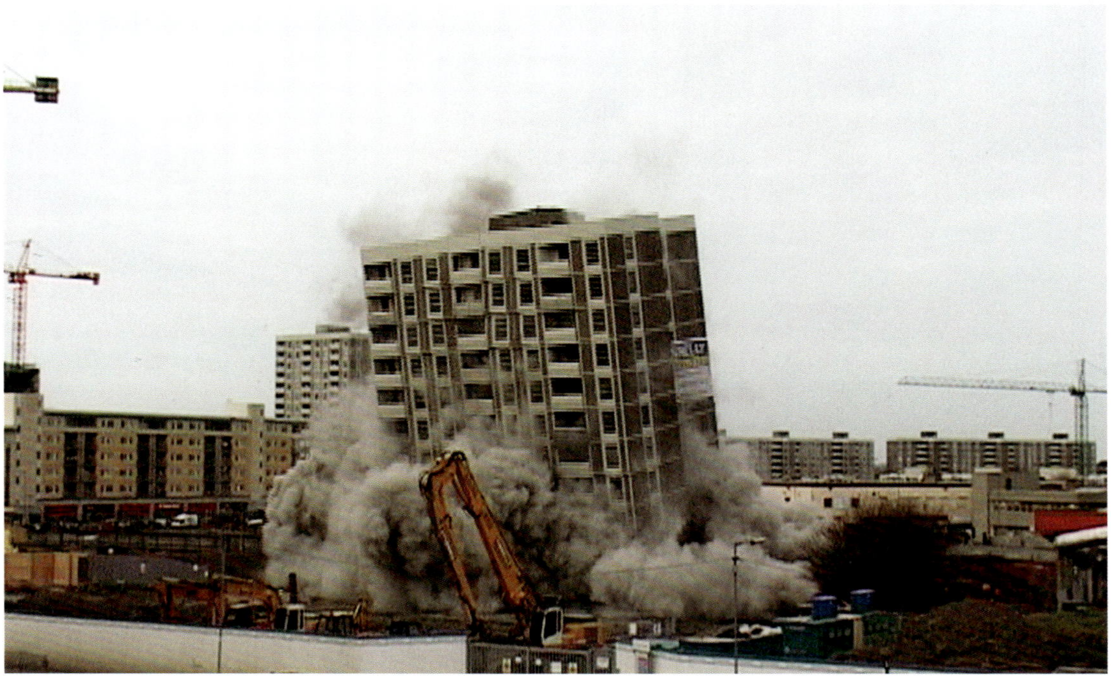

# 98

**Around** 2007

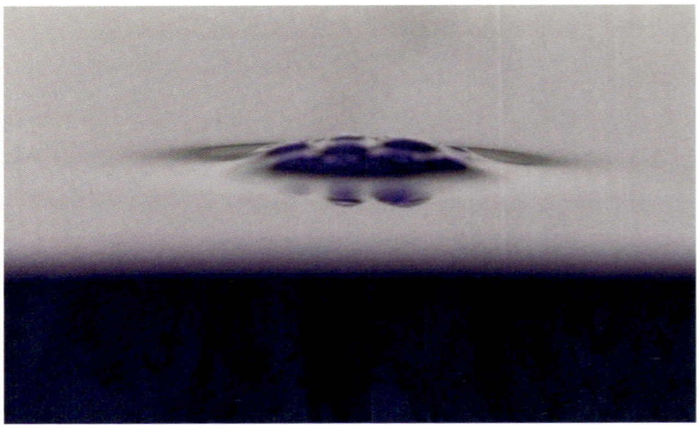

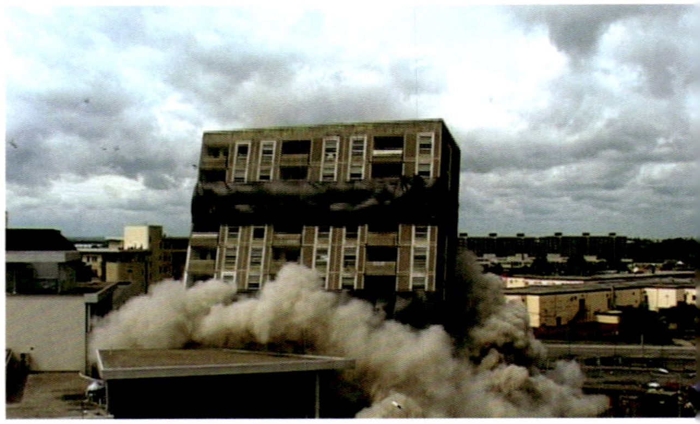

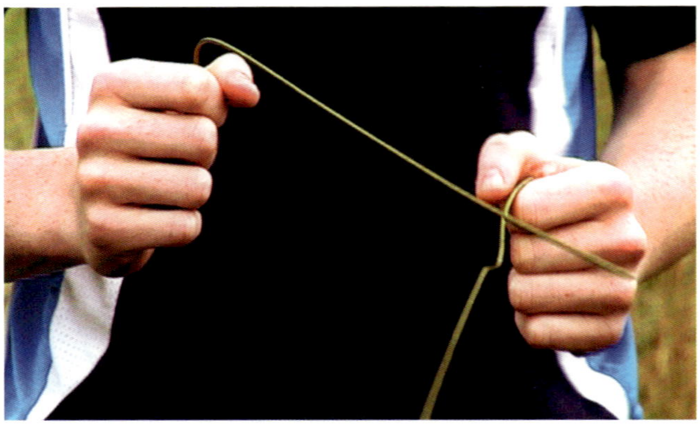

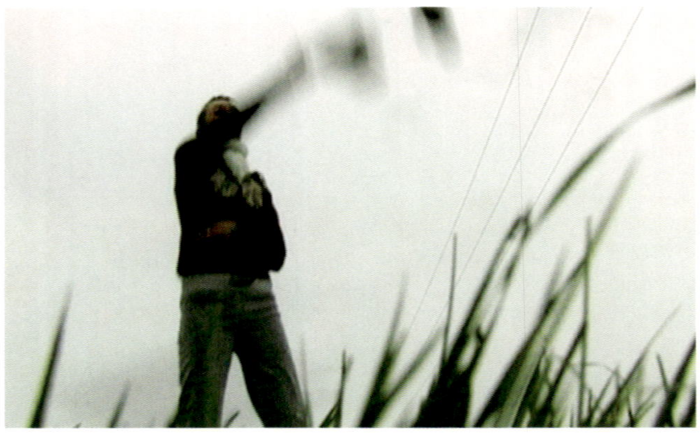

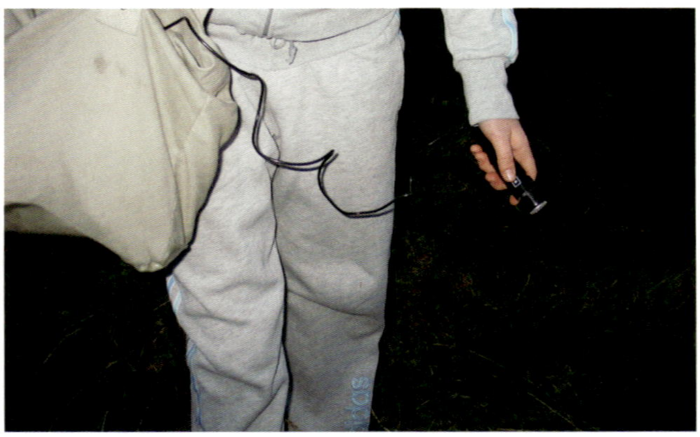

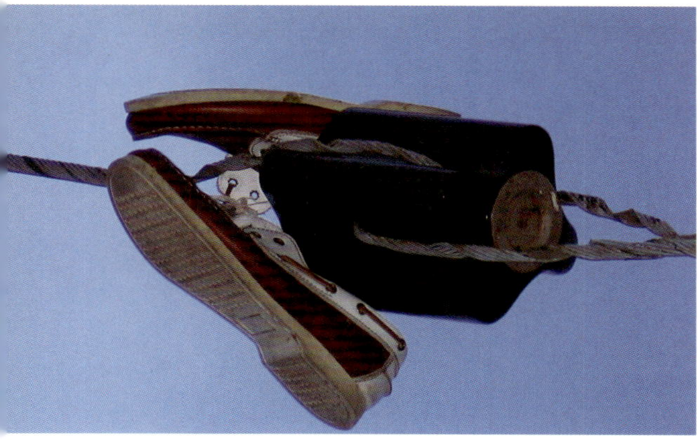
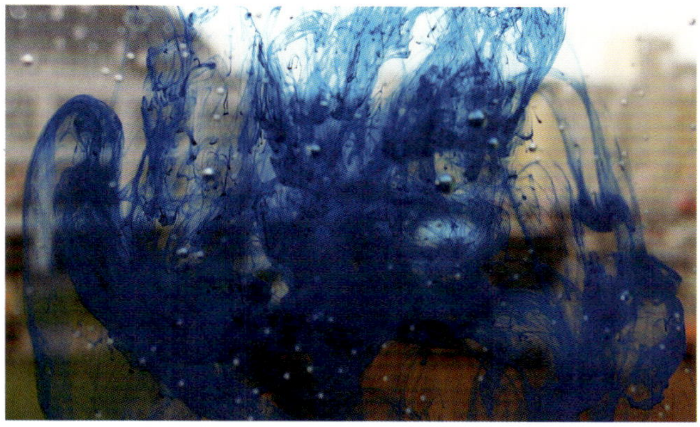
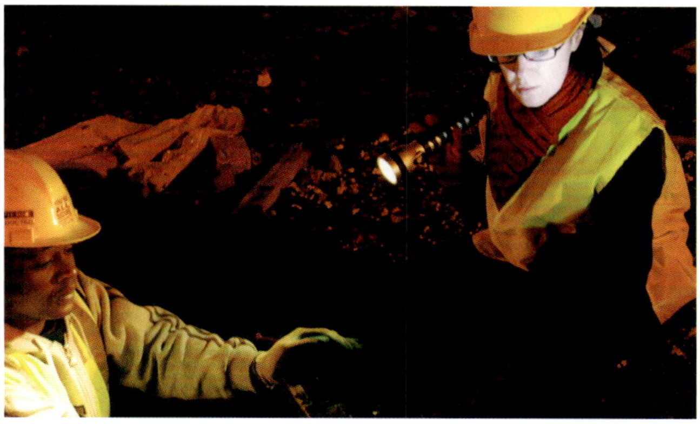
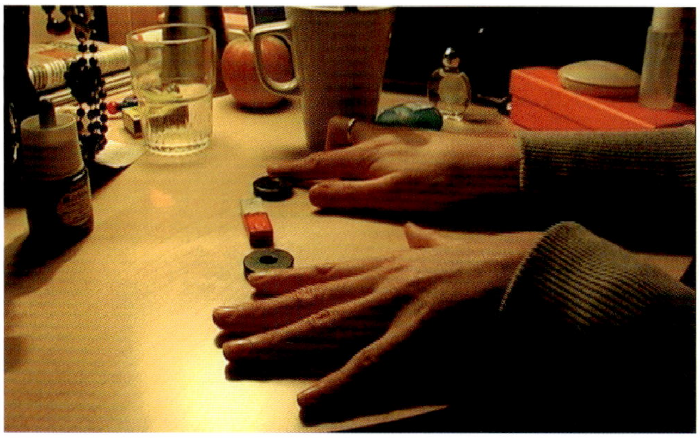
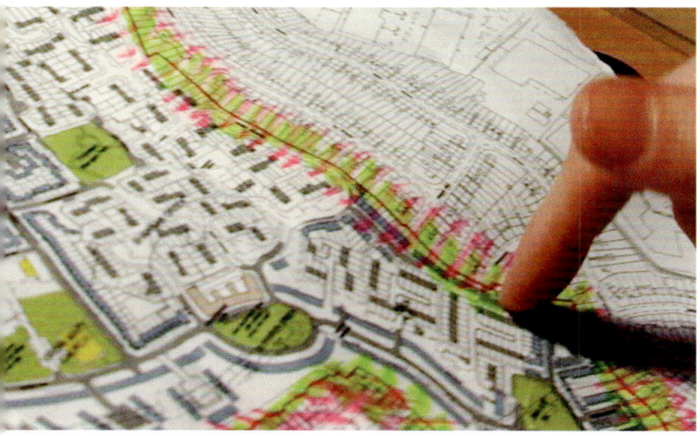
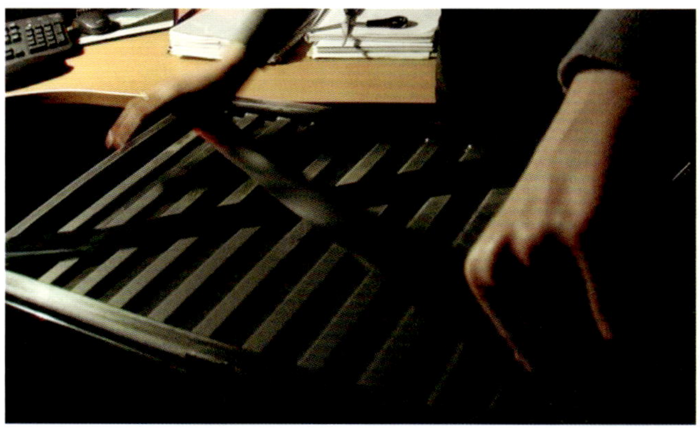

**Yet** 2005

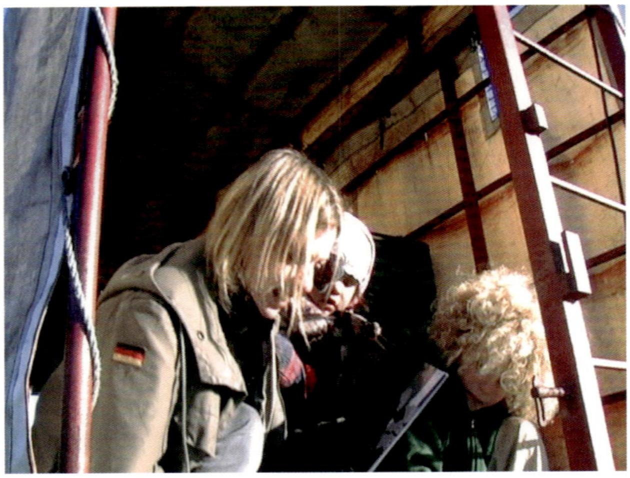

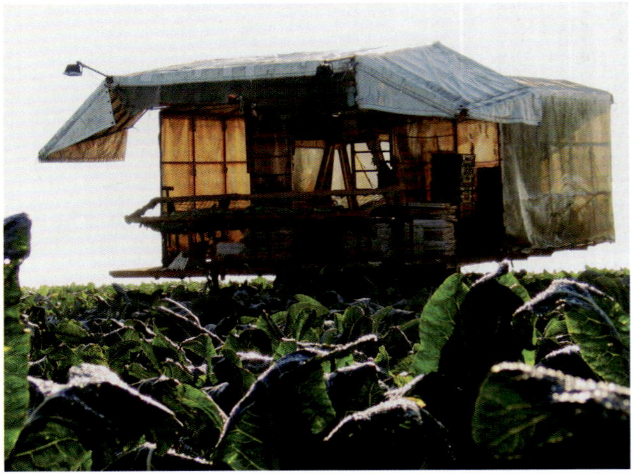

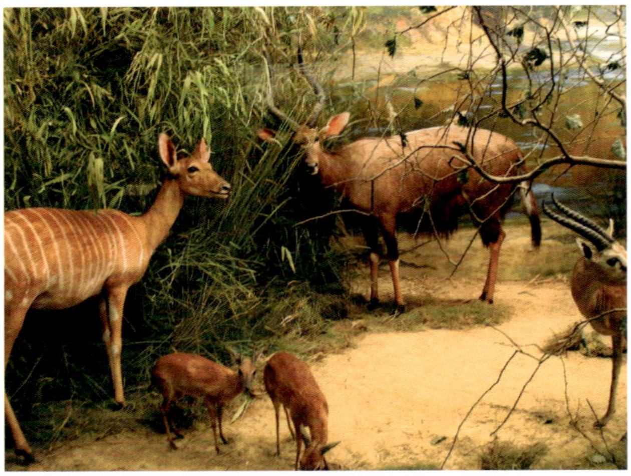

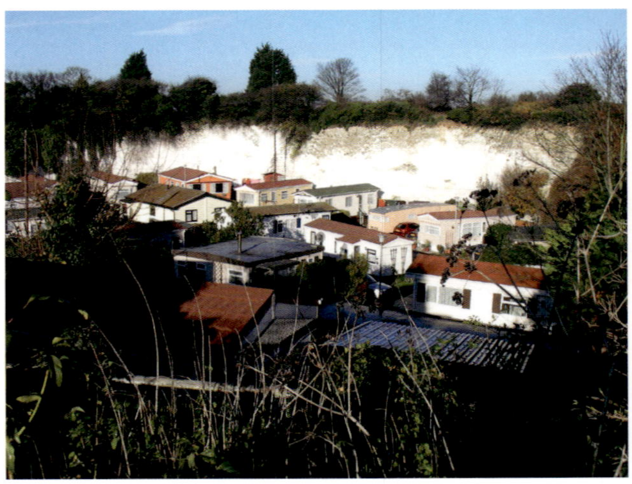

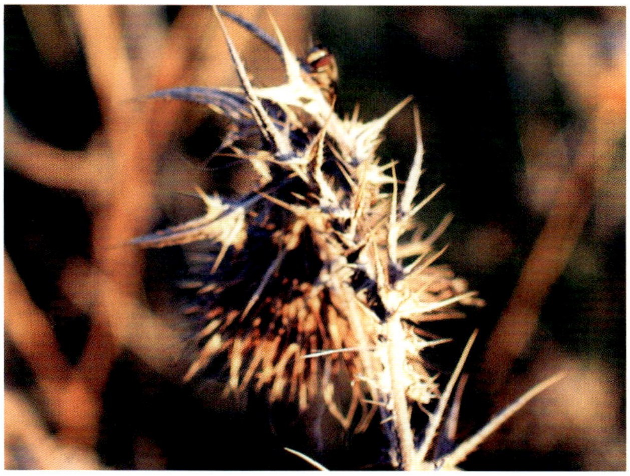

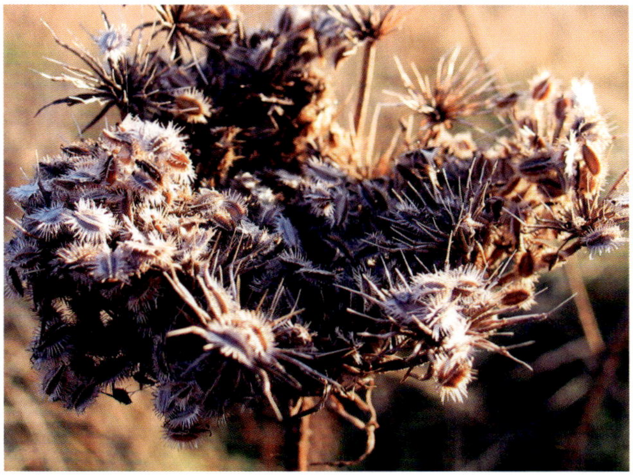

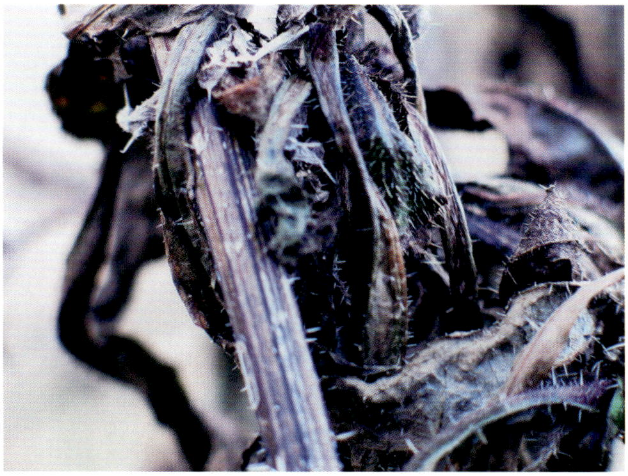

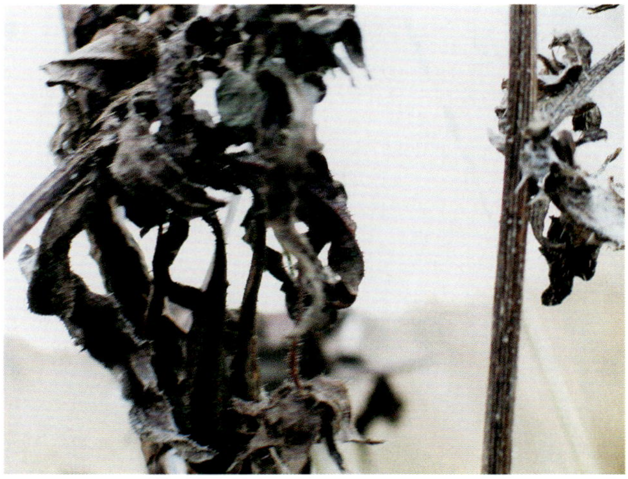

# 102

**Hole** 2007

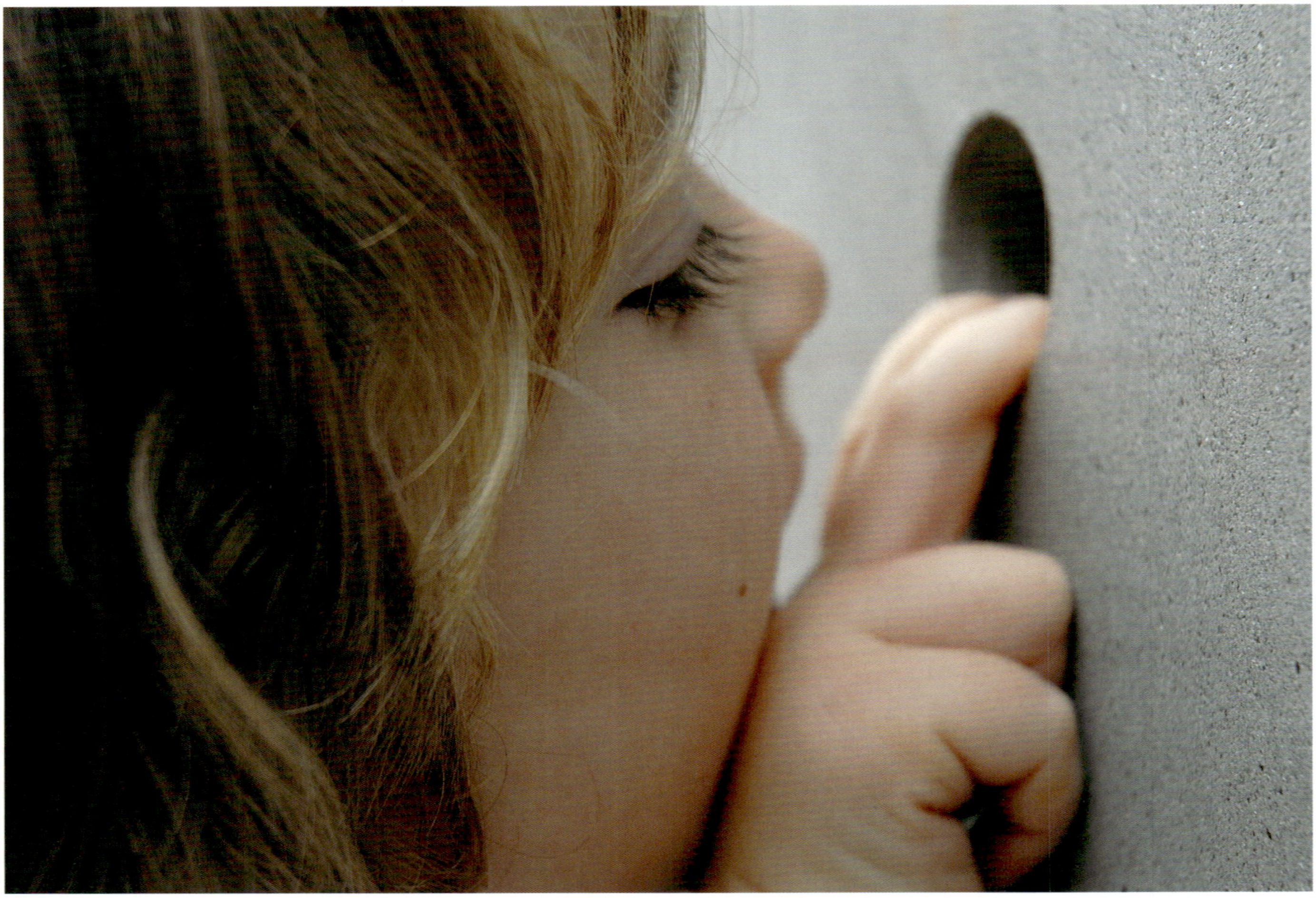

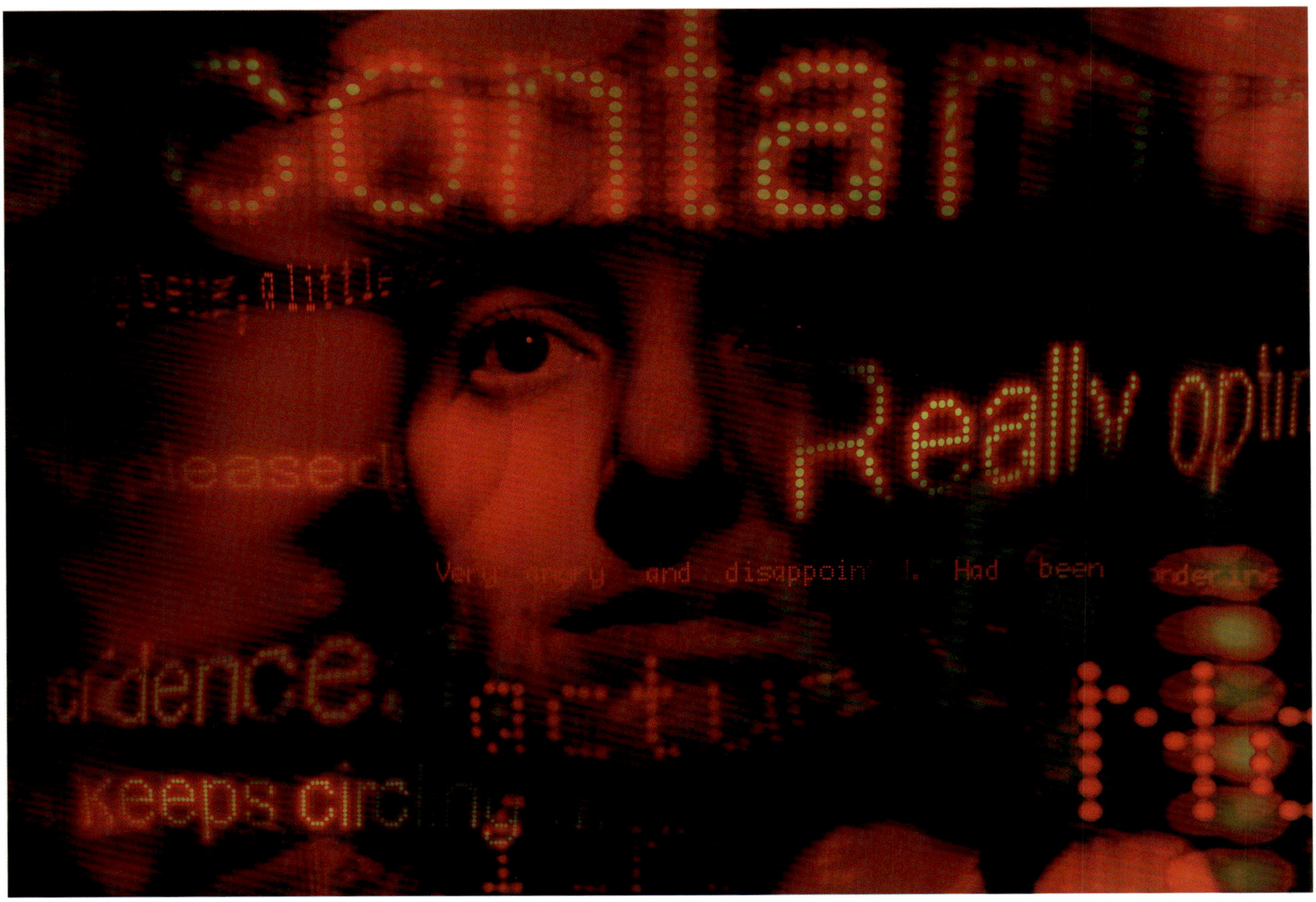

Really
Very and Had been
Keeps

# 104

**Longshore drift, early detroit techno and other processes of erosion**
2006 –

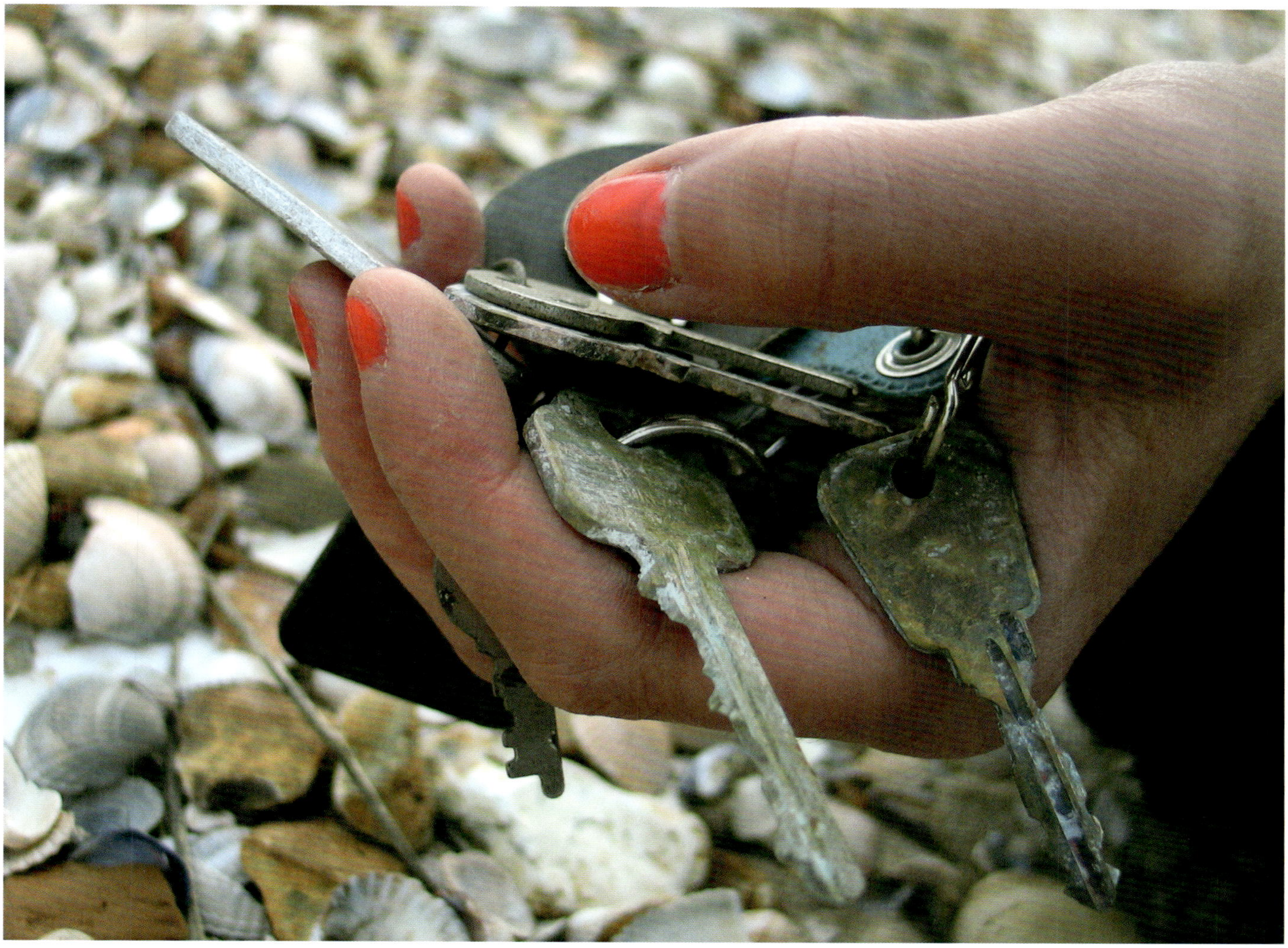

**Longshore drift, early detroit techno and other processes of erosion**
2006 –

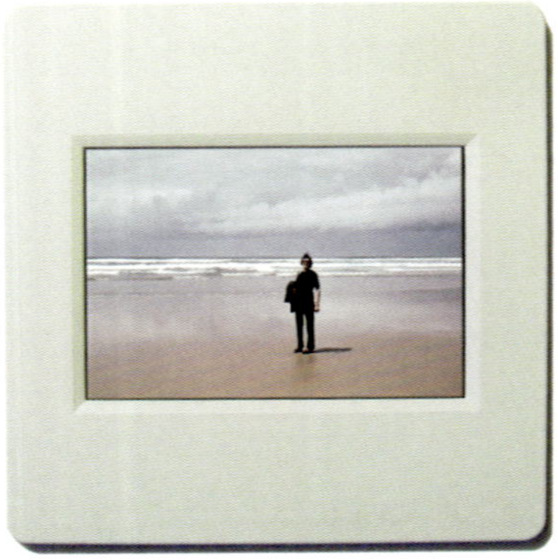

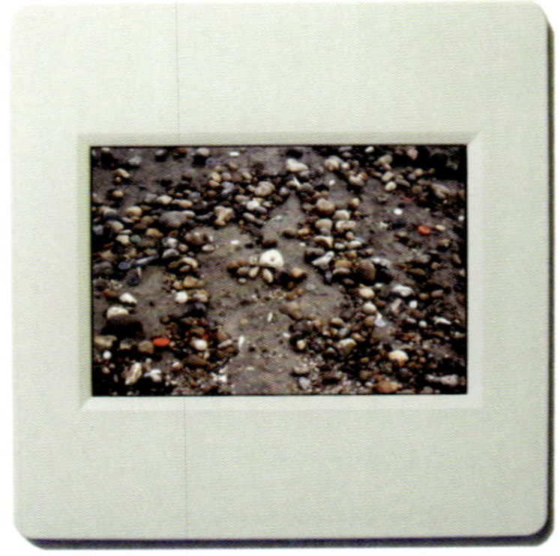

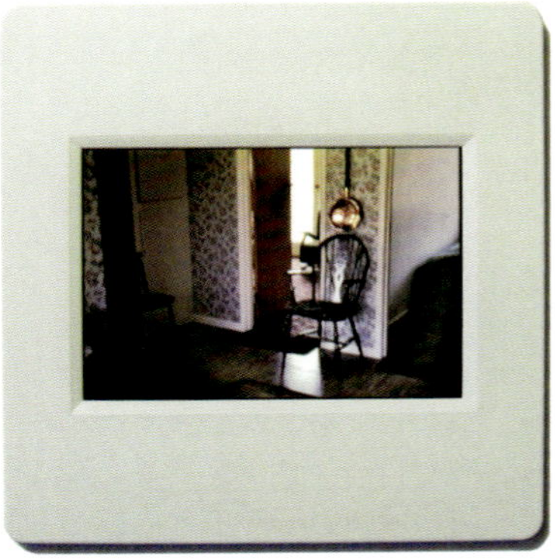

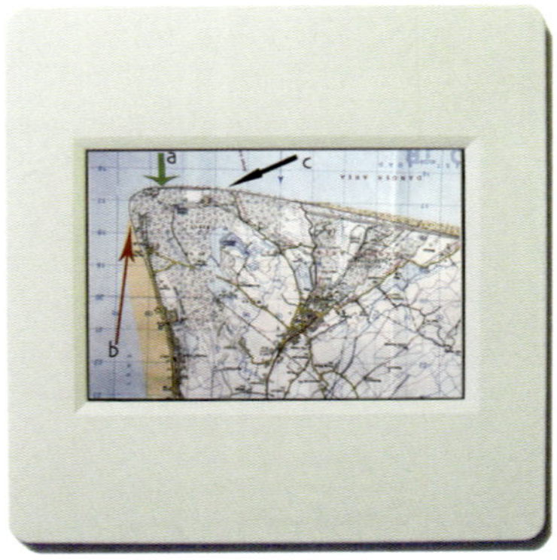


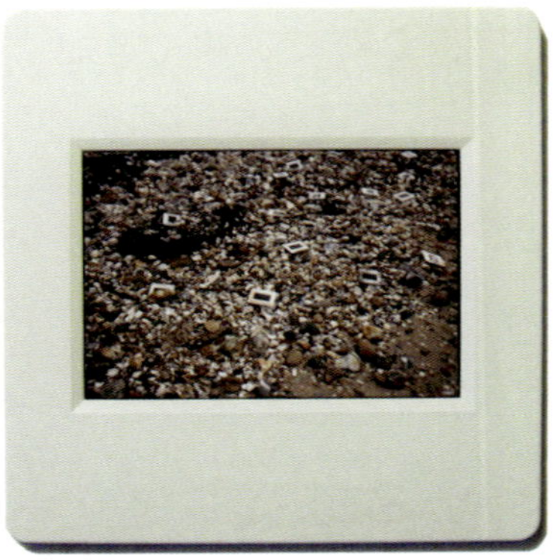

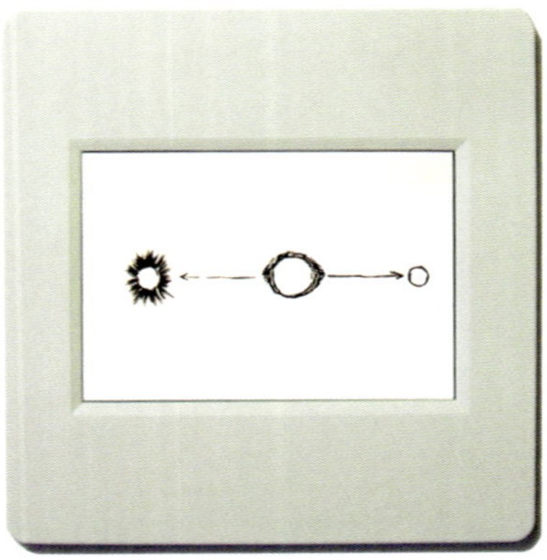

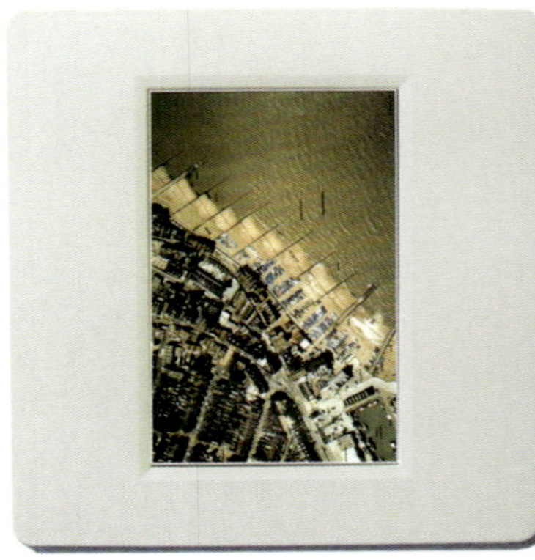

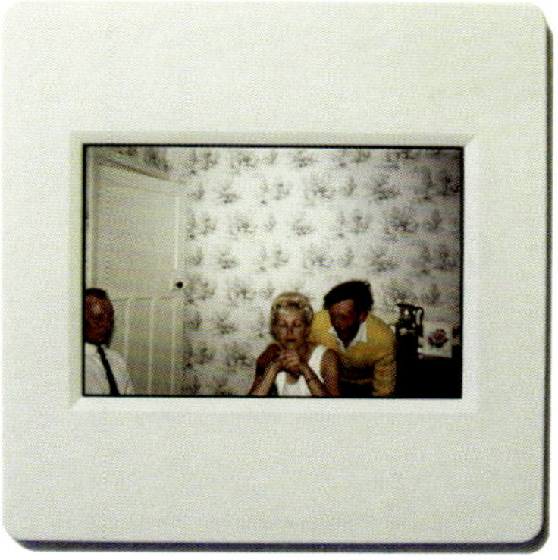

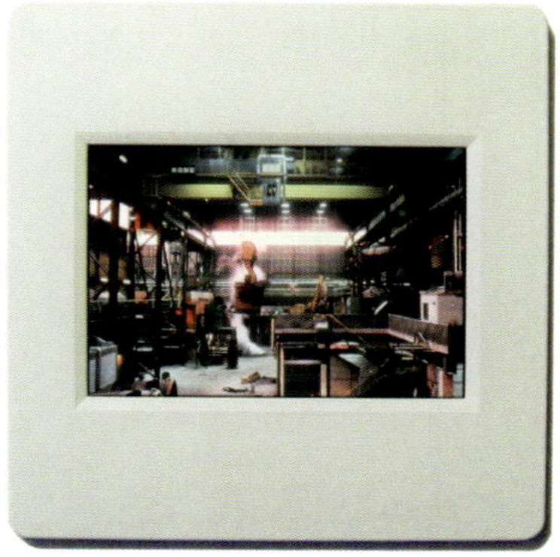

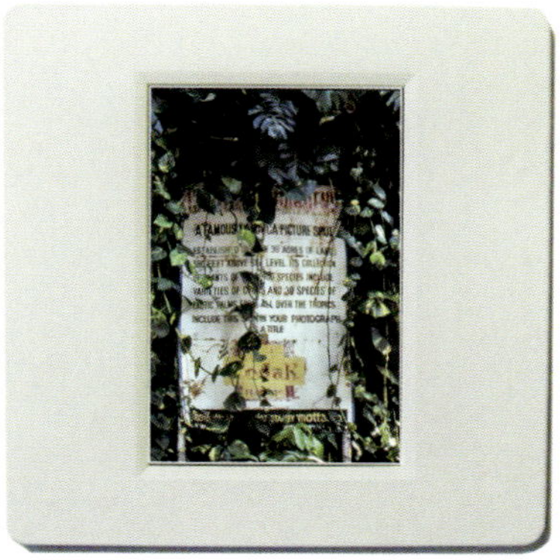

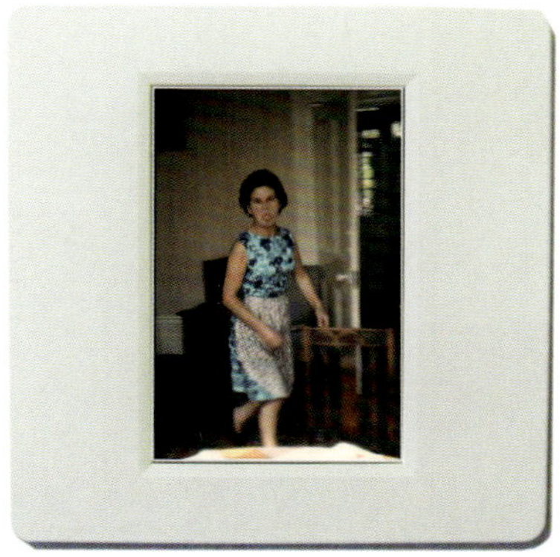

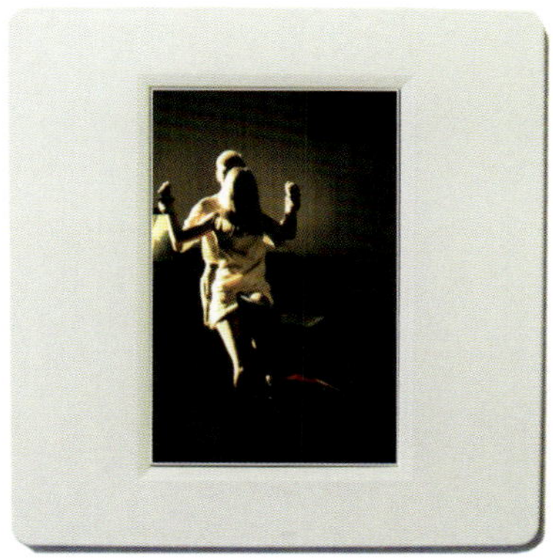

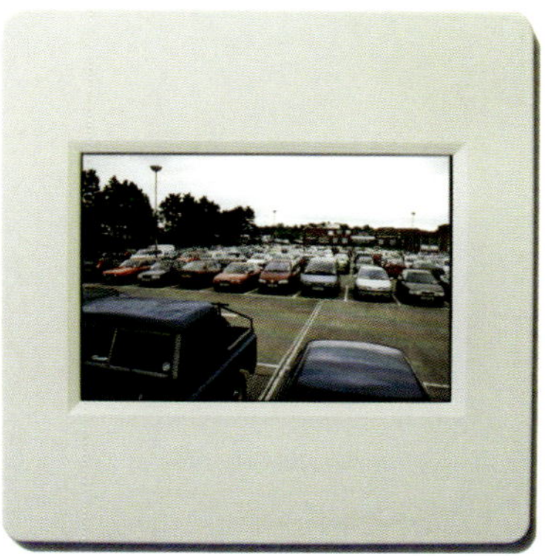

# 108

**Longshore drift, early detroit techno and other processes of erosion**
2006 –

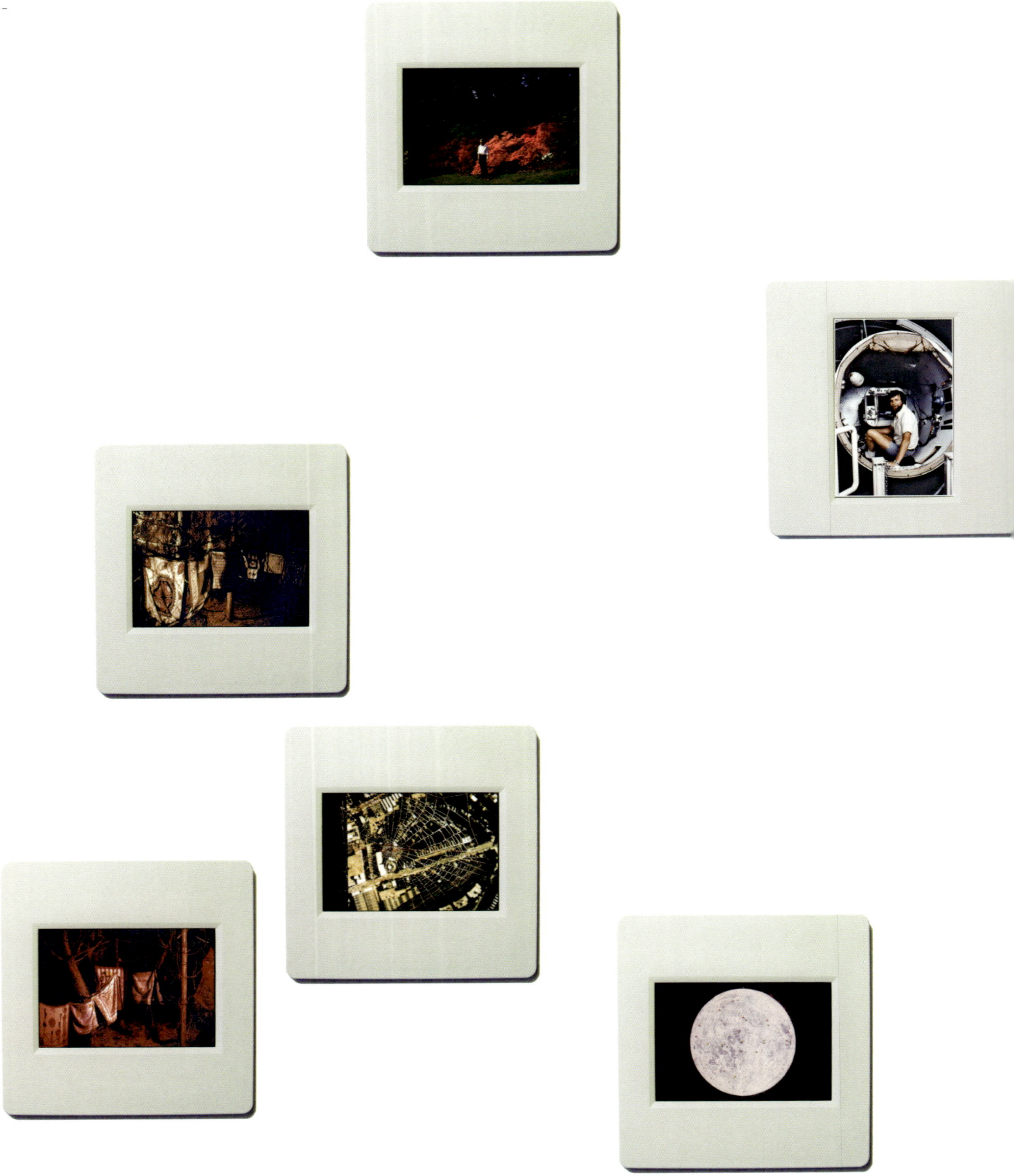

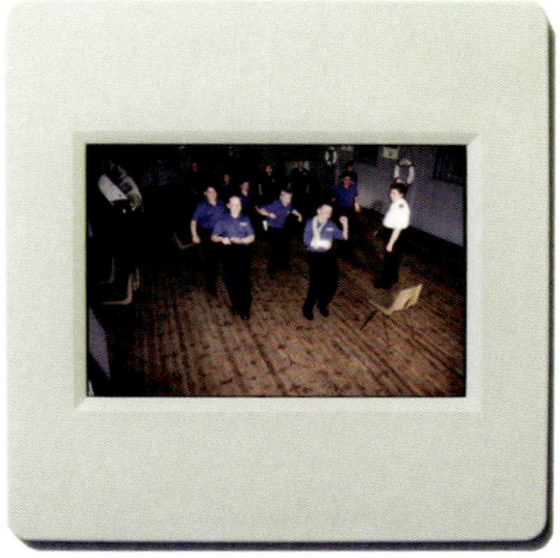

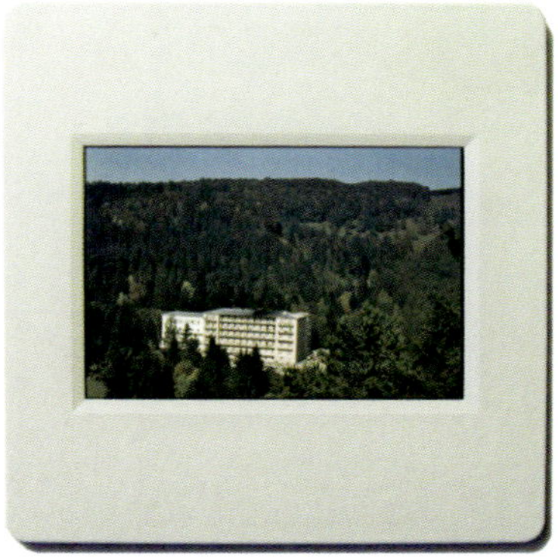

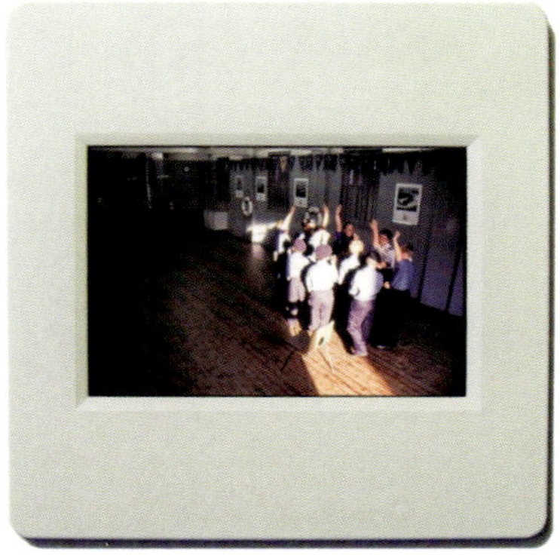

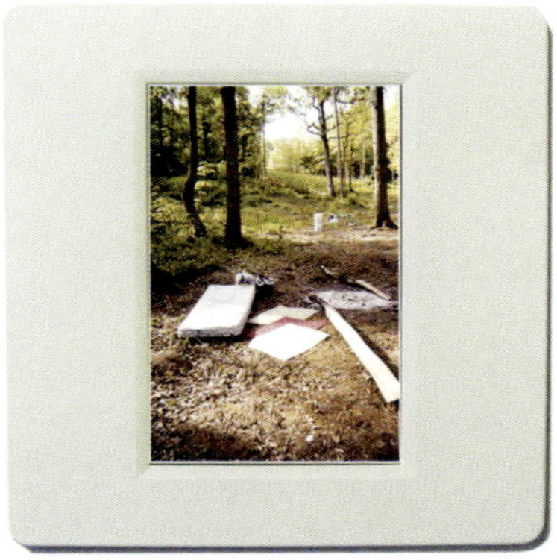

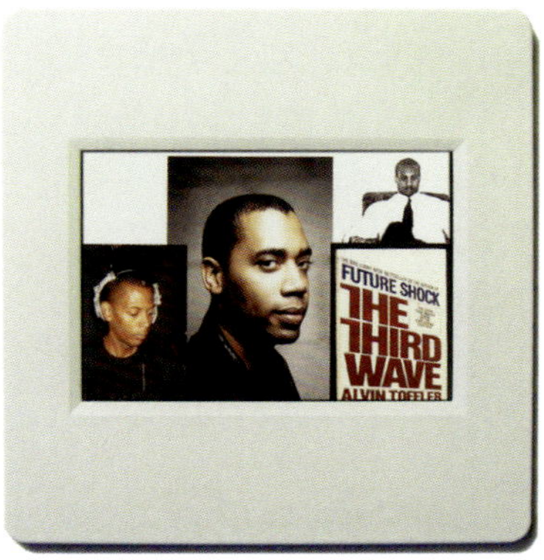
FUTURE SHOCK
THE THIRD WAVE

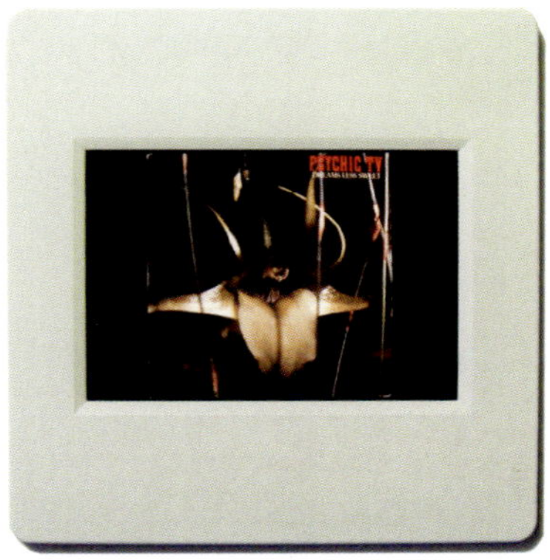
PSYCHIC TV

# 110

**Next Meeting: The car park of the plywood factory, just north of the town of Tolhóin...** 2008

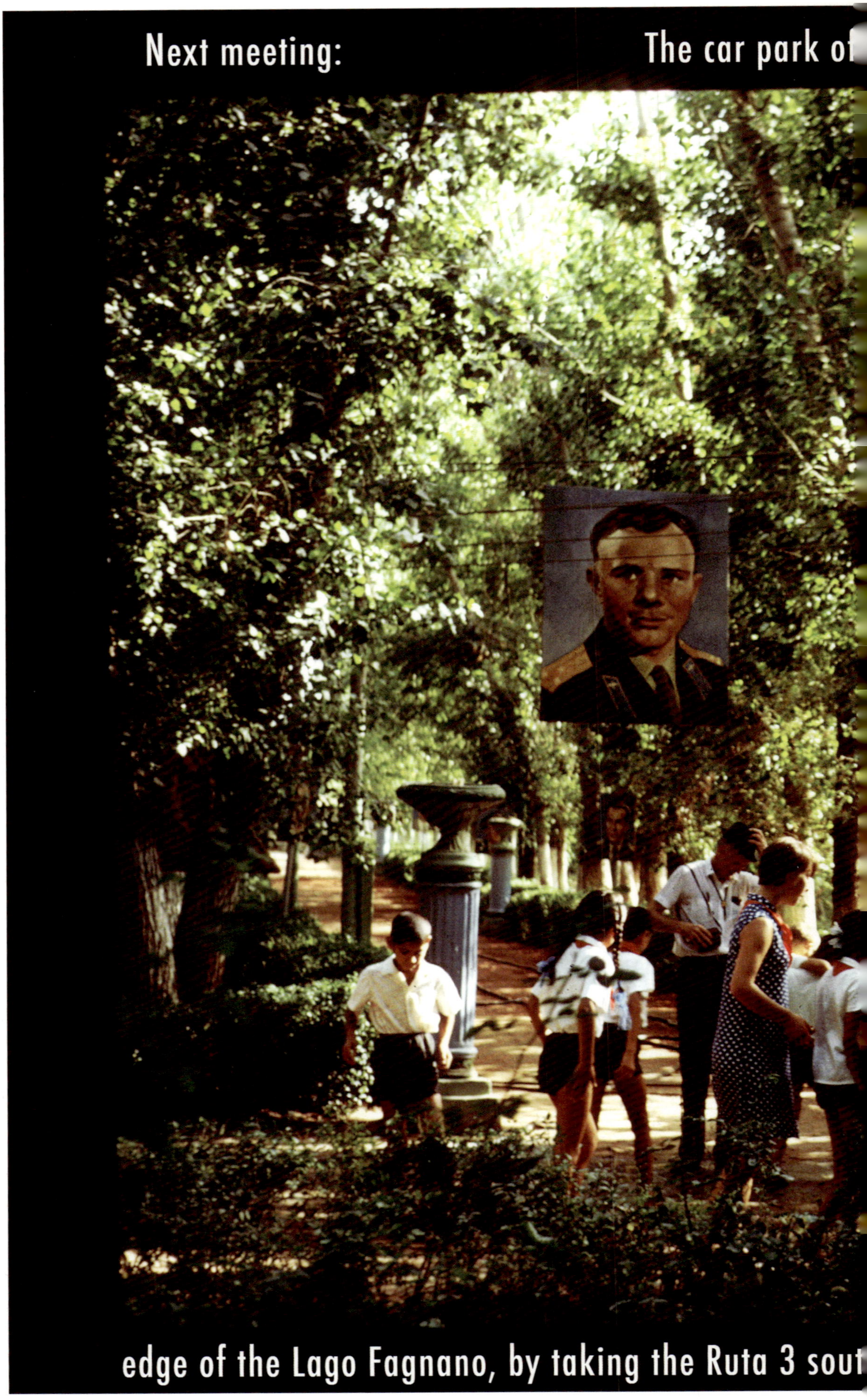

wood factory, just north of the new town of Tolhóin, on the western

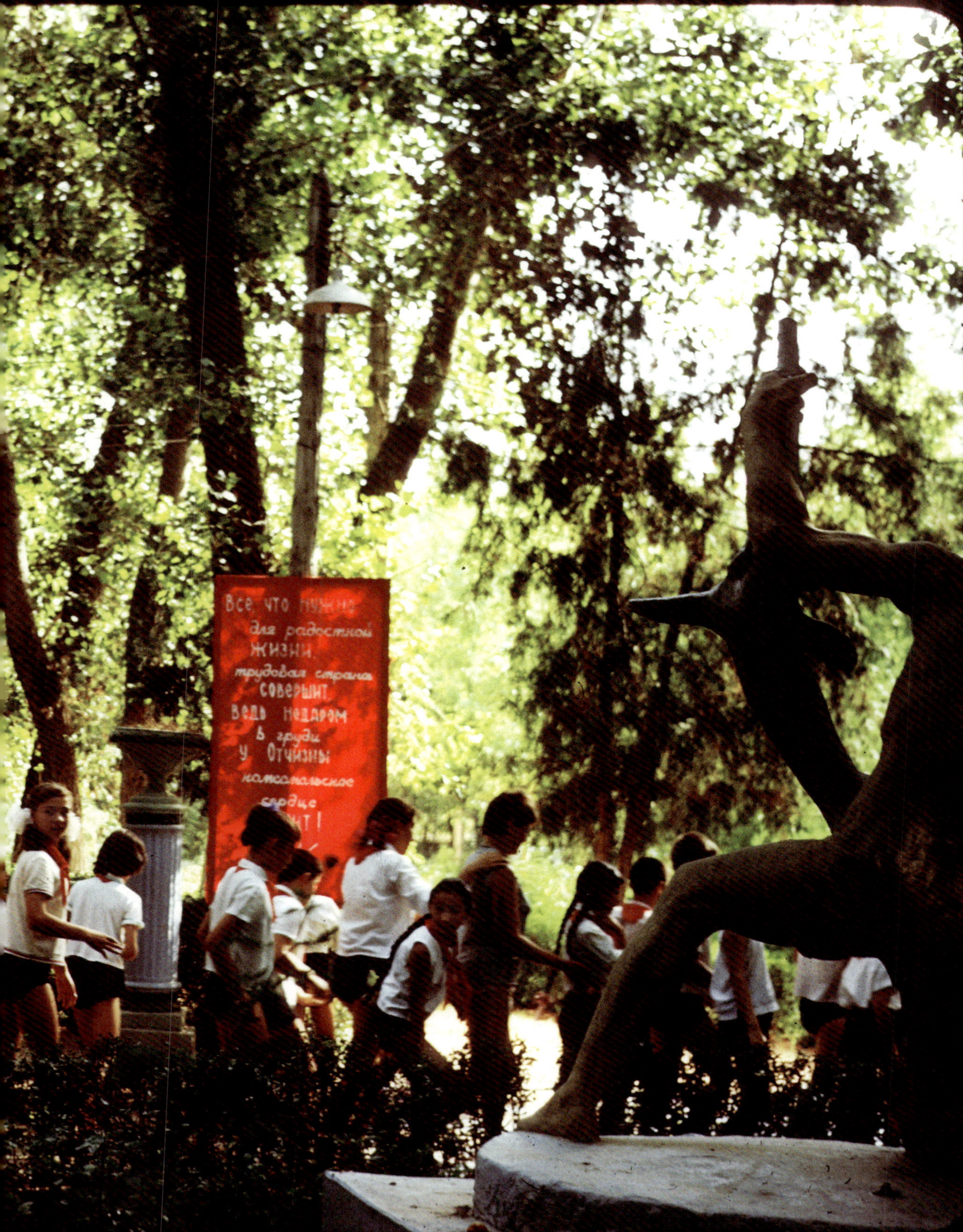


towards Ushuaia along the valley of the Río Ewan, Tierra Del Fuego.

# 112

**Better Scenery** 2002

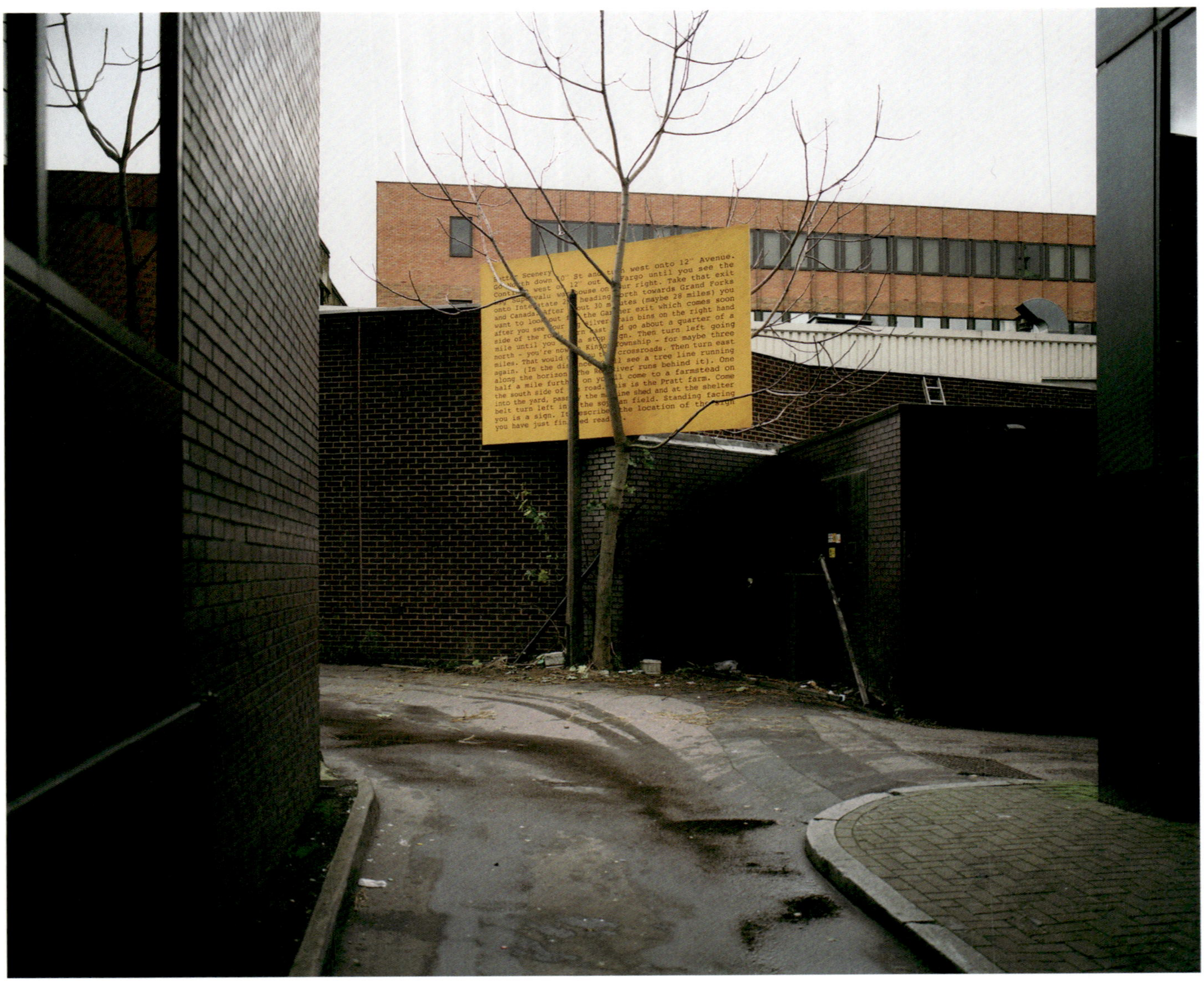

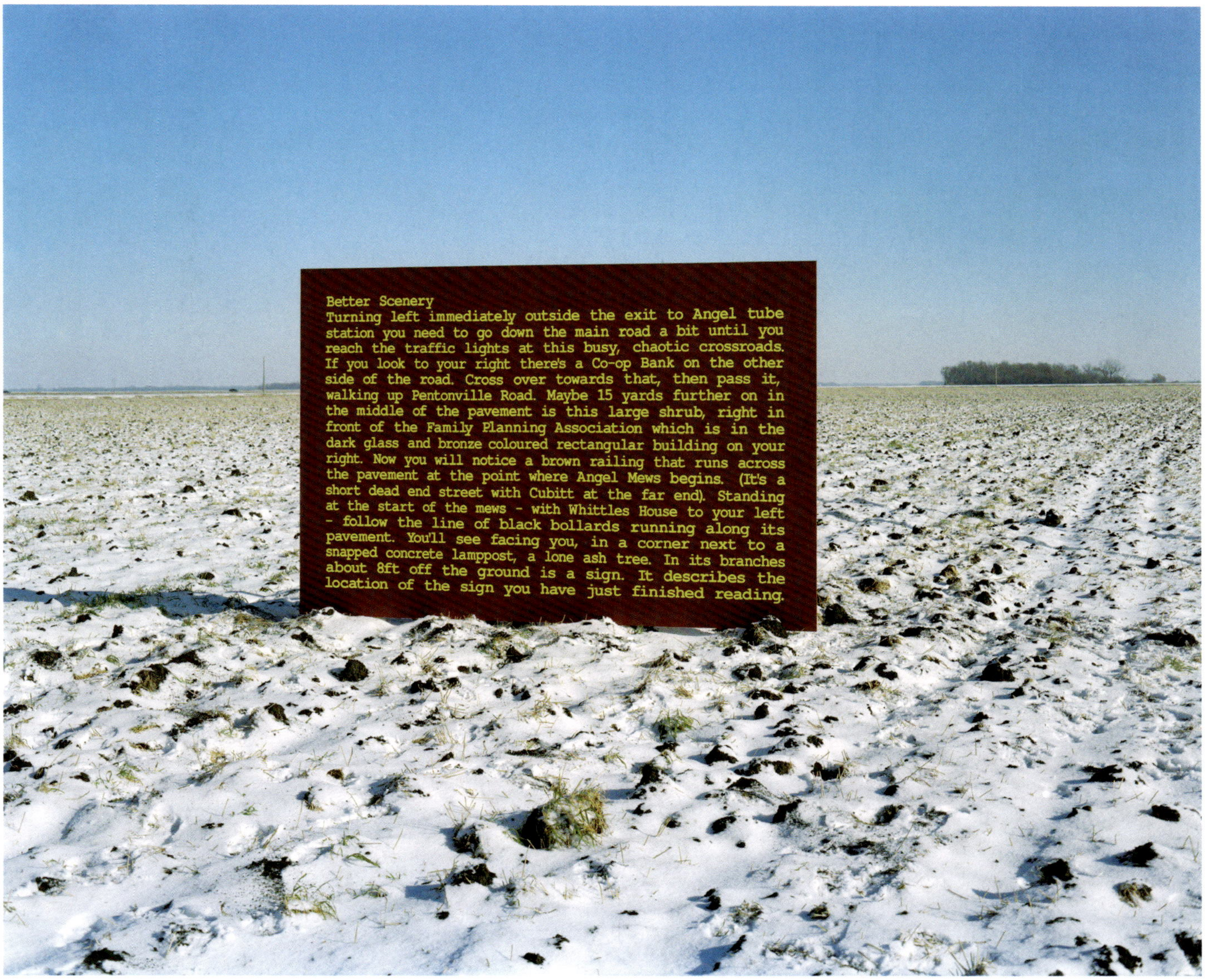
Better Scenery
Turning left immediately outside the exit to Angel tube station you need to go down the main road a bit until you reach the traffic lights at this busy, chaotic crossroads. If you look to your right there's a Co-op Bank on the other side of the road. Cross over towards that, then pass it, walking up Pentonville Road. Maybe 15 yards further on in the middle of the pavement is this large shrub, right in front of the Family Planning Association which is in the dark glass and bronze coloured rectangular building on your right. Now you will notice a brown railing that runs across the pavement at the point where Angel Mews begins. (It's a short dead end street with Cubitt at the far end). Standing at the start of the mews - with Whittles House to your left - follow the line of black bollards running along its pavement. You'll see facing you, in a corner next to a snapped concrete lamppost, a lone ash tree. In its branches about 8ft off the ground is a sign. It describes the location of the sign you have just finished reading.

114

**The God Look-Alike Contest** 1992

# THE FREE-ADS

## EDITOR'S CHOICE

100

**LOOK AT THE VARIETY! Editor's ...oice is full of advertisements ...lected from all sections of LOOT ...ch day to give you just a taste of ...at to expect in the rest of the ...per.**

**LOOT'S FREE-AD PHONE ...NES are open 24 hours a day, 7 ...ys a week. We can serve you ...st, and you can avoid the frus...ation of finding our number ...gaged, if you phone outside ...ak times. Our lines are espe...ally busy on weekday mornings ...etween 10am and 1pm and on ...eekday evenings between 6-...m. Remember, you can mail ...d FAX your free ads to us too!**

**...Alto recorder,** £25. Descant recorder, £5. ...th excellent condition. 081-909 2077 NW.

**...Alton Towers,** 2 tickets for 9th June, and ...ickets for 10th June, swap for 2 tickets for ...other dates. 081-367 8045 North.

**...Bed settee,** 3 seater, good quality, modern ...terial, with fitted sheets, matching quilt cover ...2 pillows, £100. 0375 394655 Essex.

**...Bedford Midi Diesel** Van, 1989, LWB, full ...vice history, floor change, windows, seats 8, ...dge bar, sunroof, 53,000 miles, MOT & tax, ...,000. 081-641 5572 SW.

**...Body Sculpture Rowing** machine, ...draulic action, adjustable resistance, com...ter monitors time, strokes, tempo, calories, ...dded seat, hardly used, original packaging, ...st £70, will accept, £45 ono. 081-769 7953 ...V.

**...Boxer's speed ball,** punching rig, sturdy, ...ofessional item, for wall mounting minus ...nch ball, £35. 071-833 3522 North.

**...Bros fans,** Coke-size can, embossed with ...tt, Luke and Craig, was to be UK launch but ...aig left group, 1 only, £250 ono. 071-431 ...93 NW.

**...Building land, 60,000sqm,** located in ...ntastic French Mediteranean area for sale or ...change with interesting property abroad. ...ease write to M. Fromage Lesternes 23140 ...onnat France.

**...Buttons,** thousands, new and unused, lots ...different kinds, colours, buyer collects, £20 ...o. 081-672 9227 after 6pm SW.

• **BMW 325i,** 1986, dolphin grey metallic, 4 door switchable Auto, black leather interior, PAS, all electrics, computer, spares etc, new MOT, tax, excellent condition, £4,600. 081-518 5611 or 081-505 5311 East.

• **BMW 520i Auto,** 1985, 1 previous owner, fsh, MOT January 1994, good condition, sunroof, power steering, electric windows, mirrors and aerial, metallic bronze, AA inspection welcome, £1,995 ono. 081-764 3732 after 6pm SW.

• **Canada, Nova Scotia,** 140ha, wooded, with lake frontage. Suitable for development. CAN $107,000. Tel +46-16-29261, Fax +46-16-121420, Dishart.

• **Canoe,** slalom, with paddle and spray deck, fair condition, £60 ono. Wet suit and life jacket. £45. 0702 294100 Essex.

• **Cash register,** electronic, control lock, all features, perfect order, £85. 0708 737885 Essex.

• **Cast iron bath,** white, roll top, deep, old fashioned, chrome taps, shower attachment, freestanding / conventional panel, basin and pedestal with taps, good condition, £90. 081-884 1111 N/E.

• **Chairs, cane, folding,** set of 6, dark wood, good condition, £40. 081-524 8078 East.

• **Cigars wanted,** reasonable price paid. 081-461 2790 SE.

• **Clapham Common,** beautiful 1 bed flat, Georgian garden square, fully furnished, stripped pine floors, fully fitted kitchen, DSS welcome, £120pw. Hayley 0895 431735.

• **Coca Cola lampshade,** old, lead and shell, 2ft round, offers over £500. 0708 476136 Essex.

• **Cordon Bleu** mini kitchen, 2 rings, oven and grill, plugs into mains, vgc, new £130, will accept £60. 0708 722585 Essex.

• **Designer wall light,** Italian, lead crystal, 100W halogen bulb & diffuser, as new, £25. 081-690 5103 SE.

• **Diamond solitaire,** .60 carat diamond in white gold ring, antique setting, not perfect quality but large with good colour, £650 ono. 071-498 1756 eves & weekends SW.

• **Eight berth static** caravan in rural Sussex close to sea, mains, electric, & water, vgc throughout, large kitchen with cooker & fridge, ground rent paid til 1994, genuine reason for sale, £1,995 ono. 081-855 5574 SE.

• **Engagement rings,** 2, one ruby, two diamonds in silver, £55 ono. Other emerald, 3 diamonds in silver, £70 ono. Cultured pearl necklaces, 10, 16in length, silver clasps, £11 each. 081-671 5406 SW.

• **Everything you need** for home brewing - wine & beer, including over 30 bottles, £30 ono. Michelle 081-424 0285 eves NW.

• **E3,** spacious 6 bed house, 2 bathrooms, patio, 23 x 13ft kitchen / diner, swimming pool, jacuzzi, gym, all mod cons, 5 mins tube, £350 pw. 081-985 4678 / 081-983 1513.

• **Fontana CD collection,** very limited edition, serial number 000025, set of 12 singles, shrink wrapped, includes Walker Brothers, Scott Walker, The Herd, Pretty Things, The Troggs, Jimmy Page, offers. 071-275 9175 City/SE.

• **Ford Escort XR3i,** 1984, B reg, white, 2 new tyres, new clutch and brake pads, MOT until October, tax until July, £925. 081-992 7345 evenings West.

• **Ford Escort 1100,** X reg, 11 months MOT, tax 5 months, very reliable, £650 ono. 071-359 7936 after 6pm North.

• **Ford Escort 1400,** 1989, G reg, dark blue, grey interior, sunroof, stereo, rear belts, 36,000 miles from new, full service history, MOT & tax, immaculate, must be seen, £3,695. 081-894 2522 W/SW.

• **Ford Granada 2.3,** C reg, new MOT, new tax, radio cassette, central locking, vgc, £499. 081-442 1795 North.

• **French Alps,** Morillon, Geneva 13 mins, 1 bed fully furnished chalet style apartment, garage, ski locker, next to ski lift, vgc, summer / winter resort, FF420,000 ono. 081-861 4063.

• **Futon sofabed,** double, 6 months old, vgc, £85 ono. 081-946 0299 after 7pm SW.

• **Gents racer,** 10 speed, 27in wheels, good condition, £30. 0708 227903 Essex.

• **Harlesden,** 5 double bedroom, first floor maisonette, newly converted, 2 luxury bathrooms, new kitchen, close to all amenities, gch, double glazing, month in advance & deposit, £225 pw. 081-452 8908.

• **Kit car,** 1991 reg, Spartan 2+2 Roadster, Ford based, 2.0 OHC, 130bhp, high performance components, many s/s parts, MOT & tax, relocating, must sell, cost over £6,500, accept £2,950 for quick sale. 0206 330269 Essex.

• **Ladies foldaway shopper,** many extras, excellent condition, £25. 0708 227903 Essex.

• **Levis 501s,** stonewash, size 30-32in waist, new with label still on, £20 pair. 081-653 2347 SW.

• **Life model prints,** set, black and white, taken by Koo Stark in 1987, commissioned by Highlands, proof cards included, serious offers only. 081-671 5406 SW.

• **Look-alike contest,** artist seeks people who think that they look like God, for interesting project. Adam 071-737 0651 SW.

• **Mamas & Papas Anniversary** pushchair, as good as new, with sun canopy, rain cover in plastic, also changing bag, all to match, cost £400, only 5 months old, £180 ono. 081-697 4334 after 6pm Catford.

• **MV Augusta 350** Sports, 1976, Italian import, excellent and original condition, runs beautifully, 13,000km only, not yet registered hence £1,400. 081-851 2066 SE.

• **Negretti & Zambra clock,** 8 day, and anaroid barometer, in Deco style marble plate on metal base, £70. 0737 554824 Surrey.

• **Nikayo 35mm camera,** fully automatic, auto focus, brand new, quick sale require... £25. 081-841 9781 North.

• **Nintendo Super Famicon,** with PA... adaptor, and Super Magicom with 38 game... £500. Steve 081-841 7561 any time days Wes...

• **Old mangle,** approx 1920s model, han... operated, with wooden shears, cast iron, fre... standing, timber pull-out draw, £100 ono. 08... 830 1392 Willesden.

• **Panasonic bread maker,** mixe... kneads, rises & bakes, 3 months old, still und... guarantee, £120 ono. 071-221 7948 West.

• **Philips mini oven,** electric. with grill, 3 p... plug, 1 shelf, glass door drops down, white, ... new, 36.5 x 20cm x 23cm high, perfect for be... sit, £35. 071-624 6262 NW.

• **Postcard collection,** includes many ra... items in old album, £100. 0737 554824 Surre...

• **Quantam Calculight-X,** digital exposu... meter, vgc, £70. 081-390 7650 SW.

• **Reggae,** 12in singles, 1978 to 1992, ... good condition, some Jamaican labels, most ... UK, 27 records, £20 the lot. 081-471 43... East.

• **Shergold Custom Masquerader,** ... string electric solid bodied guitar, classi... superb action, refretted and restrung, £2... ovno. 081-337 3157 SW.

• **Small family car** wanted, smaller than 1 ... litre engine, less than eight years old, must ... Auto, with electric windows and good worki... order, pay up to £5,000. 081-202 2387 NW.

• **Turbo/Brooks saddle...** Campagnolo/Laprade seat pins, Cinelli handl... bars/stems, Miche/Shimano peda... Stronglite/Rival/SR chain setsand botto... brackets, Bell/Brancale helmets, everythi... good condition. 071-247 5948 City.

◆ **THE COPYDATE FOR ALL AD... APPEARING IN LOOT is 12 NOO... TUESDAY for Friday's PINK editio... 12 NOON WEDNESDAY for Mo... day's GOLD edition, 12 NOO... THURSDAY for Tuesday's RED ed... tion, 12 NOON FRIDAY for Wedne... day's GREEN edition and 12 NOO... MONDAY for Thursday's BLUE ed... tion. The best classified service ... London COMPLETELY FREE to ... private advertisers!**

• **Wedding dress,** beautiful ivory crinolin... Gone With The Wind style, size 12, shawl coll... Bo-peep skirt, price includes hoop, £225. 08... 203 8418 NW.

• **Windsurf board,** hardly used, storm s... sitting waiting in the garage, suit beginner, £2... 081-550 0372 Ilford.

• **XWD Prismatic binoculars,** from 194... by REL of Canada, 6 x 30, with .5 degree grat... ule and height judgement guide, £25. 07... 554824 Surrey.

• **Yves St Laurent** dogtooth suit, nea... new, black and white, waist 32in, chest 38... £20. 081-340 2788 North.

*CONTINUED BACK PAG...*

# 116

**The God Look-Alike Contest** 1992

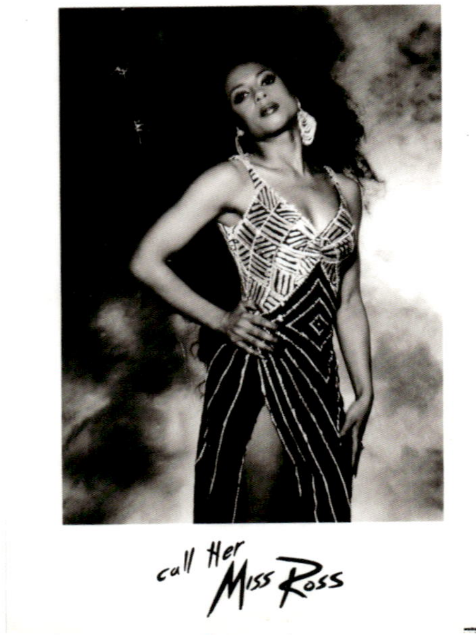


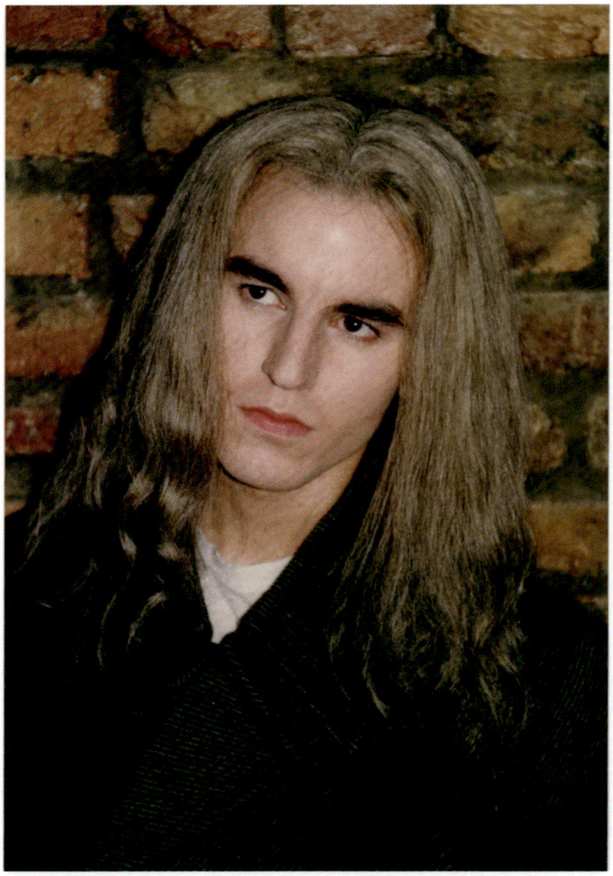

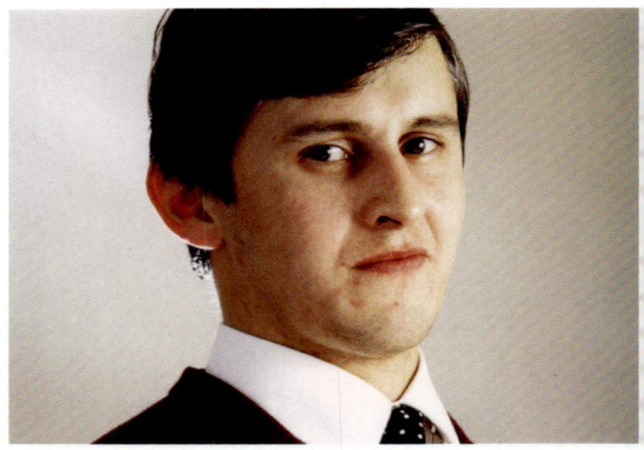

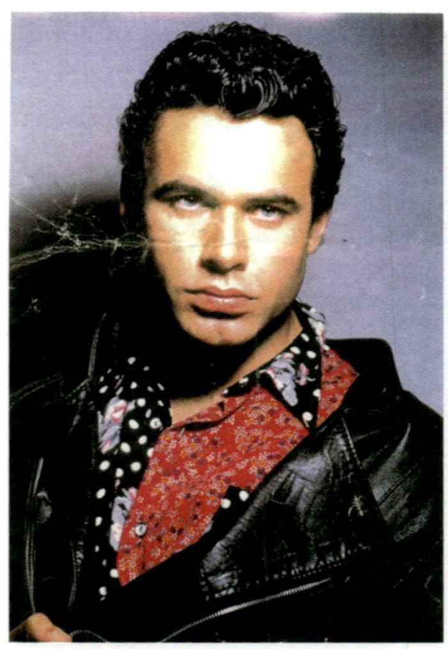

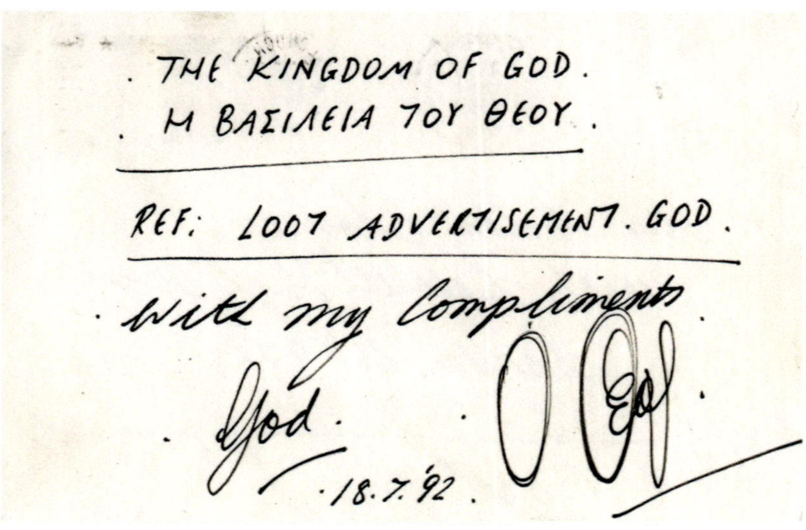

. THE KINGDOM OF GOD .
. Η ΒΑΣΙΛΕΙΑ ΤΟΥ ΘΕΟΥ .

REF: LOOT ADVERTISEMENT. GOD .

. With my Compliments .

. God .

. 18.7.92 .

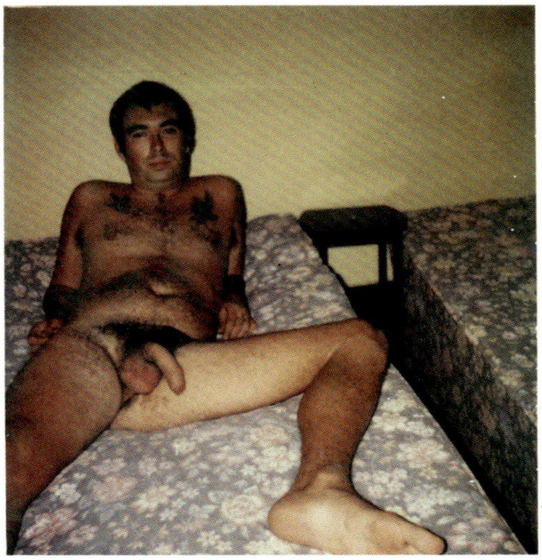

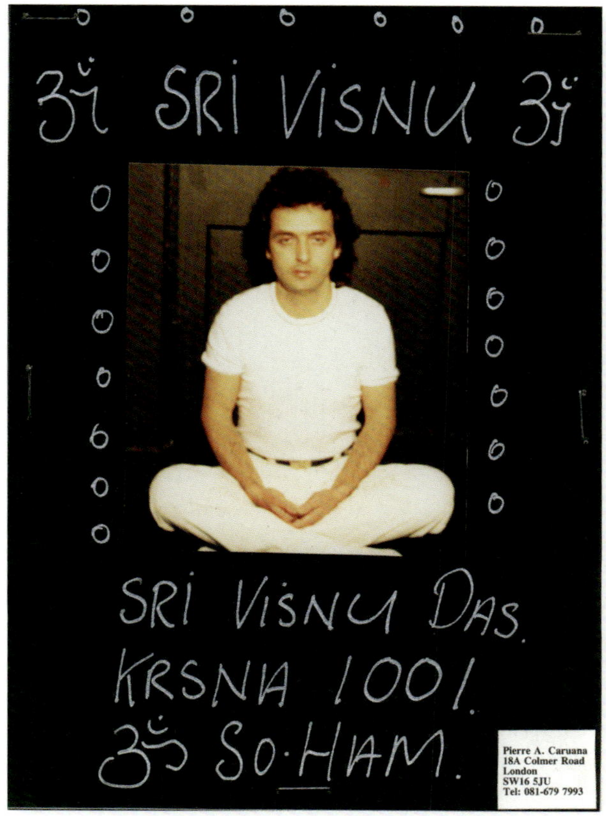
SRI VISNU
SRI VISNU DAS.
KRSNA 1001.
SO·HAM.
Pierre A. Caruana
18A Colmer Road
London
SW16 5JU
Tel: 081-679 7993

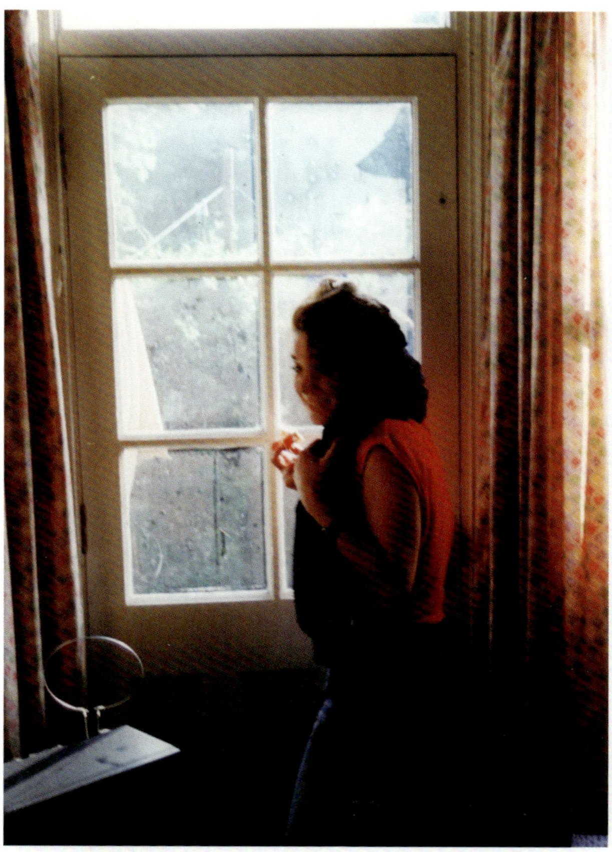

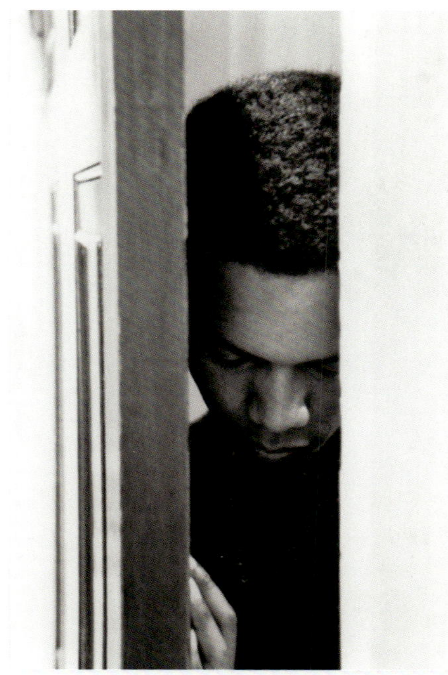

**Better Scenery** 2002

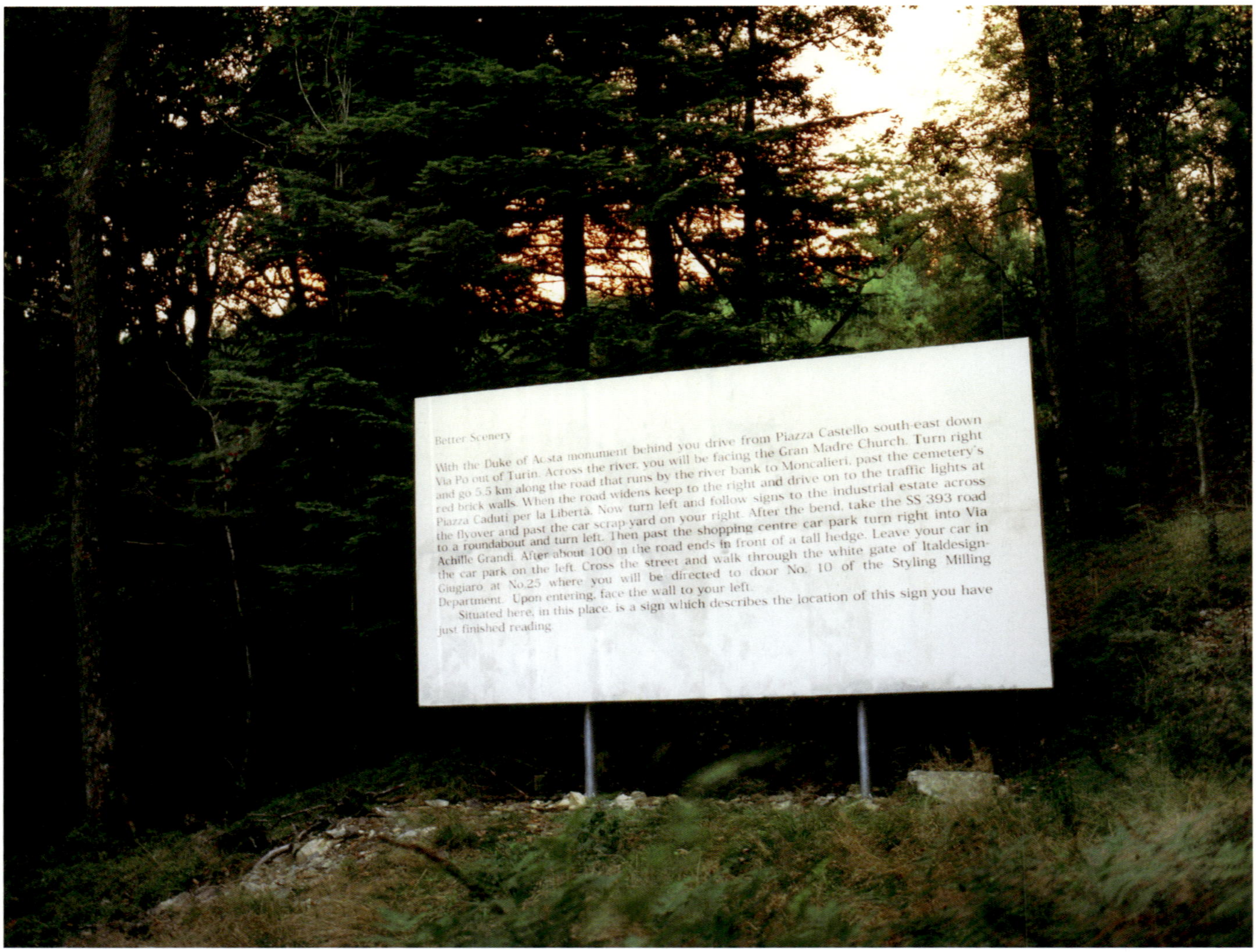

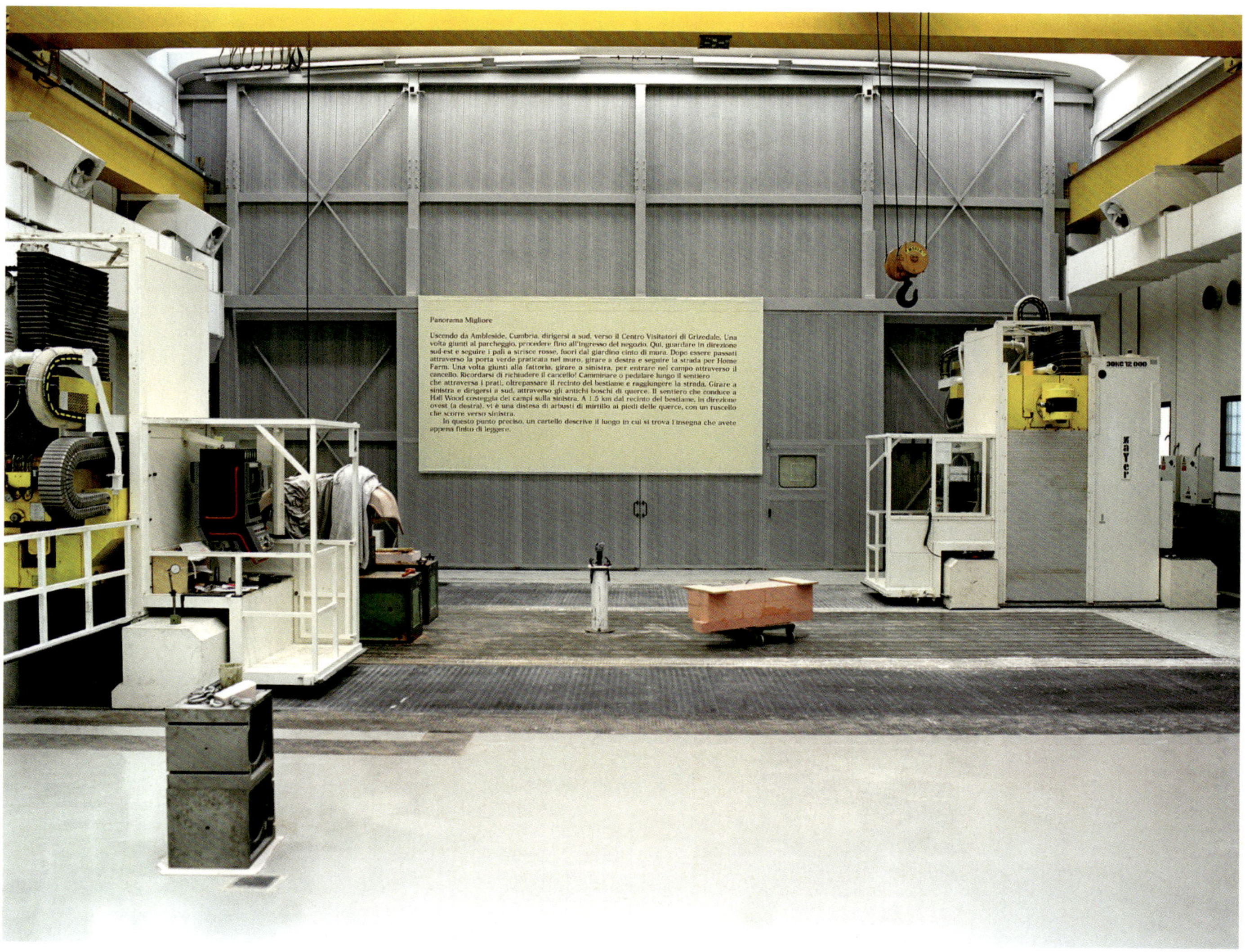
Panorama Migliore
Uscendo da Ambleside, Cumbria, dirigersi a sud, verso il Centro Visitatori di Grizedale. Una volta giunti al parcheggio, procedere fino all'ingresso del negozio. Qui, guardare in direzione sud-est e seguire i pali a strisce rosse, fuori dal giardino cinto di mura. Dopo essere passati attraverso la porta verde praticata nel muro, girare a destra e seguire la strada per Home Farm. Una volta giunti alla fattoria, girare a sinistra, per entrare nel campo attraverso il cancello. Ricordarsi di richiudere il cancello! Camminare o pedalare lungo il sentiero che attraversa i prati, oltrepassare il recinto del bestiame e raggiungere la strada. Girare a sinistra e dirigersi a sud, attraverso gli antichi boschi di querce. Il sentiero che conduce a Hall Wood costeggia dei campi sulla sinistra. A 1.5 km dal recinto del bestiame, in direzione ovest (a destra), vi è una distesa di arbusti di mirtillo ai piedi delle querce, con un ruscello che scorre verso sinistra.
In questo punto preciso, un cartello descrive il luogo in cui si trova l'insegna che avete appena finito di leggere.

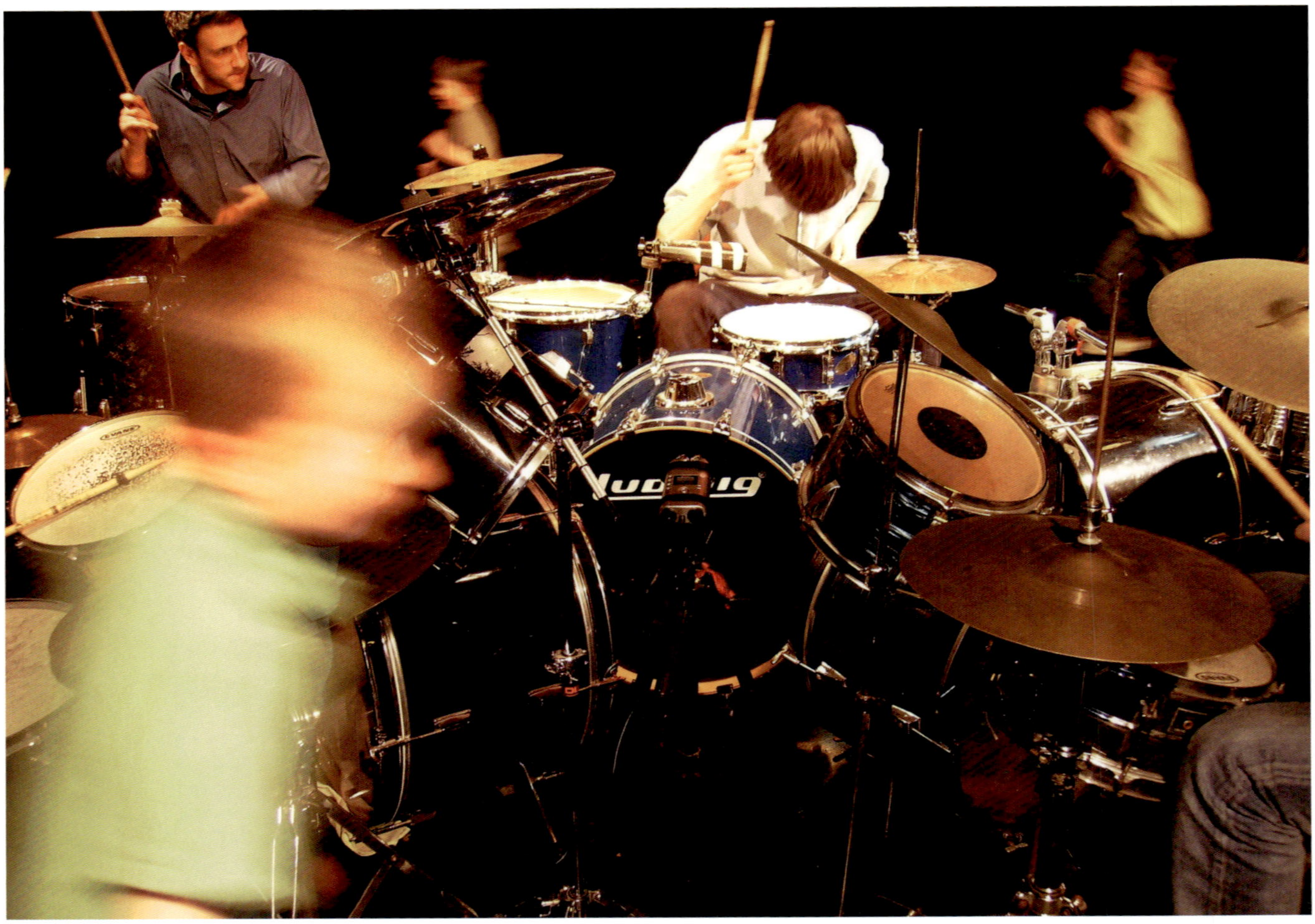

Pyramid 2008

## A Conversation between Adam Chodzko and Martin Clark

**Martin Clark** OK, maybe we can begin by talking a bit about the show at Tate St Ives. You have made some new works for the exhibition here, but you've also responded quite specifically to the location - and this very particular building - in the way that you have both conceived and structured the exhibition.

**Adam Chodzko** Well, St Ives itself is pretty extraordinary anyway, and on top of that there is one of the UK's four Tate galleries in this remote little seaside town, at the very westerly tip of the country. In some senses, living in Whitstable – another small, coastal town – means that St Ives is an environment I feel quite familiar with. Both are seemingly at odds with 21st-century metropolitan life and yet also manage to inhabit small but vital roles within that culture and its identity, maybe as its respite. But the Tate's existence in St Ives seems extraordinary. We know the historical reasons why it's there but that doesn't quite dispel the experience of its almost surreal presence, like the ship on the mountain in Herzog's Fitzcarraldo. Its significance and scale makes it feel immensely solid but at the same time there is a lingering suspicion that it occupies a different reality; that at any moment the sea might crash through and remove it altogether. Or that it's the town's collective dream, and after a good deep sleep they might just begin dreaming up something else.

**MC** It's odd that you should respond to it as incongruous, because the architects designed Tate St Ives with the idea of it mirroring or evoking a walk through the town. Some of the spaces refer to quite specific locations, and their arrangement and scale is meant to echo the experience of the place. In a sense the town very much defined the shape, particularly with respect to the interior spaces.

**AC** When I first visited, a few months back, the architecture really threw me. For instance, the experience of the awkwardness of the Loggia - that large circular space on the front of the building. I couldn't understand its design. I was totally confused as to how I was expected to enter the building. I felt wrong-footed from the start. You're put through these complicated angles and offered some strange approach options.

**MC** It's interesting that you have these immediate, quite intense reactions to architecture and space. I remember the book you did a few years ago, Whitstable Interiors, where you would become very perplexed about peoples' skirting boards, or light switches or a particular kind of cupboard.

**AC** Well, there is a way of looking which seems to empty out any assumptions of history, design, usage and so on and leaves matter as some kind of pure presence. So I'm experiencing that each time I set about wondering about these spaces through staring at them. Anyway, I wanted to use that experience of the Loggia space in some way, and I was thinking about a work I made in 2006, Test Tone for Landscape. It operates as a kind of kit that can be transposed to a place in order to harmonise it. Mostly I imagined it working across wide expanses (kilometres apart) so the Loggia is a comparatively confined space. The work has five speaker positions that create various test-tones as the viewer progresses through the space that might lead to an ideal (but temporary) situation or solution for that space. But, as with much of the work in the show, a use-value is implied although its role remains ambiguous.

**MC** The space of the Loggia is also used in another of the new works in the show, one that doesn't physically appear in the building or the galleries but instead occupies a double-page spread in the current issue of Tate Etc. magazine. This is something you've done before - locating work in other kinds of spaces, including magazines or newspapers. Could you speak a little bit about this work, Memory Theatre (reproduced in this book as the endpapers) whose subtitle has lent the exhibition its title and which you've talked about as being, in a sense, the first work in the show.

**AC** As I said, I was thinking to some extent about the apparent vulnerability of the building, perched on the edge of the ocean. And then the shape of the building, with that drum of the Loggia which immediately suggested to me the form of a slide carousel. I'm interested in how a 35mm slide relates to memory, because – think of the flashback in cinema - we always seem to like our reflections mediated through older technology, and the slide-show itself was used in the past as a way for a family to recollect their excursions, both to themselves and to others. Also, the circular form of the carousel is like the circular architecture of memory theatres too – amphitheatre-type spaces that contain chambers holding mnemonic images ...

**MC** Tell me about memory theatres ...

**AC** Well, the art of memory was supposedly invented by the Greek poet Simonides – Francis Yates's book The Art of Memory is a brilliant history of this – but anyway, the story goes that Simonides was in a temple, and the roof collapsed, killing everyone inside. Somehow, through the grace of the gods, Simonides escaped. The bodies of the dead were unrecognisable, but because he could remember with perfect accuracy where everyone had been sitting in the space, he was able to identify all of the bodies. So the Greeks created a system whereby architectural spaces acted as prompts to memory, so you would mentally allocate specific motifs to existing spaces and places, and the motifs would trigger particular memories. A motif might be something like an anchor covered in blood – these things were often sprayed with blood in order to make them more vivid – and you would imagine this motif in a certain chamber or room. Using this technique orators or poets were able to tell these incredibly long, complex stories, mentally moving through the spaces with each remembered event triggering the next.

These amphitheatre-type architectures were both conceptual and, sometimes, built structures. The Globe Theatre in London was supposedly designed along these lines. So you have this idea of an architecture of the mind, formed from an organised system of memories, being realised as a building. And Tate St Ives, with its whorl-like progression of chambers, for me, seemed to have a similar resonance. At the same time the gallery functions to process the memories of a particular cultural moment for its community.

**MC** That idea of a procession or sequence of images around a space is very evocative of a carousel of slides, and of the way that you have used slide projections in a number of your works, from Cell–a and The Gorgies Centre, to Turning Point, and the three masked parade proposal works included in this exhibition. It also makes me think of the performance work, Longshore Drift, which you are presenting toward the end of the show ...

**AC** Yes, it's strange, in relation to memory, because I have done this slide-lecture performance once before, two years ago. I did it without notes and I have virtually no recollection of what I said then. Which is odd, and it's also really frustrating because I'll have to build the bridges between the images again from scratch. So it will be a very different piece. Its full title is Longshore Drift, early Detroit techno and other forms of erosion, which helps only a little. I know I start by trying to understand tidal flow and its lunar relations and this collapses into an anecdote about finding a slide collection washed up on a beach. I explain a way that I've figured out an order to these images, through their sequence of deposition on the beach, and then weave them together. They vary from images from the 1960s of garden enthusiasts posing in front of rhododendron bushes to pictures from the 1990s of factories that specialise in distressing denim for jeans. Associations are built up between impossibly disparate material while simultaneously undermining any possible connections. Ultimately it is a public sharing of a remembering and forgetting.

**MC** In the way you've been thinking about your show as a whole, there is a sense that the works are the traces left behind, washed up by surges of production over the years. But then there is also this more literal, yet poetic idea that they might have been physically washed into the building after one of these extreme tides - that the show is made up of the detritus left behind as the water recedes. Certainly, these ideas of impossible conjunctions, memory and flow - especially the removal of evidence – are going on in the Tate Etc. Memory Theatre work.

**AC** Yes, as a mnemonic there is this suitably traumatic and ludicrous event suggested: something - a gallery visitor, possibly - is combusted on the steps of the Loggia by a sunbeam that's been horrifically magnified by an adapted lens in the roof. This event has been precisely calculated to coincide with the moment of an extreme Proxigean Spring Tide - a very high tide that occurs once every 40 or 50 years, when the sun and moon are in direct alignment - which washes into the Loggia and carries the charred remains away, out to sea. Or possibly the timing has gone wrong in an assembly of events and the extreme tide was meant to extinguish the incineration instantly; the two working simultaneously to cancel each other out, in order to create a form of ecstasy for the 'sitter'. The architecture of the building is reimagined with this entirely other, apparently insidious – even sinister – function inscribed within it. The Loggia becomes a sacrificial sun temple and the awkwardness or illegibility of the design is revealed to be due to its adherence to a previously unknown set of principles, which access another kind of use or knowledge.

**MC** In Hole (2007) there is this account of a visitor going into the newly opened Museum of Modern Art in Bologna, and then mysteriously disappearing into the fabric of the building never to be seen again. So in both of these works there is this idea that these places, these buildings, are charged with a much greater power than we might expect, or perhaps a very different kind of power.

**AC** Yes, Hole is one of a trilogy of videos with Around (2007) and Pyramid (2008) that further explore this, and the works share the notion of a public space being invested with particular expectations that are seen to collapse in the future. This collapse, in each case because of a lack of acknowledgement of other realities, inadvertently creates something fantastic that washes back a series of fragments or ruins into the present. These ruins appear, or emerge from these recent video works in the final gallery of Tate St Ives.

**MC** I wanted to ask you about landscape because it is pictured, in one way or another, in a number of your works both in terms of geography and also a kind of collective memory or cultural history of landscape.

**AC** Hmmm, I'm a bit squeamish about talking about 'landscape' in relation to my work because in art it seems too easily seductive, acceptable, consensual or something. My embarrassment about it isn't necessarily a bad, or an uninteresting, thing though ...

**MC** It's certainly not a clichéd or romantic or even dystopian idea of landscape. It's much more about a point where things meet or collide; an interest in borders, limits, edges – both literally and metaphorically ... the place where the town or the suburbs peter out into the woods or the wasteland. Maybe it's not so much about landscape but about place, although there is this interest in the materiality of the world and its processes to some extent.

**AC** For me, the vista is almost a red herring, functioning instead as a backdrop or relief to an event that has led to that image, that view. For instance, in Gus van Sant's Gerry you have a film which appears to be about the awesome power of a landscape but really, I think, is about a very occasional, peculiar and intimate conversation that takes place in front of this scenery. Maybe more pertinently though, Atom Egoyan's Calendar shows a series of Armenian landscapes being photographed, but the subject is really about what is hidden behind the camera, the awkwardness of the photographer who documents these panoramas, which is, of course, also the place that the audience occupies.

I've certainly been interested in a kind of space from where you might watch the urban, which might sometimes invoke the rural. This zone often becomes a place of preparation for working out how to approach the urban again, poetically, but this time avoid falling into its habits and clichés. It's an interest in quite fragile landscapes that only just manage to be there, perhaps because they have been overlooked by cultural development – so yes, it's more about a kind of wasteland. I think it's partly to do with growing up in the inertia of the outer London suburbs. When I was about seven or eight we lived in a house that backed on to some woods. The woods were actually really small, surrounded on all sides by houses, so they became a sort of unused, surplus space for these homes. For five or six years I spent most of my time alone there, building camps and traps, hanging out, talking to myself, getting to know twigs, making fires. And when local kids did appear, they really believed that I lived among the trees, because I was just always there.

It was essentially a kind of back-stage space that I inhabited, a very serene kind of isolation where your identity begins to meld with its surroundings. It's a similar space that Simon occupies, alone and mesmerised by the pig's head in Lord of the Flies; a zone formed or defined by the edges of the illusory spaces we inhabit and construct in our everyday life and so the only place where the play of other realities can be perceived from. It is a place of preparation, of waiting; a place where you can transform, change costumes, turn into something else – any kind of fixity of identity no longer holds.

**MC** There's a way in which your work appears to arise out of a weaving together of a kind of absolute pragmatism – using the 'ordinariness' of your immediate situation or circumstances – and a surreal or absurd fantasy. And this seems to be the case again in the new work you are producing for the Heron Mall, Borrowed Cold Lodge. In the work for Tate Etc. you have reimagined the Loggia as a sun temple, and from that space, as a visitor, you move directly into the Heron Mall where you have created a fantasy of cold weather, a winter store.

**AC** For me, the Heron Mall is an odd room. It feels a bit like a Methodist chapel mixed with a cycle storage area. I wanted to change the status of that first public space of the gallery into that of a staff cloakroom or locker room – something which the visitor would pass through feeling they were somehow bypassing the normal entrance. Instead they were accessing a private space; a chamber beyond the bounds of the self-conscious desire for scrutiny that the gallery normally encourages.

In the past year or so I had made M-path, a threshold that proposed that visitors make a physical and symbolic transformation by changing into second hand footwear, to enhance their perception of the spaces beyond it. And also Sowmat, at Signal Galleri, Malmö, where I made a mud trough in place of a doormat, so that gallery visitors brought in dirt as they entered the space. Sowmat's mud was made up of very specific ingredients: clay dug out from a deep excavation made for a transport terminal that would create a new centre for Malmö; rainwater from the leaking roof of the abandoned Rooseum (previously the home of a great art collection) and 1 million wormwood seeds. But Sowmat was also specifically a winter work where visitors turning up to a pristine gallery through the January sludge would actually become dirtier upon entering, but dirtier with a material that suggested some alchemical potential. Borrowed Cold Lodge for the Heron Mall stems from these ideas of entrances and transformation, and of making a beginning that is somehow 'wrong' ('starting off on the wrong foot' again). You kept on reminding me when I visited that it will be summer when the show is open, and many of the visitors will come in straight off the beach ...

**MC** That's right, lots do. We get sand drifting into the gallery from people's flip-flops, and lots of them will be looking at the art in their swimwear.

**AC** Exactly, so this is why I began thinking about creating a sign of the opposite season, by borrowing a large quantity of very warm, protective clothing to store in this space. There is something very disturbing about looking at a thick coat in semi-darkness on a hot sunny day. In Yet (showing in gallery 5) the narrative, which speaks of a crisis, begins with another misapprehension. A landscape is seen as being set in early summer, yet all the vegetation is dying. 'Time has accelerated', and a problem needs solving! But the narrator has just got the timing of the visual evidence wrong, and really it is winter. All is as it should be. I'm conscious that making work that uses the 'wrong season' as a device seems a bit trite, and I think that triteness needs to be offered at the start of the work as a false expectation of what is to follow. But there is that British preoccupation with the weather, much increased by current anxieties about global warming – 'The weather has gone crazy!'. JG Ballard's stories often begin with a subject noticing a subtle shift in landscape or weather, and this again precipitates this apocalyptic slippage into another reality.

**MC** I guess the Heron Mall itself is quite bunker-like, with its peculiar exterior pebbledash finish on those interior walls; an uncertain kind of space, neither convincingly inside nor outside the building. It also has this very austere atmosphere, as you say, like a chapel, or maybe more like a tomb. When you first started talking about Borrowed Cold Lodge, I was picturing the installation as almost like an Egyptian tomb, a hidden chamber that exists in a kind of twilight between two spaces or states: the world and the underworld - full of the possessions and equipment necessary for the next life, all held in a kind of stasis, again a space that is about a transition, a journey, a preparation.

**AC** Yes, but all these amazing ideas then get punctured by this very dominant, almost authoritarian, icon of the Heron glass, the stained-glass window that Patrick Heron made for the building. It turns what could be a relatively neutral space into a very charged space. So I wondered if I could shift it from glowing abstraction to a highly specific, short-term, pragmatic functional object (other than as a window!). Therefore the Heron Glass became, for me, a map or plan of how the borrowed winter clothes could be recovered by the lenders, the day after the show ends. Different types of clothing are allocated to different sections of the glass, only becoming activated when the exhibition closes.

**MC** I like the way that the Heron window suddenly starts to have this really strong formal relationship with the colours and patterns of the winter gear. It starts to look a bit like the design on a ski jacket or something.

**AC** Yes, and again, like the ingredients of Sowmat (or indeed the material used for the Mask-Filters or the elements in Plan for a Spell), Borrowed Cold Lodge uses the glass to request an array of elements that is peculiarly exact: 27 items of cold-weather, protective, outer clothing for water use ... 27 winter stable rugs ... 97 winter coats from primary school children ... and so on. It seems to suggest the build-up of a code that will solve or resolve something, but like a lot of the work, it's all based on putting things in the wrong place at the wrong time. So together with the impression of accumulating meaning is the feeling that at any minute it might all unravel, or be washed out to sea again.

## Biography / Bibliography

Adam Chodzko lives and works in Whitstable, Kent
Born in London, 1965
University of Manchester, BA (Hons) History of Art, 1985–88
Goldsmiths College, London, MA Fine Art, 1992–94

Selected One-Person Exhibitions

2008 *Proxigean Tide*, Tate St Ives
2007 Signal, Malmö, Sweden
*Then*, Dublin City Gallery The Hugh Lane and various sites across Dublin
MAMbo - Museo d'Arte Moderna di Bologna, Bologna
2004 Carlier Gebauer, Berlin
Els Hanappe Underground, Athens
2003 Herbert Read Gallery, KIAD, Canterbury
2002 Fabrica, Brighton
Arizona State University Art Museum, Tempe, Arizona
Plains Art Museum, Fargo, North Dakota
Cubitt, London
2001 Sandroni.Rey Gallery, Venice, California
Galleria Franco Noero, Turin
Els Hanappe Underground, Athens
2000 Accademia Britannica, Roma
1999 Galleria Franco Noero, Turin
Ikon Gallery, Birmingham
1998 Gallery II, Bradford
Northern Gallery of Contemporary Art, Sunderland
Viewpoint Gallery, Salford
1996 Lotta Hammer, London

Selected Group Exhibitions

2008 *Martian Museum of Terrestrial Art*, Barbican Art Gallery, London*
*Tales of Time and Space*, Folkestone Triennial, Folkestone, Kent*
*Print the Legend*, Fruitmarket Gallery, Edinburgh*
*Fact or Friction*, Vox Populi, Philadelphia
2007 *Breaking Step*, Museum of Contemporary Art, Belgrade*
*Gallery Exchange*, Neue Alte Brücke, Frankfurt
*Beyond the Country*, Glucksman Gallery, Cork
2006 *One Brief Moment*, apexart, New York*
*Responding to Rome*, Estorick Collection, London*
*Please close the gate*, Roche Court, Wiltshire
*From There*, Bloomberg Space, London
*Unfinished Business*, Museum of Contemporary Art, Belgrade
*Fire*, Galleria Franco Noero, Turin
*Belief and Doubt*, The Aspen Art Museum, Colorado*
2005 *Showcase*, City Art Centre, Edinburgh*
*Documentary Creations*, Kunstmuseum Luzern, Switzerland*
*Dance of the Seven Veils*, Cooper Gallery, University of Dundee
*Monuments for the USA*, CCA Wattis Institute for Contemporary Arts, San Francisco and White Columns, New York*
*Displacements: British Art 1900–2005*, Tate Britain
*British Art Show 6*, Baltic, Newcastle, touring to Manchester, Nottingham and Bristol*
*General Ideas.* CCA Wattis Institute for Contemporary Arts, San Francisco
*Video Spirit: Mysteries, Myths, Meditations & the Moving Image.* Cheekwood, Nashville
*Seeing God*, Museum of Fine Arts of Thurgau, Kartause Ittingen, Warth, Switzerland*
*Le Voyage Interieur*, Espace EDF-Electra, Paris*
*Pasolini e noi*, Archivio di Stato in the Royal Palace, Turin and the Istituto Nazionale Per La Grafica, Rome*
*Moving Home: Six Artists, Six Rooms*, Towner Art Gallery, Eastbourne
2004 *Off the Beaten Track*, Longside Gallery, Yorkshire Sculpture Park
*Tonight*, Studio Voltaire, London, Sandroni.Rey, LA
*Perfectly Placed*, South London Gallery
*Romantic Detachment*, PS1, NY, touring to Chapter Art Gallery, Cardiff*
2003 *Electric Earth*, British Council curated, the State Russian Museum, St Petersburg, then touring Russia, and Lithuania through 2004*
*Micro/Macro: British Art 1996–2002*, British Council curated, Mucsarnok Kunsthalle, Budapest*
Visionary Landscapes, Cecil Sharpe House, London
*Independence*, South London Gallery
*In Good Form*, Longside Gallery, Yorkshire Sculpture Park
*Bad Behaviour*, Longside Gallery, Yorkshire Sculpture Park, touring to other venues across the UK
2002 *Life is Beautiful*, Laing Art Gallery, Newcastle upon Tyne*
*Tabu*, Kunsthaus Baselland, Switzerland*
*Location*, UK, Gimpel Fils, London
*Fabrications*, Cube Gallery, Manchester*
*On a Clear Day*, Sophienholm, Lyngby-Taarbæk, Denmark*
*Networks*, Chapter Art

Centre, Cardiff and touring to Fruitmarket Gallery, Edinburgh* and other venues across the UK

2001 *The seat with the clearest view*, Grey Matter Contemporary Art, Sydney
*Bright Paradise*, 1st Auckland Triennial, Auckland Art Gallery, New Zealand*
*Night on Earth*, Städtische Ausstellungshalle Am Hawerkamp, Münster*
*Liquor*, Trafo Galeria, Budapest*
*Helle Nächt*, Bottmingen, Baselland
*Sacred and Profane*, Mappin Art Gallery, Sheffield*

2000 *Dreammachines*, (curated by Susan Hiller), Dundee Centre for Contemporary Art, touring to Mappin Gallery, Sheffield; Camden Art Centre, London; Glyn Vivian Art Gallery, Swansea*
*Found Wanting*, The Contemporary, Atlanta
*Somewhere Near Vada*, Project Art Centre, Dublin*
*Artifice*, Deste Foundation, Athens*
*Waiting*, Mjellby Konstgård, Sweden*
*Black Box Recorder*, Museum Ludwig, Cologne, touring to Croatia, and Czech Republic*
*Tabley*, Tabley House, Cheshire
*Face On*, Site Gallery, Sheffield touring to Milton Keynes Gallery; Open Eye Gallery, Liverpool; Stills, Edinburgh*
*Better Scenery* (with Peter Liversidge), Pand Paulus Gallery, Schiedam, Holland
*Places in Mind*, Ormeau Baths Gallery, (with Stan Douglas and Elizabeth Macgill), Belfast

1999 *Holding Court*, Entwistle, London
*Sleuth*, ffotogallery, Cardiff, touring to Oriel Mostyn, Llandudno, Wales; Barbican Centre, London
*The Poster Show*, Gavin Brown Enterprises, New York

1998 *A to Z*, Approach Gallery, London
*Real Life*, Gallery SALES, Rome
*Wrapped*, Vestjælands Kunstmuseum, Sorø, Denmark*

1997 *It Always Jumps Back and Finds its Own Way*, Stichting de Appel, Amsterdam*
*3 wege zum see*, Künstlerhaus Klagenfurt, Austria*
*Sensation*, Royal Academy, London* touring to Museum für Gegenwart, Berlin; Brooklyn Museum of Art, New York
At one remove, Henry Moore Institute, Leeds*

1996 *Brilliant*, Contemporary Art Museum, Houston, Texas
*21 Days of Darkness*, Transmission Gallery, Glasgow
*Perfect*, Jan Mot and Oscar van den Boogaard, Brussels
*British Waves*, curated by Mario Condognato, Rome

1995 *Zombie Golf*, Bank, London
*General Release*, British Council selection for Venice Biennale, Scuola San Pasquale, Venice*
*Brilliant*, Walker Arts Center, Minneapolis*

1994 *High Fidelity*, Kohji Ogura Gallery, (with Simon Patterson), Nagoya (January 1994); tour to Röntgen Kunst Institut, Tokyo*
*Remote Control*, Royal College of Art, London

1993 *Making People Disappear*, Cubitt Street Gallery, London
*Okay Behaviour*, 303 Gallery, New York
*Wonderful Life*, Lisson Gallery, London

1992–93 *Instructions Received*, Gio Marconi, Milan*

1991 *City Racing*, London

* exhibition publication

Selected Projects

2008 *Memory Theatre*, *Tate Etc.* (double-page spread magazine project), issue no.13, pp.26, 27

2007 Poster project, Mercer Union, Toronto

2005 *M-path*, British Art Show 6, Baltic, Newcastle; Cornerhouse, Manchester; Nottingham; Arnolfini, Bristol

2004 *Night Shift*, Frieze Art Fair, London, publication and event

2003 *Looper*, billboard project for centre of Turin, Italy, as part of the city's '*manifesTO*' series accompanying 'Artissima', Turin art fair

2001 *Zu spät*, Material, no. 3, Summer, pp.7–9
*Cell Pace, Lo-Fi*, website
*Slipstream*, Film & Video Umbrella website www.slipstream.uk.net/
*Art for All.* (edited by Mark Wallinger and Mary Warnock), Peer, pp.64, 94
*Nothing*, edited by Graham Gussin, August Publications, pp.98–99
*Saturday*, edited by Polly Staple, issue 1, pp.16–18

1999 *Moonstruck*, *Tate*, no.18, Summer, pp.34–36
*A Place for The End*, Birmingham, off-site project for Ikon Gallery, Birmingham*
*Better Scenery*, (Camden, London and Arizona desert, USA) off-site project for Camden Art Centre, London

1997 *Le Petit Prince Recall*, with Pierre Huyghe,

Mobile TV, Dijon
1996 *Involva* in Jake and Dinos Fine Arts Inc., *Dazed and Confused*, no.16, pp.78, 84
Interview with *Georgina Starr*, *Tate*, issue no.6, Spring 1996, pp.35–38 and '3+3' p.45
Cover of *frieze*, November
Red Herring, artist's project, *Dazed and Confused*, no.27, pp.60–65
1995 *Involva*, *Experience*, vol. 25, no.3
1994 *Slow Down Skin Shed*, in 'British Art Special', *The Face*, no.68, May, pp.56–72
1993 *Untelevision*, project for *frieze*, Summer, no.11, p.21


Bibliography
Selected Books and Catalogues

2008 *Proxigean Tide*, essays by Martin Herbert, Lisa Le Feuvre, Andrew Wilson, Tate Publishing
*Hey Hey Glossolalia (BEFORE/AFTER)*, editor Mark Beasley, Creative Time Books, New York City/ Article Press, Birmingham, cover
2007 *Adam Chodzko*, texts by Lisa Le Feuvre, Alex Farquharson, Mark Godfrey, Andrea Villani, Skira, Italy
*Then*, essays by Jaki Irvine, Andrew Wilson, Caoimhín Mac Giolla Léith, edited by Rosa Ainley, Breaking Ground, Dublin
*Breaking Step - U raskoraku*, Museum of Contemporary Art Belgrade, British Council, pp.32–41
*Print the Legend*, Patricia Bickers, Fruitmarket Gallery, Edinburgh, pp.48–53
*Aernout Mik*, files notes, Camden Art Centre
2006 *Frieze Projects*, Polly Staple, Jorg Heiser, Frieze, pp.13, 20, 22, 68–69,
2005 *1+1+1, double agents*, Jitka Hanzlova, Central Saint Martins College of Art and Design (exhibition and publication)
2004 'Imagine this doughnut ...' artist's project in *Wonderful: Visions of the Near Future*, pp.33–44, 99–101
*Arttracks*, Mathew Arnatt, pp.12–17, 35
*Frieze Art Fair Yearbook*, pp.1–2
Resonance FM broadcast
*Annual*, Kent Institute of Art and Design, pp.19–34
2003 Blog on www.thecentreofattention.org/
*Whitstable Interiors* fanzine
2002 *Plans and Spells: Adam Chodzko*, Film & Video Umbrella, texts by Chris Darke, Jeremy Millar, Polly Staple, Will Bradley
*Romanov*, Adam Chodzko, Bookworks
*Speaking and Listening*, Sheffield Hallam University and Site Gallery, pp.184–193.
2001 *Bright Paradise*, 1st Auckland Triennial, Auckland Art Gallery, New Zealand, texts by Allan Smith, etc
*Out of the Bubble*, edited by John Carson and Susannah Silver, pp.32–36
*Night on Earth*, Städtische Ausstellungshalle Am Hawerkamp, Münster
2000 *Dream Machines*, National Touring Exhibitions, text by Susan Hiller
*Face On*, Black Dog Publishing, text by Craig Richardson etc
*The Saatchi Gift to the Arts Council Collection*, South Bank Centre
'*Somewhere Near Vada*', Project Art Centre, Dublin, texts by Jaki Irvine and Shirley MacWilliam
1999 *Adam Chodzko*, texts by Jennifer Higgie and Michael Bracewell, August Publications
1998 *Wrapped*, Vestjælands Kunstmuseum, Sorø, Denmark
1997 *It Always Jumps Back and Finds its Own Way*, Stichting de Appel, Amsterdam, texts by K. Schippers and Cosima Rainer
*3 Wege zum See*, Künstlerhaus Klagenfurt, Austria
*Sensation*, Royal Academy
*at one remove*, Henry Moore Institute, Leeds, text by Penelope Curtis
1996 *British Waves*, British Festival, Rome, text by Mario Condognato
1995 *General Release*, British Council, Venice Biennale, texts by Gregor Muir and James Roberts
1993 *High Fidelity*, Kohji Ogura Gallery, Nagoya, Japan, text by James Roberts (exhibition catalogue)
*Instructions Received*, Gio' Marconi, Milan (exhibition catalogue)
1992 *Innocence and Experience*, Stichting Air, Amsterdam, text by Andrew Wilson

Selected Articles and Reviews

2008 Martin Behr, 'Du sollst dir kein Bildnis machen', *Salzburger Nachrichten*, Austria, 22 March
Niamh Ann Kelly, 'Art in the Life World,' *Art Monthly*, no.315, April, pp.30, 31
Jason Oakley, 'Is that what it is going to be?' *The Visual Artists' News Sheet*, January/February
2007 Matthew Miller, *Fabrica.*

*The first 10 years*, pp. 23–27
2006 Jane Rendell, ‘Art and Architecture: A Place Between,’ I B Tauris & Co Ltd, pp. 30, 32–33
Neal Snowdon, ‘Art and sole laid bare’, *Manchester Evening News*, 1 February, pp. 22-23
2005 David Barrett, ‘From Here,’ *Art Monthly*
Patricia Bickers, *Showcase; Contemporary Art for the UK*, Contemporary Art Society, pp. 20, 34
Mark Crinson, ‘Explaining Urbanism to Wild Animals’, *Mute*, Winter/Spring, pp. 62–66
Mark Crinson, ‘Mnemotechny of the industrial city,’ *Urban Memory*, Routledge. pp. 202–208
Helen Luckett, *British Art Show 6*, Hayward Gallery Touring, pp. 204–207
Jeremy Millar and Tacita Dean, *Place*, Thames and Hudson, pp. 64, 65–67
Susanne Neubauer, *Documentary Creations*, exhibition catalogue, Museum of Art Lucerne, pp. 19–21, 30–37, 108
2004 Mark Beasley, *frieze*, no. 82, April, pp. 84–85
Gabriel Coxhead, ‘Who let the wolf out?’ *Times T2*, 13 October
Brian Dillon ‘No Right of Light or Air,’ *Annual*, Kent Institute of Art and Design, pp. 19–34
Maria Fusco, ‘Whitstable Interiors,’ *Art Monthly*, no. 280, October, p. 35
Rachel Greene, *Internet Art*, Thames and Hudson, pp. 206–207
Despina Zevkili, *Athenirama*, Athens, p. 91
2003 Michael Bird, *Modern Painters*, Spring 2003, p. 116
Martin Coomer, *Time Out*, 8–15 January, p. 51
*Foundation for Contemporary Performance Arts 2002*, NY, pp. 16–18
Dan Glaister, *The Guardian*, 23 May 23, p. 27
Pablo Lafuente, *ArtReview*, July/August, p. 49
Jeremy Millar, ‘A New Start,’ *Visualise the Future* publication
Dan Smith, *Art Monthly*, no. 263, February, pp. 29–30
2002 Dave Beech, ‘*Location; UK*’, Art Monthly, no. 259, September, p. 28
Neal Brown, ‘*Romanov*,’ Modern Painters, Winter, p. 165
Martin Clark, *Untitled*, no. 28, Summer, p. 59
Downtowner, Arizona, November, p. 2
Laura Gascoigne, ‘Fear and Laughter,’ *What's on in London*, 4–11 December, p. 23
Mark Godfrey, *Douglas Heubler*, Camden Arts Centre, p. 14
Phil Green, Memory Lanes, *The Architect's Journal*, October, p. 53
Sally O'Reilly, ‘The Games Artists Play’, *[a-n]*, November, pp. 24–25
Mick Robertson, *Flux*, no. 32, Aug/Sept, pp. 26, 27
Helen Sumpter, *Evening Standard*, Hot Tickets, 26 April
Deborah Sussman Susser, ‘Final Cut’, *New Times [Az. USA]*, 21–27 November, p. 63
John Villani, *The Arizona Republic*, 17–24 November, p. 28
Rachel Withers, ‘Critics Picks’, www.artforum.com/picks/place=London - picks3923
2001 Steven Bury, *Artists' Multiples* 1935–2000, p. 159
Jonathon Jones, ‘21st Century Arts,’ *The Guardian*, 21 September, p. 5
Jonathon Jones, ‘Drawn, quartered, hung,’ *The Guardian*, 1 November, p. 12
Emily King, *Restart: New Systems of Graphic Design*, *Thames & Hudson*, pp. 95–97
Michael Wilson, ‘These Days’, *Untitled*, no. 25, Summer, p. 7–9
2000 Massimo Carboni, ‘Adam Chodzko’ *Art Forum*, 38, no. 8, April, p. 14
Mariuccia Casadio, ‘Personal Ads’, *Vogue Italia*, no. 597, May, p. 242
Mario Codognato, ‘Cosa resta di “Sal ò,”’ *Il Sole 24 Ore*, 30 January
Richard Cork, ‘Remember kids, just say no’, *The Times*, 4 October
Michael Corris, ‘FaceOn’, Art Monthly, no. 240, October, pp. 30–31
Jerry Cullum, ‘Boredom and Disgust as Art’, *The Atlanta Journal*, 7 April
Guido Curto, ‘Art & Facts,’ *Flash Art*, April–May
Martin Herbert, ‘Sleuth’, *Time Out*, no. 1539, 16–23 February, p. 54
‘How to get back to your routes’, *Ham & High*, 14 January
Daniel Jewesbury, ‘Places in Mind’, *Art Monthly*, no. 242, November, p. 46
Jonathon Jones, ‘Arizona, NW3’, *Guardian G2*, 15 January, p. 25
Jonathon Jones, ‘Adam Chodzko’, *frieze*, May, no. 52, p. 95
Gideon C. Kennedy, ‘Filling Want’, *Atlanta Press*, 24–30 March, p. 15
Liliana Madeo, ‘La dentista reduce di “Salò”’, *La Stampa*, 18 January
Graham Parker, ‘Tabley’, *Art Monthly*, no. 240, October, p. 42
Lisa Parola, ‘L'artista che s'infila nella

cronaca', *La Stampa*, 2 March
Michael Wilson, 'Sleuth', *Art Monthly*, no. 234, March, p. 34
*ZOO*, Purple House, January, pp. 168–169

1999 David Barrett, 'Adam Chodzko', *Art Monthly*, no. 229, September, pp. 29–31
Interview with David Barrett, Art Club, *Habitat*, pp. 16–22
Laura Cherbini, 'I video crudeli di ...' *Il Giornale*, Italy, 24 May
Robert Clark, Review, *The Guardian*, 29 June, p. 13
'Commerce to Art', *Hotshoe International*, July/August
Charles Darwent, 'Who do they think they are?' *Independent on Sunday*, 4 July
Dawn Fulcher, 'Sleuth', *Contemporary Visual Art*, issue 25, pp. 78–79
'Holding Court', *What's On*, London, 27 January, pp. 20–21
Paolo Levi, 'La Mostra,' *la Repubblica*, 9 May
John E. McGrath, 'Sleuth', *Portfolio*, p. 64
Heidi Macleod, 'chodzko's children', *I-D Magazine*, August
Adam Chodzko in discussion with Robin Rimbaud', *Everything*, no. 24, pp. 16–20
'Reunion: Salò', *Blocnotes*, no. 17, Autumn, pp. 133–137
John Russell Taylor, 'The Big Show: Sleuth', *The Times: Metro*, 20–26 November, p. 42
Interview with John Slyce, 'Looking in the Wrong Place,' *Dazed and Confused*, August, no. 57, pp. 100–106
John Slyce, 'Adam Chodzko' *Flash Art International*, 32; no. 208, October, pp. 120–121
*Tema-Celeste*, 'Adam Chodzko', May–June
*Terzoocchio*, no. 91, June
Elisabetta Tolosano, 'Adam Chodzko,' *Flash Art*, October/November, no. 133
David Vincent, 'Selective Subjects', Gallery, *Express and Star*, 17 July
Rachel Withers, Preview, *Artforum*, May, p. 77
*Young British Art-The Saatchi Collection*, Booth-Clibborn, pp. 17, 40, 105

1998 Louisa Buck, *Moving Targets*, Tate, pp. 150, 156, 170, 175
Christie's *Contemporary*, London, 8/9 October, p. 172
*Dazed and Confused*, no. 49, December, pp. 148, 149
Helen Duff, 'A reunion of one', *City Life*, no. 361, 5–27 August, p. 5
Tony Godfrey, *Burlington Magazine*, 'At One Remove,' January, p. 54
*I-D Magazine*, no. 180, October, p. 165
Jonathan Jones, 'Faces of Evil', *The Guardian*, August, pp. 12, 18

1997 Hilary Alexander, 'Keeping our Cool', *The Daily Telegraph*, 3 January, p. 13
Mathew Collings, 'Blimey', 21, pp. 124, 126, 132–133
Susan Corrigan, *I-D Magazine*, December
Penelope Curtis, 'At One Remove', *Henry Moore Institute Foundation Review*, no. 5, Autumn, p. 10
Antonia Donajgrodzka, 'The naked truth', *Yorkshire Post*, Yorkshire Live, At One Remove, 3 October
Michael Gibbs, 'It Always Jumps Back and Finds Its Way', *Art Monthly*, p. 34
Mark Goodall, 'Space Invaders', *The Big Issue in the North*, At One Remove, no. 184, November, pp. 10–16
Martin Herbert, *Time Out* 'Sensation' supplement, September, p. 14
Karen Joyner, 'A highly individual view of the world', Yorkshire Evening Post, *At One Remove*, 25 September
Tom Lubbock, 'Who are they pointing at?' *Independent, Eye*, 18 September, p. 3
Teresa Macri, 'In cerco di "Salò"', *il manifesto*, 8 November
Charlotte Moore, *Elle*, October, pp. 118–122
Charlotte Mullins, 'Reality, but not as we know it', *Tate*, no. 13, Winter
*Contemporary Visual Arts*, At One Remove, no. 16, October
Johnny Shand Kydd, *Spitfire*, pp. 97, 148
Helen Sumpter, 'Are You Strange?' *Big Issue*, 13 October, p. 32
Paul Usherwood, *Art Monthly*, no. 211, October, p. 32
Godfrey Wordsdale, 'Reality Bites', *Artists' Newsletter*, February, pp. 14–16

1996 Catherine Anspon, 'brilliant', *Public News*, Houston, 6 March, pp. 8, 10
Vito Apuleo, 'Da Londra arriva a Roma un'arte post-umana, *Il Messaggero*, 10 June
Patricia Bickers, 'The Young Devils', *Art Press*, no. 214, p. 34
David Bonetti, 'Brilliant', San Franscisco Examiner, 7 April
Hans-Jurgen Buderer, 'Between Shock and Banality', *Dimensions*, Kunsthalle Mannheim, p. 82
David Burrows, *Art Monthly*, July/August, no. 198, pp. 28–29
Susan Corrigan, 'Twisted Mister', *I-D Magazine*, no. 148, January, p. 10

Shaila Dewan, 'England's Edge', *Houston Press*, 21–27 March, p.35
Kevin Jackson, 'Brit Pop Art', *Arena*, April, pp.60–66
Patricia C. Johnson, 'British exhibit shows attitude', *Houston Chronicle*, 15 February, Section D, pp.1, 6
Sarah Kent, 'Adam Chodzko', *Time Out*, 12–19 June, p.44
Katrijn Klinger, *Der Spiegel*, no.24, pp.212–213
Andrew Lambirth, 'Adam Chodzko', *What's On*, 12 June, p.19
James Roberts, 'Adult Fun', *frieze*, issue 31, pp.62–67
Kate Spicer, 'Nearly God', *The Face*, no.93, June
Andrew Wilson, Spatialised Time, Unchecked Duration', *Art and Design*, Art and Film, p.85

1995 Dave Barrett, 'Contained', Art Monthly, no.186, May, p.31
David Barratt, 'Zombie Golf', *frieze*, issue 24, Sept/October, p.74
Daniela Bezzi, 'Biennale', *L'Espresso*, no.23, 9 June, p.126
*British Council Visual Arts News*, Summer, no.38, p.6
Diane Eddisford, '>alt. zombie.golf.the.earth', *Mute*, issue 2, Summer, p.2
William Furlong, 'Venice Biennale 1995', *Audio Arts*, vol. 15, nos.1&2
Tony Godfrey, 'Venice Biennale Report,' *Untitled*, Summer, p.4
Simon Grant, 'Playing God', *Art Monthly*, issue no.189, September, pp.28, 29
Sarah Greenberg, 'Hard to Love, Impossible to Forget', *Art News*, vol. 94, no.7, NY. September, pp.130–132
Roberta Smith, 'A Show of Moderns Seeking to Shock', *New York Times*, 25 November, pp.B1/B6
Calvin Tomkin, 'London Calling', *The New Yorker*, December, p.116
Neville Wakefield, 'Quite Brilliant', *Tate*, No.7, Winter, pp.33, 39

1994 Julia Cassim, 'Chodzko, Patterson Weak on Public Participation', *The Japan Times*, Sunday, 13 February
Ekow Eshun, 'British Art Special', *The Face*, no.68, May, pp.56–72
Carl Freedman, 'Acting Out/Remote Control', *frieze*, May, issue 16
Kaori Makabe, 'London Strikes Back', *Bijutsu Techo*, Tokyo, vol. 46, no.688, pp.53–55
James Roberts, 'Out in the Real World', *Bijutsu Techo*, Japan, vol. 46, no.688, pp.36–39
Angela Vittesse, 'Domestic Violence', *frieze*, October

1993 Laura Cottingham, 'Wonderful Life', *frieze*, issue 12, October–November, pp.56–57
Richard Dorment, 'Hypnotised by a Handful of Stars', *The Daily Telegraph*, London, 11 August
'Galleries: Okay Behaviour', *The New Yorker*, July
Simon Grant, 'Making People Disappear', *What's On*, London, 21 April
Simon Grant, 'Wonderful Life', *What's On*, London, 25 August
Ruiko Harada, 'From London', *Bijutsu Techo*, vol. 45, no.678, pp.148–149
Rob Legge, 'The Faces of God', *The Independent on Sunday*, London, 19 September
K. Levin, 'Okay Behaviour', *The Village Voice*, 13 July
Tom Lubbock, 'Stupid like a Conceptualist', *The Independent*, London, 10 August
David Alan Mellor, 'Wonderful Life', *Untitled*, Winter, no.3
James Odling-Smee, 'Life', *Art Monthly*, London, October, pp.26–27
Richard Shone, 'God's Bods and Odd Bods', *The Observer*, London, 8 August
John Windsor, 'Art to Hang on the TV Screen', *The Independent*, London, 25 September

1992 Andrew Wilson, '15/1', *Art Monthly*, London, September

## Awards

2007 AHRC Creative Research Fellowship, University of Kent
2002 Paul Hamlyn Award Foundation for Contemporary Arts, NY
1998 British School in Rome, Scholarship

## Collections

Tate Gallery, GAM (Galleria d'Arte Moderna, Turin, MAMBo – Museo d'Arte Moderna di Bologna, British Council Collection, Arts Council Collection, Contemporary Art Society Collection, Saatchi Collection, South London Gallery, Frac Languedoc-Rousillon, Auckland City Art Gallery, Plains Arts Museum, North Dakota, and international private collections

First published 2008 by order of the Tate Trustees by Tate St Ives in association with Tate Publishing, a division of Tate Enterprises Ltd, Millbank, London SW1P 4RG www.tate.org.uk/publishing

On the occasion of the exhibition Adam Chodzko: Proxigean Tide at Tate St Ives 24 May – 21 September 2008

This project has been supported by:
Arts Council England
Tate St Ives Members and Tate Members



British Library Cataloguing in Publication Data:
A catalogue record of this book is available from the British Library
ISBN-13: 978 1 85437 825 5

Texts by Martin Clark, Martin Herbert, Lisa Le Feuvre and Andrew Wilson


Catalogue essays:
Lisa Le Feuvre, Martin Herbert, Andrew Wilson

Catalogue designers:
Claudia Schenk, Silke Klinnert

Catalogue editors:
Rosa Ainley, Martin Clark

Lenders:
British Council, Arts Council, Artists Pension Trust, South London Gallery

Thanks to: Catherine Herbert, Marcus Korhonen, Tim Barker, Justin Chodzko, the Arts & Humanities Research Council, and the Department of Film Studies, University of Kent and to Polly Read, Els Hanappe, Andrea Viliiani and MAMbo – Bologna, Bux Bailey, Ian Smith, Justin Westover, Adam Sutherland, Polly Staple, Simon C Grant, Steven Bode and Film & Video Umbrella, Sophie Thompson, Ryan Gander, Andrew Renton, Mark Beasley, Mark Dickenson, Jeremy Millar, Elizabeth Cowie, Laurence Coone, Rose Lord, Seth Barnard Chodzko, Clay Barnard Chodzko, Clio Barnard.

Repro and print by Cassochrome, Belgium

Cover image:
Plan for a Parade with Two Masks (Blean, Kent, UK and Sepolia, Athens, Greece) 2004
(From Design for a Carnival)
(detail)
35mm slide projection,
81 slides
6 minutes

St IVES
TATE

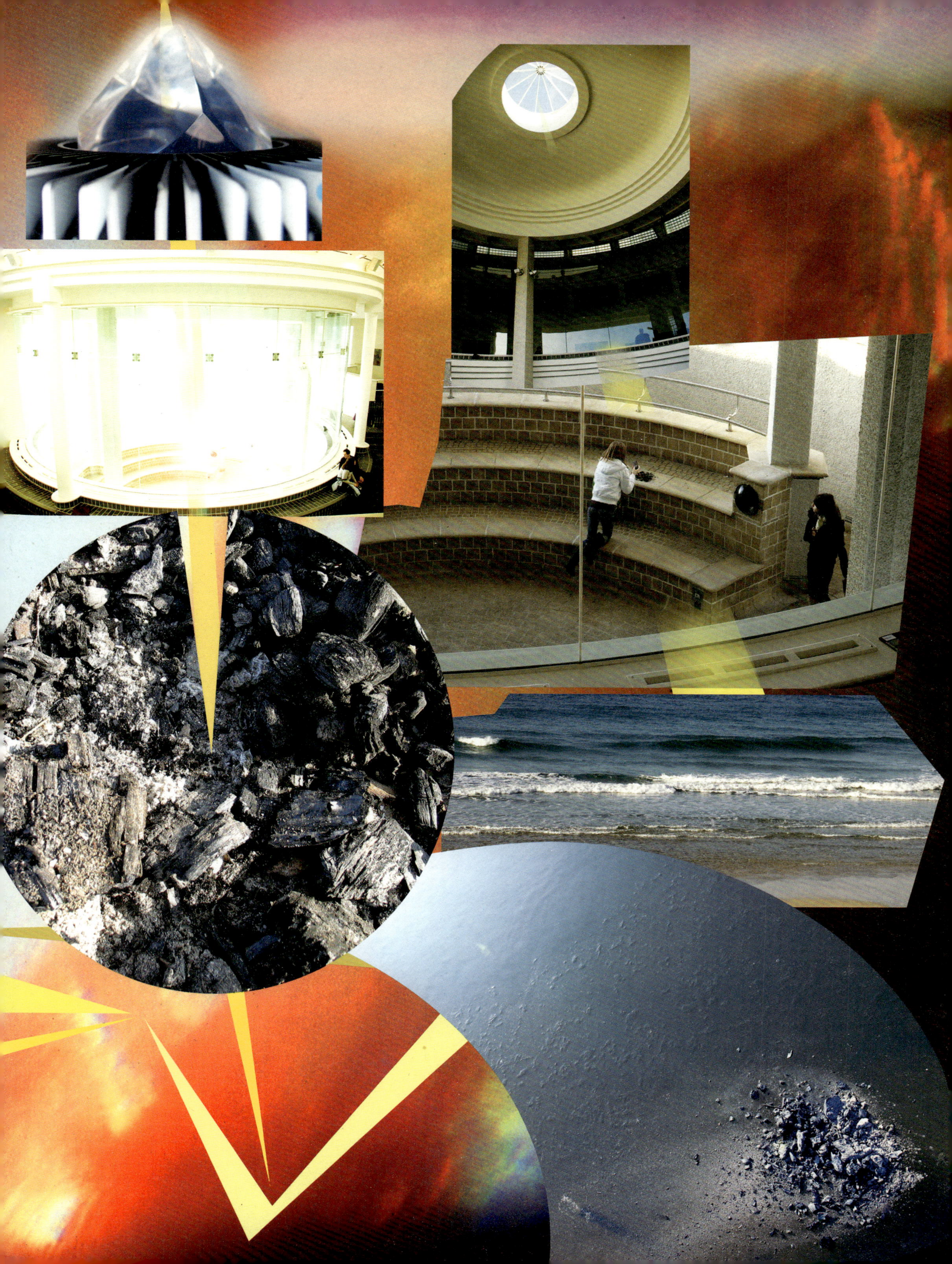

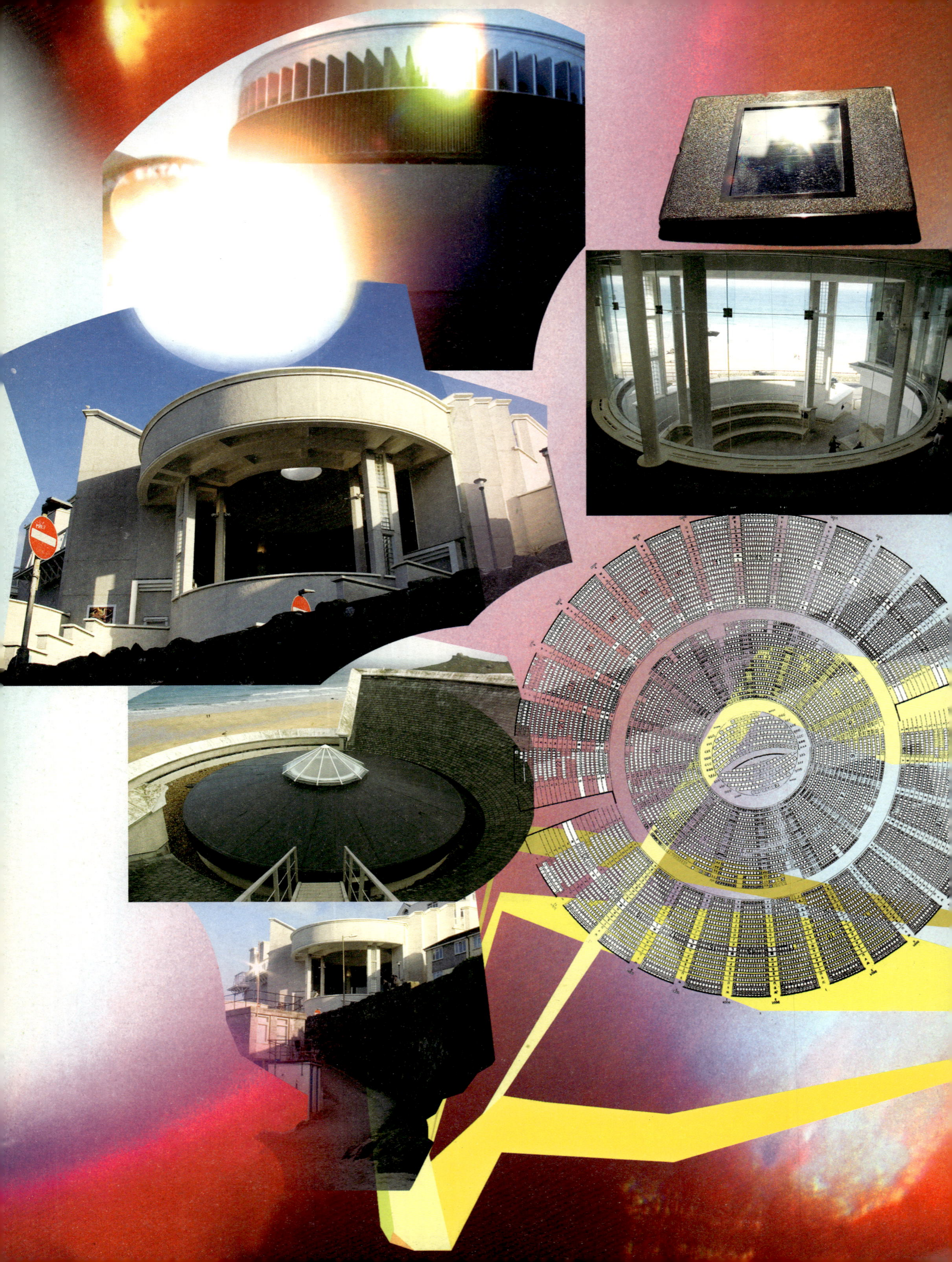

## Works

Dimensions as height × width × depth

00

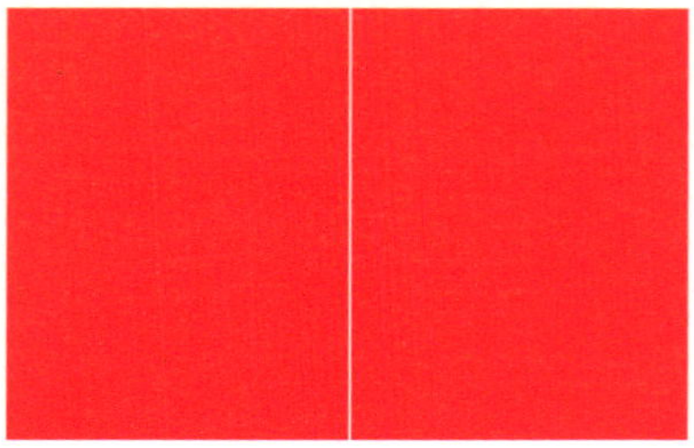

**Memory Theatre (A slide of a sun temple's sacrificial altar, a modified skylight in the Loggia's dome at Tate St Ives, an Extreme Proxigean Spring Tide, and the correct angle of the sun.)** 2008

Double-page magazine project
Tate Etc, issue no. 13, pp. 26, 27

04

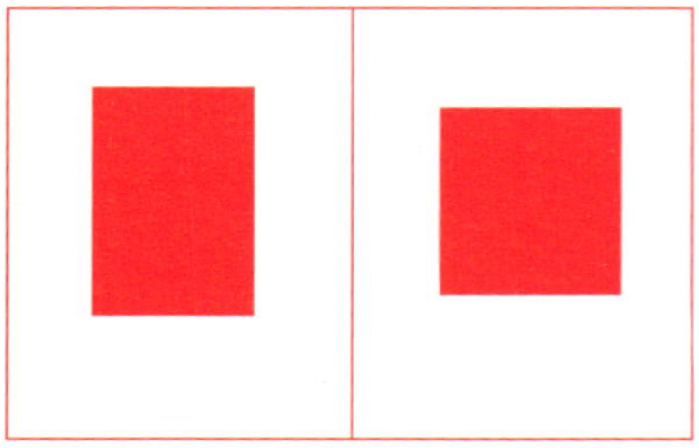

**The God Look-Alike Contest** 1992 (detail)

Thirteen framed images
Mixed media
Dimensions between 9 x 12cm and 48.5 x 21cm
Collection: Saatchi Collection

08

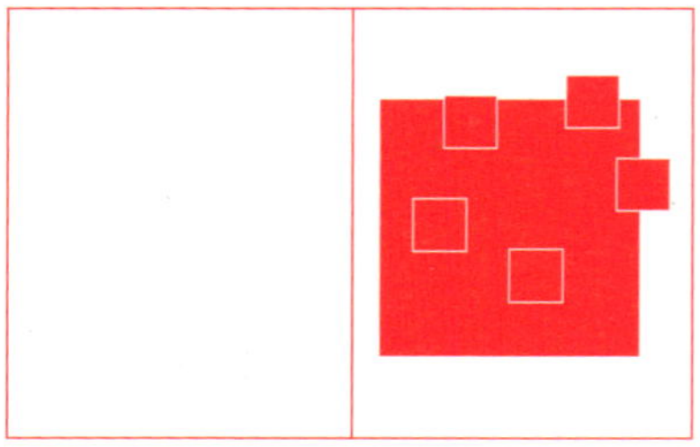

**Sketch for location of Test Tone for Landscape in Tate St Ives Loggia** 2008

Ink on paper
29.5 x 43cm

10

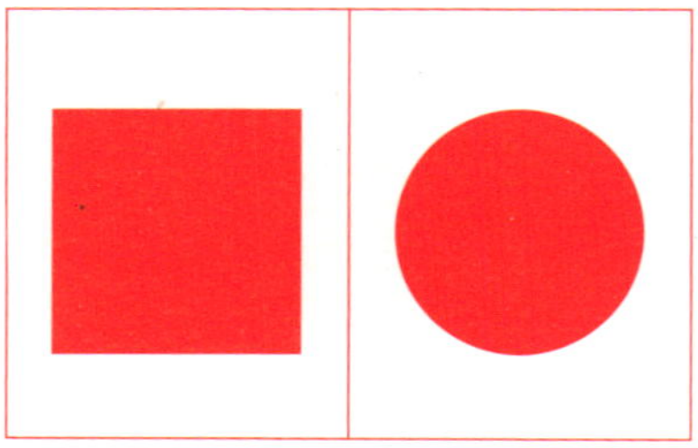

**Test Tone for Landscape** 2005 (detail)

5 Walnut veneered record sleeves
34cm x 34cm x 4cm each
5 clear vinyl 12" records and ink
No. 4: Collection: APT

Five clear vinyl records each containing five tracks. Each track is made up from domestic ambient sounds collected to create five different tones along a scale. Each of the five records is to play a separate tone simultaneously from five sound-systems placed around an environment. Various harmonies of a chord can be heard depending on the position of a listener as they move through a space in relation to these five sound-systems. For any area, of any size, the precise positions for the sound-systems can be 'located' by the markings scratched into the wood grain on each record 'sleeve,' each sleeve being fabricated from the same walnut-veneered bed headboard. Each record is allocated to five different owners.

12

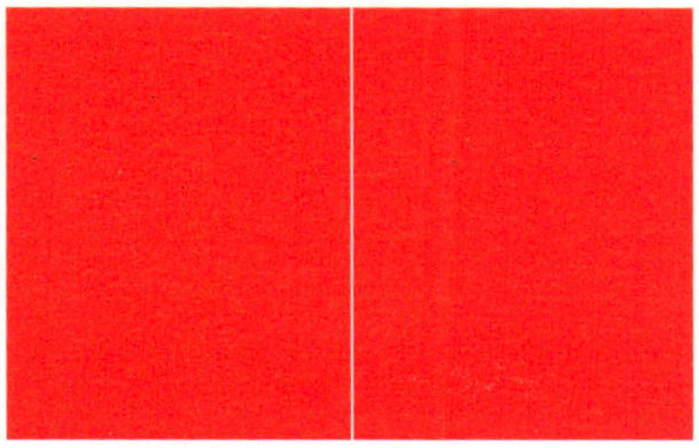

**Borrowed Cold Lodge** 2008

Installation of 286 items of cold-weather, protective, outer clothing, borrowed from St Ives and the West Penwith area
Coat rails, coat hooks, barrels and drawing
Dimensions variable
Commissioned by Tate St Ives

---

14

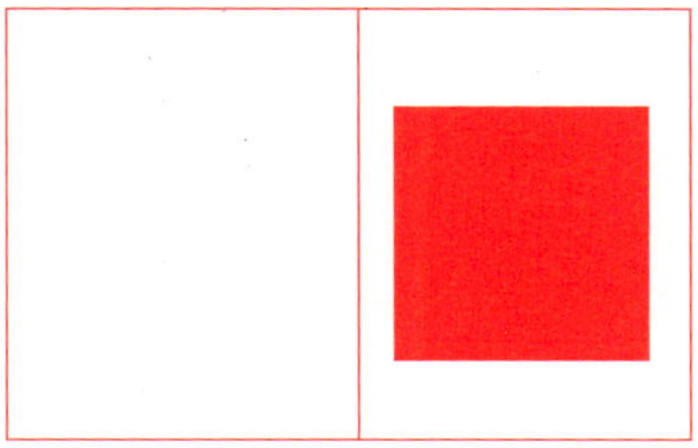

**The music from Float 17, as it stops briefly under the fly-over, as it makes its way in to the city** 2003
(From Design for a Carnival)

Dub plate, Formica, MDF, and ink
33 x 33cm

---

16

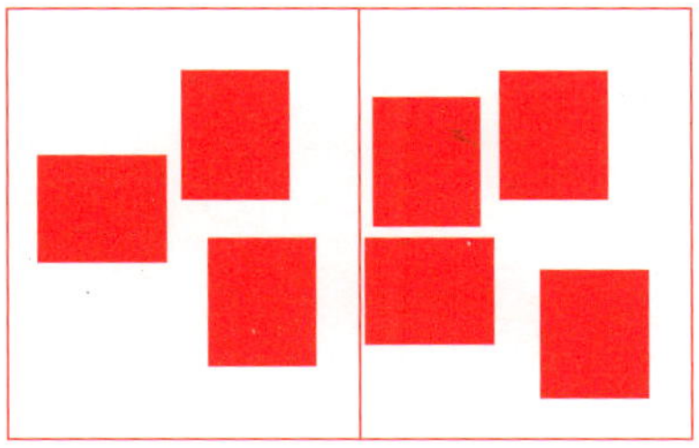

**Baseball Hat Pyre** 2003 (From Design for a Carnival)

7, from 3 sets of 7:
1) '... on every sixth thursday after a flood' 2005
2) '... whenever a bridge to the city is closed' 2006
3) '... every time the motorway is empty' 2006

21 Polaroid photographs
6 x 10cm each

---

18

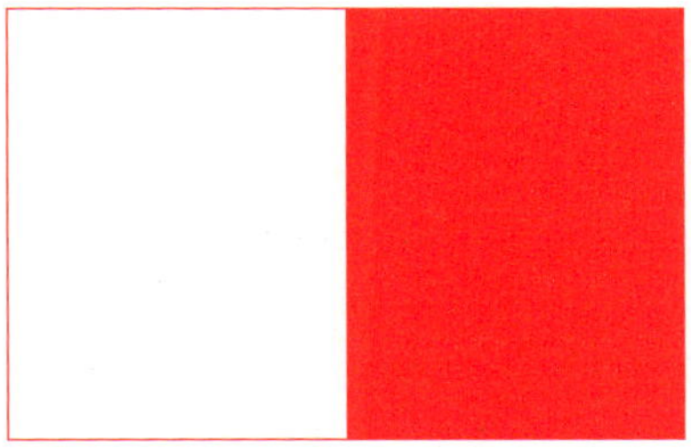

**Flasher no. 22 (Light Levellers)** 1996 –

Photograph from one-minute videos, recorded on to the end of video films rented from video stores
25.4 x 30.4cm

---

20

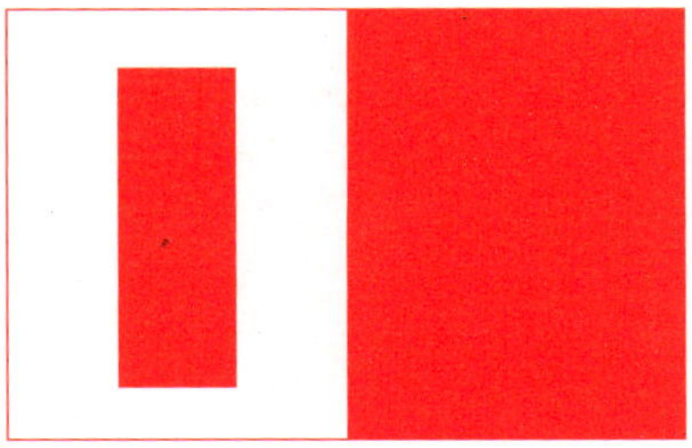

**This is it** 1992 (p.21 detail)

Polyurethane, Cherry, hornbeam and apple sticks, Ecstasy, glass, sealing wax, foam
178 x 30cm each

## 22

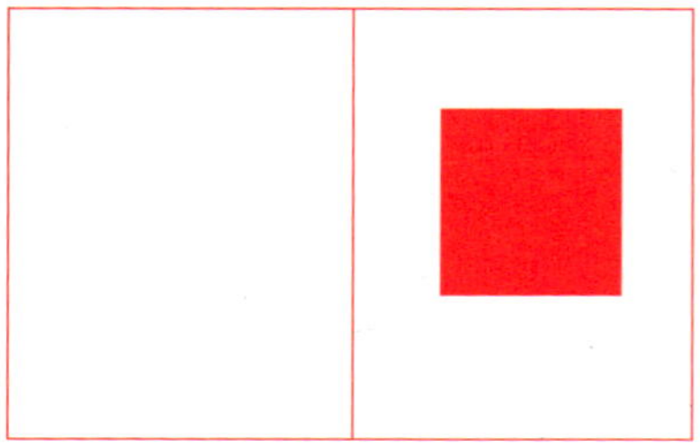

**Night Shift** 2004 (Red Deer Stag visit: 2am, 15 October) (detail)

Commission for Frieze Art Fair, 15 – 18 October 2004
7 photographs
30 x 50cm each
Ink and paper drawing
Collection: British Council

See 78 – 79

---

## 34
## 36

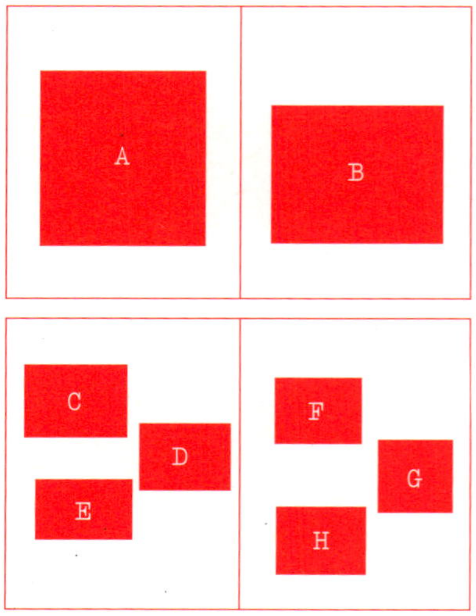


**Mask-Filter** 2004 (From Design for a Carnival)

All approx. 23 x 26 x 40cm

A. Camera lens adapter, stick, ink, peacock and gull feathers, plastic connector straws, car-body filler

B. Camera filter-holder, 'pick-up sticks', brake cable, scoubidou strings, washers, CD packaging, rings

C. Camera filter-holder, Japanese paper string, bicycle spokes, rattan chair cane no. 6, drinking straws, acrylic paint, car-body filler

D. Camera filter-holder, sterling silver, Super-8 film leader, kinder egg toys, packaging tape, poppy heads, model kit frames.

E. Camera filter-holder modem cable, porcupine quill, car body filler, chopsticks, shell, electrical wire, and African beads and paper knife

F. Camera lens adaptor, cable ties, luminous bones, gimp

G. Camera lens adapter, chopsticks, ribbon, fishing line, beads, paint

H. Camera lens adapter, plastic bi-plane kit, mohair, dinosaur stickers, raffia

---

## 38

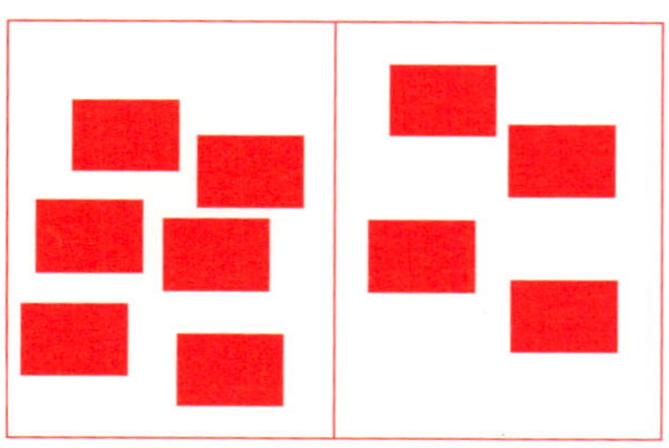

**Plan for a Parade with Two Masks (Blean, Kent, UK and Sepolia, Athens, Greece)** 2004
(From Design for a Carnival) (detail)

35mm slide projection,
81 slides
6 minutes

**Guide for a Parade with Two Masks (Alf, hamlet of Shellness, Isle of Sheppey, UK and Stefan, Roosevelt Island, New York)** 2004
(From Design for a Carnival) (detail)

35mm slide projection,
81 slides
6 minutes

40

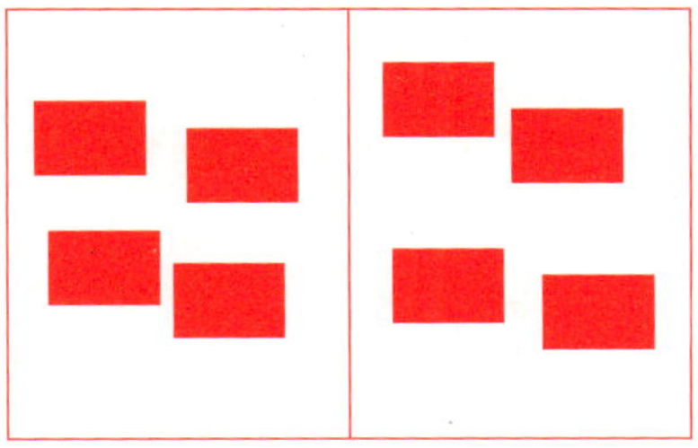

**Pattern for a Procession with Two Masks (Whitstable, Kent, and Vozdovac, Belgrade)** 2007 (From Design for a Carnival)

35mm slide projection, 81 slides
4 minutes

---

42

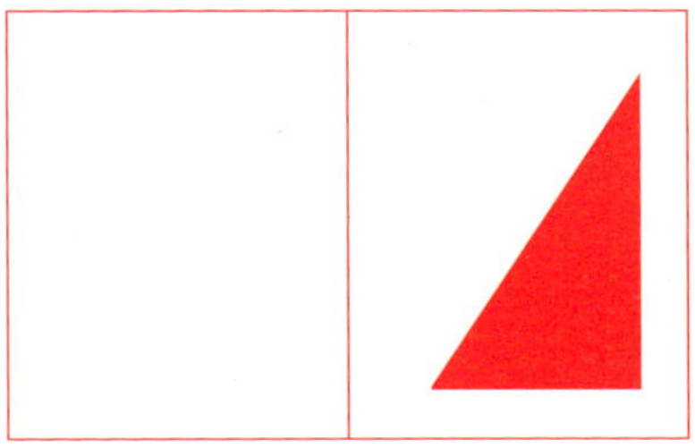

**Cleaner (a story)** 1999

Ink on contiboard
280 x 380cm
Private Collection, New York

Text reads:
*You know the way that contemporary art fans love to tell stories about the cleaning staff at this museum or that gallery, who accidentally threw away some top artist's work thinking that it was a bit of rubbish.*
*And we roll our eyes and tell our anecdote about this really interesting very new work ( a scatter piece, a ready-made, a process piece,.....) which might look like a little piece of junk but was actually made by this very happening artist; but the cleaners threw it away, ......not realising its value,........as if it was trash.*
*Well, I tried to find some of these cleaners who had unwittingly scrapped art works over the last five years in the major museums and galleries around the world.*
*I wondered if something could arise from this situation.*
*As a group we got together and they came up with something really wonderful. We had been talking a lot about the way things look and they became really interested in certain kinds of design; designing things that they really wanted to see.*
*They chose to focus on a design for horses to wear and showed me how, onto the saddle where the rider would go, they would add a beautiful large dorsal fin.*

---

44
46

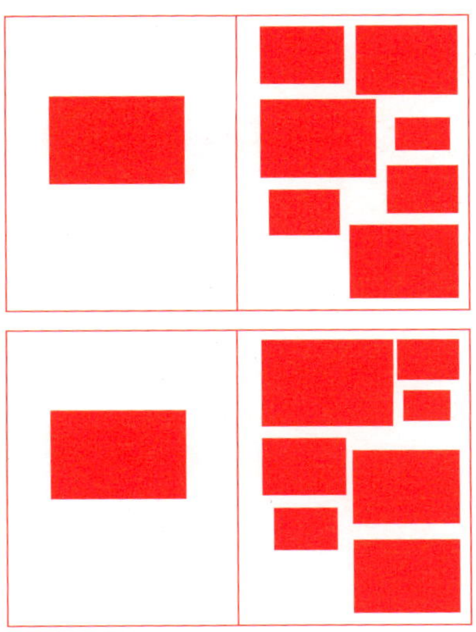

**White Magic (Kent, UK and Brooklyn, NY)** 2005 (From Design for a Carnival) (detail)

Video
3 minutes
Commissioned by Grizedale Arts

**58**

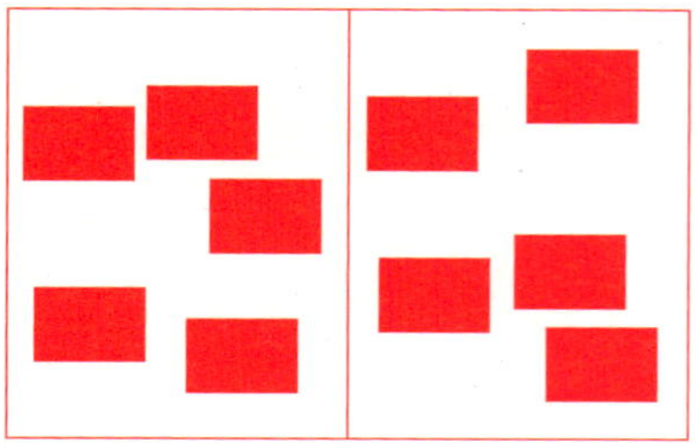

**Turning Point (A performance for drivers on a bridge)** 2007 (details)

35mm slide projection, 80 slides
5 minutes
Commissioned by Signal Galleri, Malmö

**60**

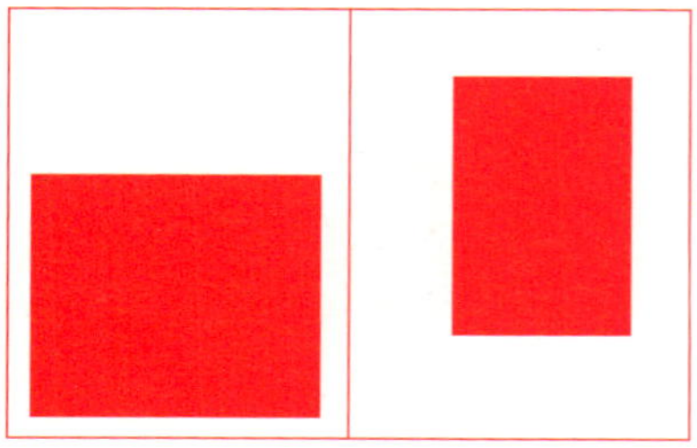

**Settlement** 2004

Production still from video with sound
9 mins 28 secs
Detail from legal contract between Kunal Singh and Southwark Council, through the solicitors Denton Wilde Sapte for 34 x 23cm of land
Collection: South London Gallery from the Contemporary Art Society

**62**

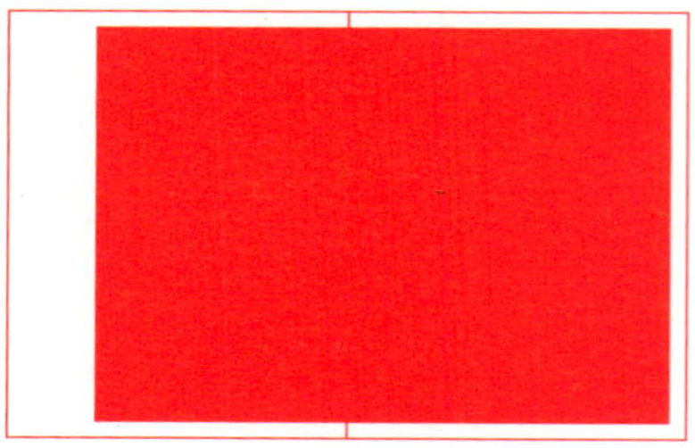

**Ants Choose Position for Sequins – 2 Seconds Intervals**
2003 (From Design for a Carnival)

Photographic diptych
76.2 x 101.6cm together

**64**

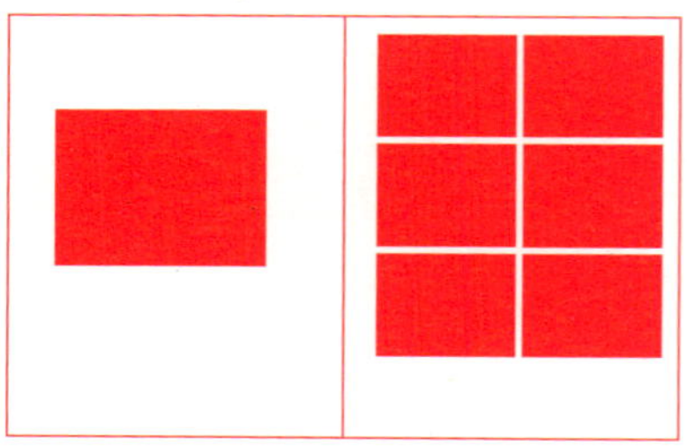

**Plan for a Spell** 2001 (details)

Video, single screen projection and 5.1 Surroundsound
Infinite duration
Commissioned by Film and Video Umbrella
Private Collection, Athens

**66**

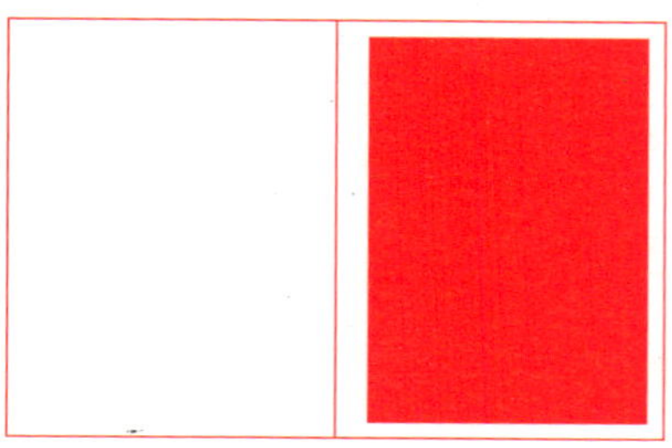

**Transmitter – (Tiny princes)** 2002 (detail)

Page from classified advertisement newspaper, crayon
30.5 x 39cm

**68**

**Transmitter – (Swing seat)** 1991 (detail)

Page from classified advertisement newspaper,
acrylic paint
30.5 x 39cm

---

**70**

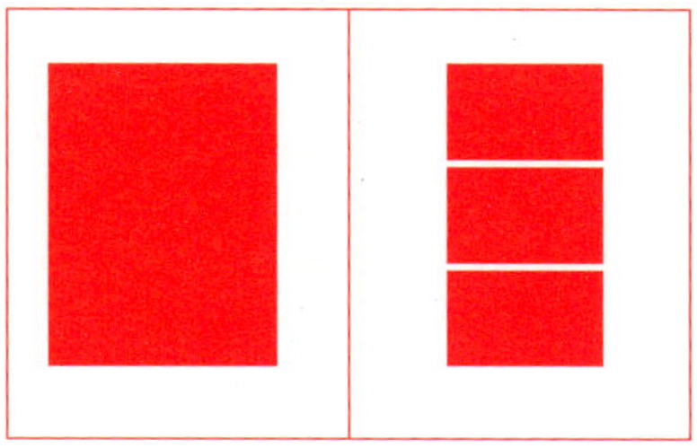

**Inverter (Clearance Sale) (No.2)** 1999

Adler advertisement, Harpers & Queen
21.3 x 28.8cm
Three advertisements from Loot, November 1998
40.5 x 10cm each
Edition produced with Paul Stolper

---

**72**

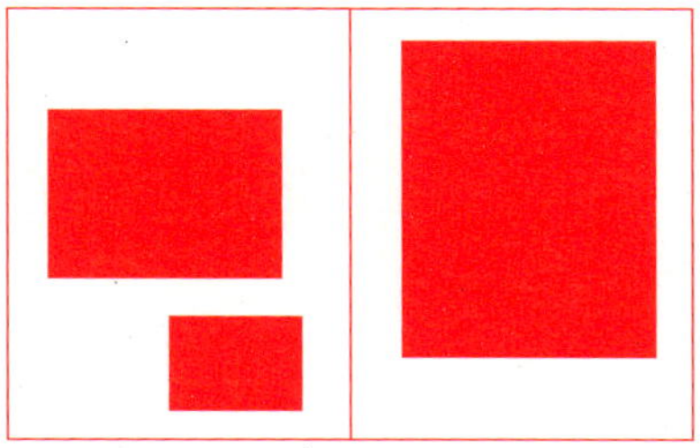

**Flasher no.5, no.4 and credits** (1996 -)

Photograph from one-minute videos, recorded on to
the end of video films rented from video stores
25.4 x 30.4cm
ink and contiboard
50.5 x 40.5cm

Text reads:
*...for a while now I've been recording bits of video footage on to the end of films that I've rented from video shops.*
*I then return the tapes to the video store so that the next person to hire the film might leave it running, and so will discover my signal.*
*There are now lots of Flashers in circulation, distributed through video shops.*
*I only record onto the section of surplus black tape that doesn't carry any image, a few seconds after the credits finish.*
*I film footage of distress-signal flares, which illuminate a dark environment for about 50 seconds. So, this secretes an intensely bright sequence into that black space; and when the flare burns out, the tape returns to darkness.*

74

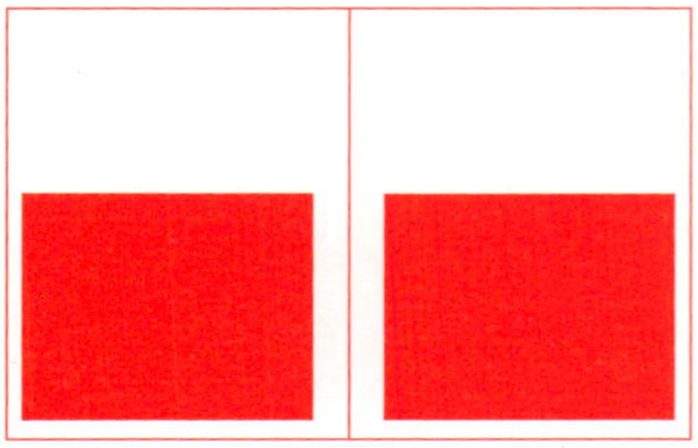

**Better Scenery** 2000

Photograph
101.6 x 76.2cm
Commissioned by Camden Art Centre
Collection: Tate

Text left [sign in Sainsbury's car park, London] reads:
Better Scenery
*From Flagstaff, Arizona take route 89 northeast, then route 510 east, then 505 northeast for 7 miles until you reach a left turn soon after passing Maroon Crater. Follow this dirt track (the 244A) for 6 miles northeast passing the volcanic formations of The Sproul and the Merriam Crater on your right. Half a mile beyond a small well take the track that heads north towards Little Roden Spring. After exactly 6.7 miles a rough, overgrown cinder track leads off to the left. Head west along this for a quarter of a mile until you reach a fence post. Then walk 100 yards 160° south SE. At this point stop and face due east (visible on the horizon are the Roden Crater and the glow of pink rocks in the Painted Desert ).*
*Situated here, in this place, is a sign which describes the location of this sign you have just finished reading.*

Text right [sign in Arizona desert] reads:
*Better Scenery*
*Heading north out of London along the west side of Regent's Park is the Finchley Road (A41). Follow it through St John's Wood and half a mile beyond to Swiss Cottage. From here, bearing north-west for a quarter-of-a-mile the Finchley Road veers towards West Hampstead. Keep Holy Trinity Church and the Laser Eye Clinic to your right and Finchley Road Underground station to your left. Then take a left turn, following the graceful curvature of the prodigious, concrete and glass, O2 building. This takes you down a steeply inclined unmarked road which opens out to an expansive tarmac car park bordered to the north and south by the tracks of railway lines.*
*Situated here, in this place, is a sign which describes the location of this sign you have just finished reading.*

---

76

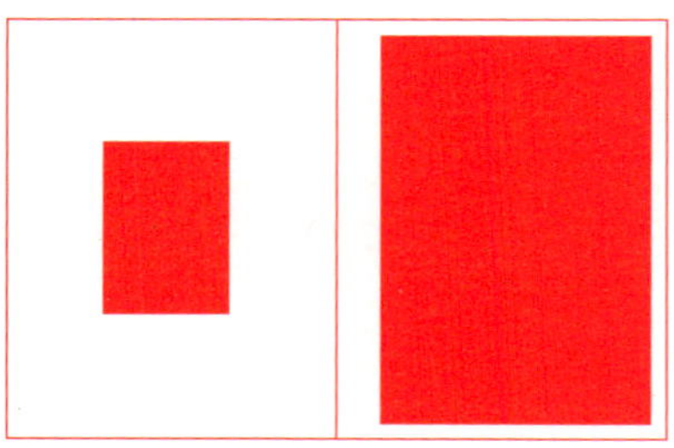

**Untitled Stile (Teenage Version)** 1991

Wood, paint and polish
130.7 x 105.4 x 74cm
Arts Council Collection, Southbank Centre, London

**Meeting** 1999 (detail)

Paper, ink and paint
59.3 x 41.7cm each

## 78
## 80

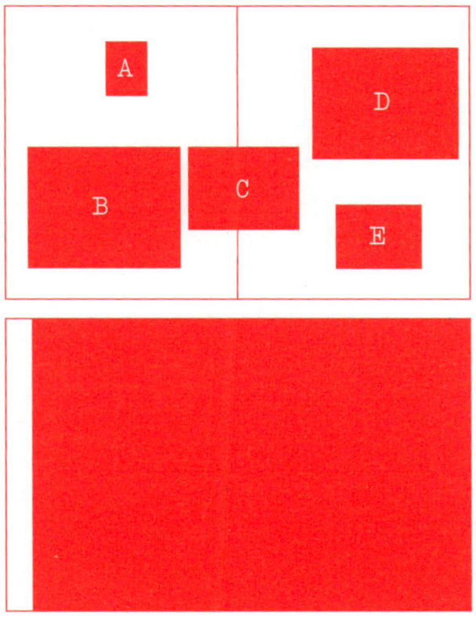


**Night Shift** 2004

Commission for Frieze Art Fair, 15 – 18 October 2004
7 photographs
30 x 50cm each
Collection: British Council

A. Burmese Python visit: 1am, 12 October (detail)
B. Timber Wolf visit: 12.30am, 14 October (detail)
C. Imperial Jungle Scorpion visit: 12.45am, 18 October (detail)
D. North American Skunk visit: 2.30am, 13 October (detail)
E. Agouti Rat visit: 1am, 16 October (detail)
F. Ink on paper drawing for printed plan of Frieze Art Fair, 15 – 18 October 2004,
42 x 61cm
British Council

Adam Chodzko was commissioned by Frieze Projects to make a poster proposing an alternative mapping of the art fair site to be distributed free to visitors.

'There's another map of the Frieze Art Fair, one for nocturnal visitors who access the tent when everyone else has left it for the night. Collectively building a sporadic carnival parade through its labyrinths; a wolf, a snake, a deer ... (London Zoo is very close). Their plotted paths are advice for the fair's daylight visitors.'

---

## 82

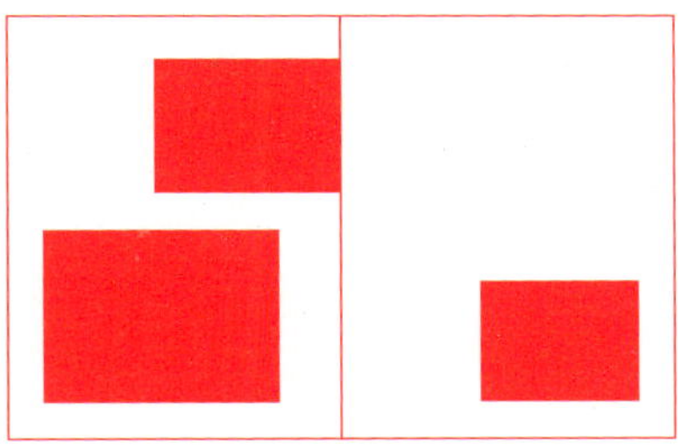

**Flasher no.17, no.29** 1996 –

Photograph from one-minute videos, recorded on to the end of video films rented from video stores
25.4 x 30.4cm

See 18

**Night Shift** 2004 (Cane Toad visit: 1.15am, 17 October) (detail)

Commission for Frieze Art Fair, 15 – 18 October 2004
7 photographs
30 x 50cm each
Collection: British Council

See 78

---

## 84

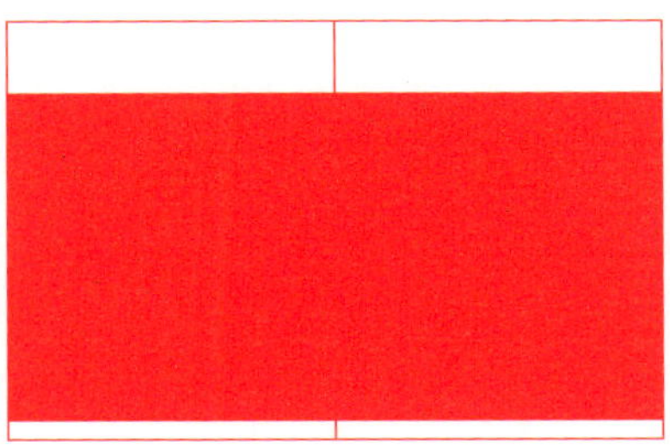

**Looper** 2003 (Billboard project, Piazza San Carlo, Turin, Italia)

Off-set lithographic poster with English translation
300 x 600cm
Commissioned as part of Turin's ManifesTO series accompanying Artissima, Turin art fair, November 2003 to February 2004

**86**

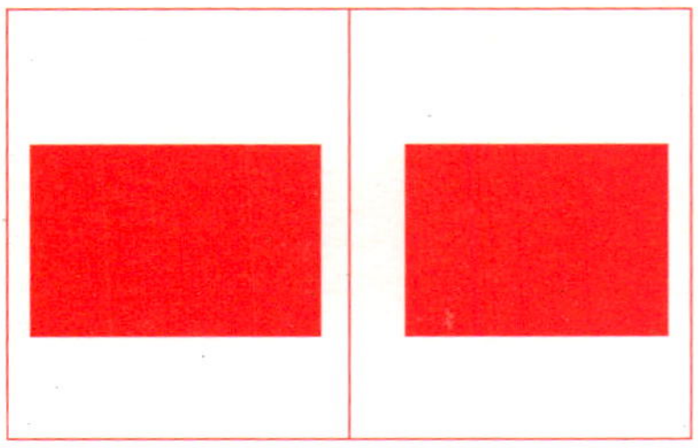

**Next Meeting: Opposite the main entrance to the Ordzhonikidze Health Centre…** 2007

Lithographic print on paper, for fly-posting in Toronto
31 x 48cm each
Commissioned by Mercer Union, Toronto

**Meeting: The foyer of the Hagens Hotel, Måløy, Sogn og Fjordane, on the island of Vågsøy…** 2007

B2 flyers on hoarding, Balbutcher Lane, Ballymun, Dublin 11
50 x 70.7cm each

---

**96**

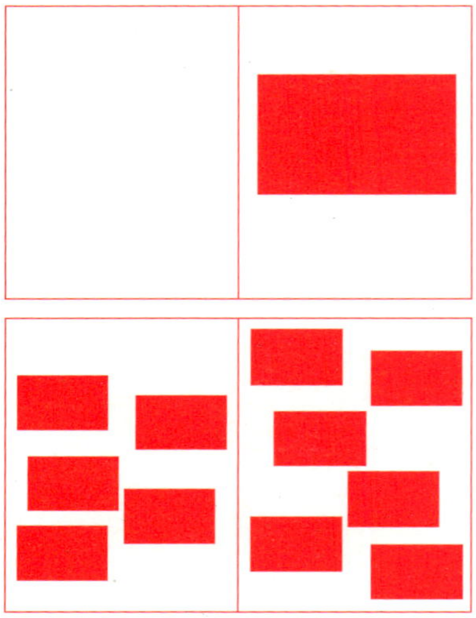

**Around** 2007

Production stills from video with sound
13 minutes 40 seconds
Commissioned by Breaking Ground, Dublin

---

**100**

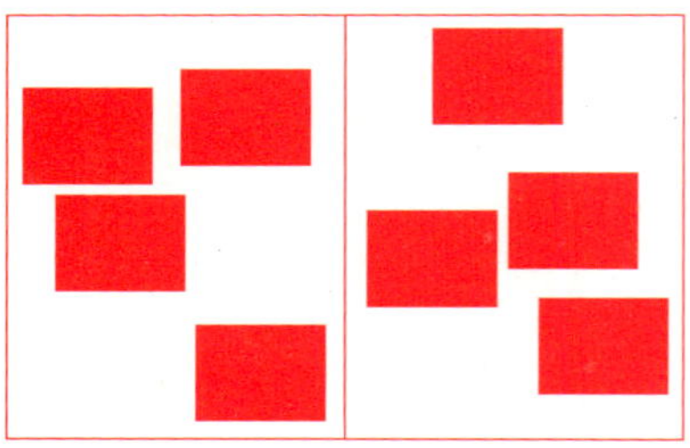

**Yet** 2005

Video and production stills from video with sound
9 minutes 10 seconds

Voice-over (in Finnish, Cantonese and English):
*'It was only early summer… but all the plants were already dying, …*
*Time had accelerated again. A small group of IKEA employees go to the local landfill site to try and retrieve some data they had accidentally thrown away. Instead they found some bags of documents which recorded the history of a place where people met and showed things to each other… Distracted from their original search they took the archive to the editing station in order to look for its questions. But… something bad happened… a disagreement… well, anyway… they fell out… They split up the information in various, but particular ways, each to take it to a separate place for safe-keeping, agreeing to reunite its parts only when they themselves had resolved their differences.*
*One took it to the ark where everything precious had been stored…*
*Another chose to entrust it to strangers, offering it to the chalkpit people… And the other took it to the comparison house. And so because of 'and yet despite all this' the plants slowly began to recover… and time… stood… still.'*

102

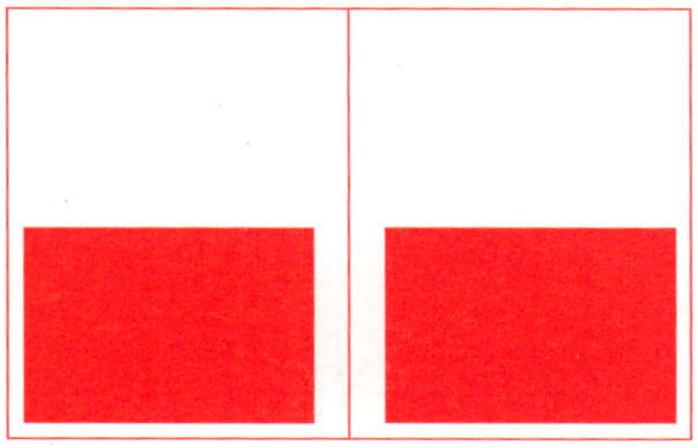

**Hole** 2007 (detail)

Production stills from video with sound
12 minutes 10 seconds
Commissioned by and collection of MAMbo, Museo d'Arte Moderna di Bologna Photograph (left) © Matteo Monti

104
106
108

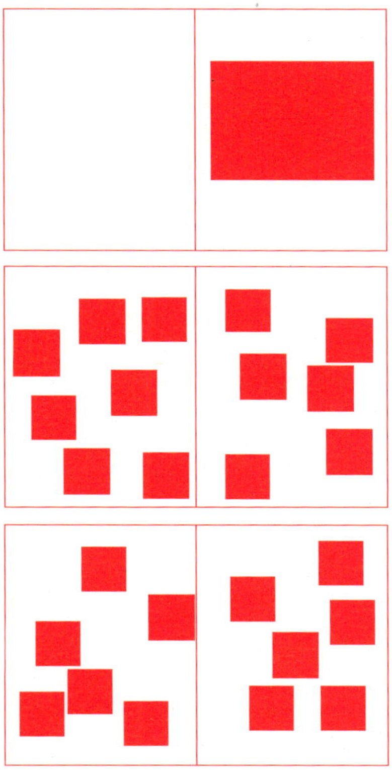

**Longshore drift, early detroit techno and other processes of erosion** 2006– (detail)

35mm slide projection, 100 slides, lecture performance at Arts Club, St Ives, Saturday 6 September 2008

110

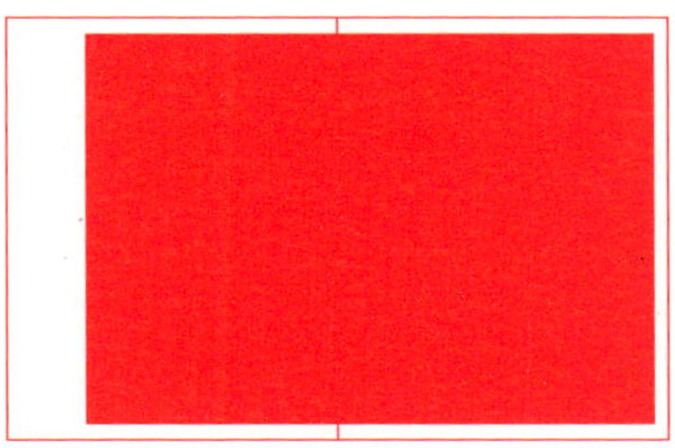

**Next Meeting: The car park of the plywood factory, just north of the town of Tolhóin ...** 2008

Billboard poster on coastal path between St Ives and Zennor, Cornwall (50°12' 53.34" N, 5°30' 52.71" W)
174.3 x 250cm
Commissioned by Tate St Ives

112

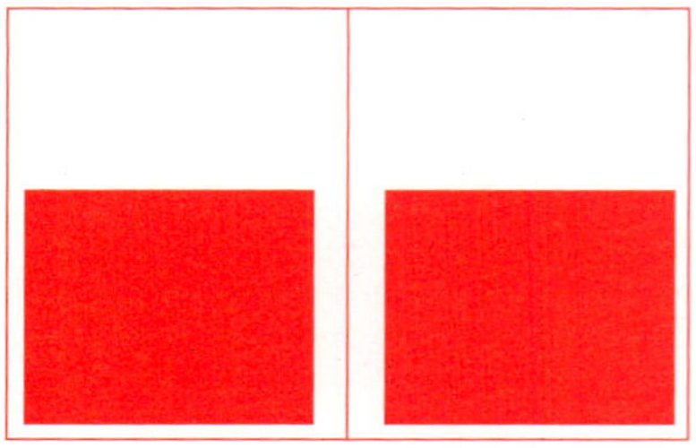

**Better Scenery** 2002

Photographic diptych
101.6 x 76.2cm each
Commissioned by Cubitt
Private Collection, London

Text left [sign in Islington, London, UK] reads:
*Better Scenery*
*Go North down 10th St and turn west onto 12th Avenue. Continue west on 12th out of Fargo until you see the big Supervalu warehouse on your right. Take that exit onto Interstate 29, heading North towards Grand Forks and Canada. After about 30 minutes (maybe 28 miles) you want to look out for the Gardner exit, which comes soon after you see four big silver grain bins on the right hand side of the road. Turn east and go about a quarter of a mile until you see a stop sign. Then turn left going north – you're now in Kinyon Township – for maybe three miles. That would get you to a crossroads. Then turn east again. (In the distance you'll see a tree line running along the horizon. The Red River runs behind it). One half a mile further on you'll come to a farmstead on the south side of the road. This is the Pratt farm. Come into the yard, pass by the machine shed and at the shelter belt turn left into the soybean field. Standing facing you is a sign. It describes the location of the sign you have just finished reading.*

Text right [Fargo] reads:
*Better Scenery*
*Turning left immediately outside the entrance to Angel tube station you need to go down the hill a bit until you reach the traffic lights at this big, chaotic cross roads. There's a Co-op bank on the other side of the road – but still on the Islington side – so cross over towards that, then pass it, walking along Pentonville Road. Maybe 15 yards along this in the middle of the pavement is a large shrub right in front of the Family Planning Association, which is in the dark glass and bronze-coloured rectangular block of a building on your right. A brown railing runs across the pavement at the point where Angel Mews begins. Stand in the entrance of this little street with Whittles House to your left. Following the line of black bollards which run along the pavement of the mews you'll see, facing you, in a corner next to a broken concrete lamp post a single ash tree. In its branches about 8ft off the ground you'll see a sign. It describes the location of the sign you have just finished reading.*

114
116

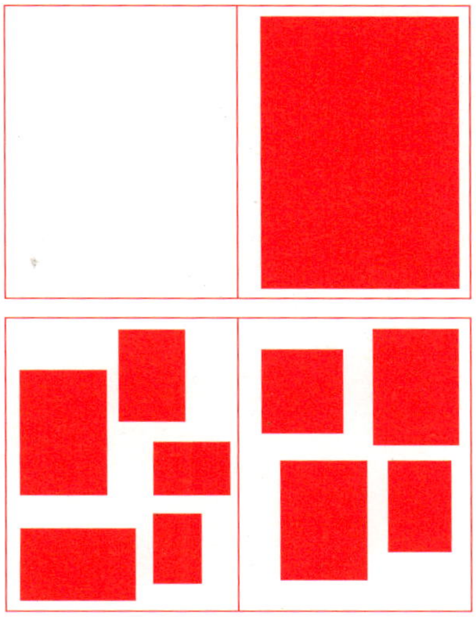

**The God Look-Alike Contest** 1992 (detail)

13 framed images
Mixed media
Dimensions between 9 x 12cm and 48.5 x 21cm
Collection: Saatchi Collection

---

118

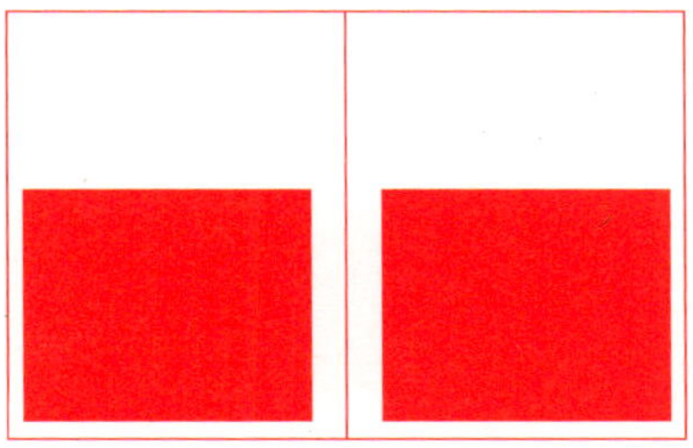

**Better Scenery** 2001

Photographic diptych
101.6 x 76.2cm each

Text left [sign in Grizedale Forest, Lake District, England] reads:
*Better Scenery*
*With the Duke of Aosta monument behind you drive from Piazza Castello south-east down Via Po out of Turin. Across the river, you will be facing the Gran Madre Church. Turn right and go 5.5km along the road that runs by the river bank to Moncalieri, past the cemetery's red brick walls. When the road widens keep to the right and drive on to the traffic lights at Piazza Caduti per la Libertà. Now turn left and follow signs to the industrial estate across the flyover and past the car scrap-yard on your right. After the bend, take the SS 393 road to a roundabout and turn left. Then past the shopping centre car park turn right into Via Achille Grandi. After about 100m the road ends in front of a tall hedge. Leave your car in the car park on the left. Cross the street and walk through the white gate of Italdesign-Giugiaro at No. 25 where you will be directed to door No. 10 of the Styling Milling Department. Upon entering, face the wall to your left. Situated here, in this place, is a sign which describes the location of this sign you have just finished reading.*

Text right [sign in car factory, Turin, Italy] reads:
*Panorama Migliore*
*Uscendo da Ambleside, Cumbria, dirigersi a sud, verso il Centro Visitatori di Grizedale. Una volta giunti al parcheggio, procedere fino all'ingresso del negozio. Qui, guardare in direzione sud-est e seguire i pali a strisce rosse, fuori dal giardino cinto di mura. Dopo essere passati attraverso la porta verde praticata nel muro, girare a destra e seguire la strada per Home Farm. Una volta giunti alla fattoria, girare a sinistra, per entrare nel campo attraverso il cancello. Ricordarsi di richiudere il cancello! Camminare o pedalare lungo il sentiero in salita che attraversa i prati, oltrepassare il recinto del bestiame e raggiungere la strada. Girare a sinistra e dirigersi a sud, attraverso gli antichi*

*boschi di querce. Il sentiero che conduce a Hall Wood costeggia dei campi sulla sinistra. A 1,5km dal recinto del bestiame, in direzione ovest (a destra), vi è una distesa di arbusti di mirtillo ai piedi delle querce, con un ruscello che scorre verso sinistra.*
*In questo punto preciso, un cartello descrive il luogo in cui si trova l'insegna che avete appena finito di leggere.*

## List of illustrations in essays